"This highly acclaimed travel memoir, *Europe with Two Kids and a Van*, was a best seller in 1973. With new detailed updates, it is as relevant today as it was a half-century ago as a travel guide for intrepid families exploring Europe. A must-have guide that even the kids will appreciate."

—Jan Baross, award-winning author of *Bye-Bye Bakersfield*

5.0 out of 5 stars I read this book back in the 70's and the concept is still valid--and it inspired our 6-week trip!

This book served as our inspiration for a 6-week trip via VW Pop-Top Van around Europe in 1976. What a glorious adventure it was! The concept still has relevant, many decades later. The more we travel around the world, the more we understand how important it is to make friends around the world when we travel, and to better understand cultures other than our own. Can't recommend it enough, even after all these years as international travelers!

—Reviewed by Amazon Reader in the United States on October 21, 2022

Original book cover published in 1973
Design © Bill Oetinger

50TH ANNIVERSARY EDITION

EUROPE WITH TWO KIDS AND A VAN

Travel Memoir and Guide

SHER DAVIDSON

LA PAGE
PRESS

To our friends and family
around the world

Contents

Gary, Sher and the kids waving good-bye at the airport

2023 Introduction

In 1972, my husband Gary and I decided to do what seemed like a pretty daring step: to camp in Europe with our two kids in a Volkswagen van. Now, looking back, it seems like just one of a string of many wonderful adventures we've shared during our fifty-seven years of marriage.

We were at a crossroads. We had two small daughters, ages three and five, when Gary decided he wasn't happy in his previously chosen career path and wanted to return to school. Gary's father had just died suddenly at the young age of fifty-three without ever having the chance to realize his dream of travel, putting it off until retirement. He didn't live long enough to retire. We decided then and there not to postpone our dreams.

I said, "Why not sell the house and all our possessions, buy a VW camper van and take the kids to Europe?" After a long pause Gary said, "Why not? Let's do it." Actually, our trip was just one facet of a conscious choice we made to change our lifestyle. We reached a point in our lives when we wanted to live more simply in a rural community, rather than in the rat race of an urban environment, like the Bay Area of California where we grew up. Our trip to Europe became the first stage of that shift.

I didn't exactly relate to our suburban San Jose, California neighborhood, and to the mundane routine of coffee dates with the neighbors. Having had quite an adventuresome post graduate career working in France for two years before meeting Gary, marrying and becoming a parent, I longed to return to France to see friends. Gary, too, wanted to see Europe. He traveled extensively in Asia while in the United States Navy, but now he picked up my enthusiasm for visiting my relatives in Sweden, meeting my French friends and having an adventure with the family. Together, we hoped not only to see Europe but also to learn from our experiences in other cultures to live on less and to live more slowly. As a consequence of our decision, a "for sale" sign went up on our house and, after paying the bills, we scraped together $4000 for our trip. We packed up the few possessions we owned, storing them with friends and family, and headed for the great continent of Europe. We had purchased the VW van through our American Automobile Association (AAA). You'll read more about that in our first chapter.

MAKING PLANS

While our house was on the market, we researched campgrounds in all the countries we hoped to visit. Remember, this was 1971 before the age of the home computer. I wrote letters to Chambers of Commerce all over Europe and haunted the library's collection of travel books. This was the year of guides with titles like *Europe on 5 Dollars a Day* by Arthur Frommer, but not much else, especially about camping in Europe or traveling with kids. Rick Steves, considered today to be one of the most respected authorities on European travel, was not yet known to the public and *Lonely Planet*, another great travel guide, was also not yet on the market. I took a myriad of notes, while Gary perused maps and made lists of things we would need to have along, like camping equipment, tools in case he needed to fix a problem with the VW van, rainy weather gear, etc. I made my own lists: things to take for the kids to keep them entertained, recipes for simple meals to fix on a two-burner camp stove, all-weather, no-iron clothing we would need. The space in a VW van would be limited as we couldn't afford the one with the pop-top, so we had to be "minimalists" and take only the bare necessities. To save money, I sewed travel outfits for me and the children in lots of mix-and-match, coordinated colors. The only clothing purchases we made were good, warm parka jackets for all four of us. On the girls' navy-blue jackets, my dad insisted I sew bright yellow labels on which he wrote with a fabric-friendly waterproof pen: "If I am lost please return me to the nearest American Express Office." Soon we were on our way to Europe with two kids to pick up our VW van and let the adventure begin!

THEN AND NOW

In 1972, we could travel Europe with two kids and a van on a budget of $10 per day, including gas. We know you might be asking yourself with a great deal of skepticism: would that really be possible to do now, fifty years later? Our flat-out answer is "No, but yes!" Now, I'm *sure* you're scratching your head, with a skeptical look on your face and saying: "Well, we sure couldn't do it on the $10 per day they talk about." You're right. In fact, we just got back from another trip to Europe without a van and children, and with more economic security than we ever had in our earlier days of marriage. We traveled to many of the same places we had gone to in 1971–72. But we didn't camp and that's one crux of the matter. There are still wonderful campgrounds in Europe in beautiful places, by lakes, mountains and streams, natural places of beauty, also campgrounds in and near the cities, but you'll pay more than what we paid in 1972 at our daily stopover campsites.

During our recent European travels, we kept asking ourselves how today's young families could go to Europe like we did, experience the joys of foreign adventures, discover new places, not to mention offer their kids the educational benefits that travel presents such as cultural awareness, possible language development, and a sense of geography that one does not get in schools today? On a darker side, how could the kids see the world before the existential threats of climate change really make travel impossible or, at least, not wise? Could it still be done? The answer we came up with was a resounding "Yes," with some exceptions.

11

A family of one to four children could travel in Europe, but not see all the countries we saw in one six-month period unless, they were exceptionally well-to-do and had unlimited time. For those with limited budget and time, we suggest choosing one country for two to three weeks, maybe during the kids' summer breaks. Van camping is still possible if you have the budget for renting camping vehicles or buying one and shipping it home, but there's now the existence of Airbnb, VRBO rentals and private vacation homes that locals rent out (in France they're called "*Gites*"). Depending on your travel budget you can do a 1- to 3-week stay in your country of choice and, with a rental car, travel around to different regions benefitting in the same way we did. It's possible and all it takes is some research, saving the money (it's a good lesson for the kids, 7- to 12-year-olds, to save in their own travel adventure piggy banks—do kids still use that term?) Learning to save for what you really want is a life-skill. Of course, if they see a parent or parents excited about an adventure in a foreign country, chances are the kids will get the "travel bug," too.

Our final suggestion is to choose kid-friendly destinations, not just where the adults want to go, but places that will have attractions for kids (see **information for today's travelers in the Appendix**). Encourage the kids to keep their own travel journals with places for drawings and gluing found stuff and stickers they may collect. Certain museums, for example, are set up to be fun and educational for kids, but not all. If you're a two-adult family unit, you can always do what we did: if one adult wants to peruse an art museum with renaissance paintings, the other can take the kids to a local park and toss the ball or frisbee. Parks are prolific in most European cities where you'll find amazing museums, too.

Secondly, start your family's foreign travels early in your kids' lives. If your finances allow, ages 7–12 are ideal. We loved traveling with our two girls of three and five, the real advantage being they were always happy to be with us. The downside is they don't remember much of the adventure now as adults. The closer to teenagers the kids are the more they may find traveling with parents or other adults a bore—they'll want to be with their peers and maybe complain about being dragged off to Europe. The more annual trips with the kids you can make between 7 and 12 the more they will be educated, world-wise and apt to enjoy the experiences they're having. These experiences also may possibly allow them to qualify for more scholarships to higher learning institutions, if this is what they want, and you seek for them as their parents. At the very least they will be more broadminded and world-wise, something that won't hurt them in adult life wherever their paths take them. In the meantime, they may also have picked up a foreign language, an asset for living and working anywhere. Case in point: both of our daughters wanted to study French after the many wonderful experiences we had with French friends, ones they *did r*emember, having had French playmates for part of our European visits.

So, to wrap up this part of our *50ᵗʰ Anniversary Edition of Europe with Two Kid's and a Van*, we hope you will enjoy reading "the story" of our adventures in 1972 and 1973, places we visited and what we learned. Mostly we hope that it will encourage and help you and your family to plan your own travels abroad, fifty years later. Your experiences will be different from ours, but, we can assure you, they will be fun and educationally rich!

We added a few new sections to the original book, deleted those that are no longer relevant and also included black and white photos of our 1972–73 travels that we hope you will enjoy. This is not only a personal travel memoir but a "how-to" guide for you, our readers. We hope you'll write us at https://sherdavidson.com about your adventures with kids traveling in Europe.

2023 NOTE: We have left the original text intact with a few added "Notes." We have updated specific site information in the Appendix at the end of the book. You will be able to compare it to the Summing Up sections at the end of each country chapter. Specific things mentioned in the original Summing Up sections like phone numbers, and even addresses may have changed.

1973 Introduction

For a long time, the idea of European travel has been attractive to North Americans. Each summer floods of travelers cross the Atlantic by air and sea. At one time it was only the rich, who could make the trek, but in recent years with the advent of less expensive means of travel such as special rates on transatlantic airlines and Eurail passes more and more people have been making the journey. Even more recently there is the possibility of camping, thus cutting expenses until one can truly envision traveling in Europe on an economy-budget. Our dream to travel, learn about other cultures and have some adventures in life before our bones were too old and rickety to allow it, started our mental wheels working on how to make the visit with our two preschoolers, five-year-old Dawn and three-year-old Tiffany. This book represents what we learned.

It is possible to take a three-to-six-month trip to Europe with two young children on a budget of $10 per day, to see something, learn a lot and have fun doing it. Don't be discouraged by those who may say, "You'll just have to wait; there will be plenty of time for travel when the children are grown," or give skeptical warnings such as, "Children require routine; traveling is just too hard on them." We heard the same thing, but fortunately had the encouragement of our families who said, "Great idea, wish we had done it," and the assurance of the family doctor that it wouldn't hurt the kids at all. "In fact," he said, "they will adjust better than you will." Most important of all, though, was our determination to turn the dream into reality. We didn't want to wait; we wanted to go now when it could be an adventure shared with our children, a time of carefree discovery for all four of us.

One thing that was lacking when planning our adventure was good books giving detailed information on what to bring and what costs really are in Europe. Arthur Frommer's well-known book, "Europe on $5 a Day," is great but not always applicable when one is thinking of four mouths to feed or what the kids might want to see and how long it will take to see it, considering their needs. Also, we could not find much on camping. It was easy to find a European guide to camp-sites, but they rarely told us what was good and bad about them, were there play facilities, where to find launderettes when you just could not stand the smelly pillow slips any longer or bear the cold-water washing you had been doing, what kinds of meals provide a balanced diet for a family of four on a tiny two-burner camp stove and what kinds of games you can play in the car with two preschoolers. These are the questions we want to answer so that some of those big hurdles you've been putting up for yourself can be eliminated.

Just a few notes are in order on how the book is organized to make it not only an account of our adventure, but also a handy guide for yours. Chapter 3 is about our decision to camp, the purchase of our vehicle, what plans to make prior to the trip, when to travel and what to take. Following this chapter is an extensive section, which includes a detailed equipment and wardrobe list, toys to take for the children, information on matters concerning your vehicle and addresses to write prior to your trip for information. Chapters 6 through 15 are accounts of our adventures along the way from Scandinavia to England, France, Spain, the French Riviera and Northern Italy, Switzerland, and Germany. In these chapters we tried to suggest a few places to camp, places to see with special attention to what children will like and incidental things that happened to us and may happen to you. A section titled "Summing Up" follows each of these chapters with suggested itineraries, addresses of campgrounds, launderettes, post offices, tourist information, etc. At the end of the book is information on driving regulations in Europe and some suggestions for activities to do while traveling.

So, if you want to travel, can save enough money for a $10-a-day budget, have young children who you enjoy sharing adventures with, and have always dreamed of going to Europe, just do it!

Making Plans

One of the first things we did upon deciding to go to Europe with our children was purchase a small, loose-leaf binder in which we recorded information from articles on European travel. It was organized by country with sections on food specialties, things to buy and interesting places to visit. This later became not only an invaluable guide, but also a travel journal in which to record each day's major events.

ORDERING A VEHICLE AND WHEN TO GO

To realize our dream of travel it would have to be done on limited funds. After some research we quickly agreed the best way to go would be with a camper van. Not only would it be the most economical, but also the best means of getting around with two small children who would need naps and midday snacks. A camper would give us the mobility we wanted, plus a play area, nap area and eating area on wheels. We could cook most of our own meals, avoiding the costs of eating out and, by shopping in the European markets, still learn about foreign cuisines. Our friends who had traveled in Volkswagen campers recommended them highly.

If you decide on a Volkswagen camper, the expense can be cut down considerably by not ordering the pop-top and tent. We found the car adequate without these options for our family of four. There were times, however, in cold winter months when more time was spent inside, that the increased space for standup room would have been appreciated. Of course, then we would have had to cope with increased cold. All possibilities should be weighed. In our case, greatest economy was the deciding factor.

The next step was to order our car to be picked up in Germany upon our arrival. This led to the question of when to go. We knew the weather would be best in early spring, but because we were going for six months this would mean a good part of our trip would be in the summer, a very bad time to travel. This is the time when most foreign visitors come to Europe and one really gets little chance to see the European cities as they are most of the year, or to meet the Europeans who escape the tourists during the summer and go off on their own vacations. The costs in the summer are higher, too, and we soon discovered that off-season rates would be far less for everything from airfares to museum fees. This left the fall and winter open as the best time for our trip. We would take a chance on the weather, knowing that there would be at least two and a half months (September and October) to see the northern countries before winter temperatures set in and we headed to southern Spain, a region of moderate temperature in the winter. If traveling with school-age kids, of course, you will have to consider if their losing out on a few months school will work.

We ordered our Volkswagen camping van through our local American Automobile Association dealer. Though it could have been ordered through the Volkswagen of America dealer at the same cost, we felt the advantage was with AAA as they provided not only financing but a free European Camping Carnet, a good identification card that also permits price reductions in some campgrounds. Always watch for small print on your contract alerting you to possible price changes. Upon our arrival in Germany we learned that our VW had been raised in price a total of $600 from that originally quoted. We had ordered a 1972 model in 1971, and there were the structural changes of a larger engine, Michelin radial tires and disk brakes in the 1972 that merited the increased price. Budget for this and it will not be the shock it was for us. The total price came to $4100. An additional feature offered by AAA is maps and booklets with general information and restaurant suggestions on each major section of Europe. You might want to browse through these to get ideas when making up your itinerary.

HOW TO GO

Our next step was to look into transportation across the Atlantic. Due to the cost, commercial airlines and ship travel were out of the question. Some research into freighter lines revealed that it is almost as expensive to travel by freighter (in fact sometimes more), as it is to travel by commercial shipping lines. Also, the children would become tired of being at sea for too long, thus making the journey unpleasant for them and for us.

2023 Note: We left out the remainder of this section from the 1973 version of our book, as it is no longer relevant. Charter flights either no longer exist or are way more expensive than booking your own flight for the family on a regular airline. Make sure to research and compare prices and itineraries that match your chosen country of arrival. If you have earned mileage on a specific airline you might be pleasantly surprised to learn how many earned miles you have but beware: the amount needed for travel to Europe is far greater now, especially after the COVID pandemic.

WRITING FOR INFORMATION

There was much to do in the last month to insure a smooth journey. First, we wrote to organizations offering various kinds of discounts for European travelers. For example, the Italian Government Office will, at the cost of $1 (no charge for children), send you a discount card for all state-run museums, a great savings when traveling in

Italy. They will also send information on purchasing coupons at the Italian borders, which allow you to buy gas in Italy at a 30 percent savings. This is something you should take advantage of, for gas is a major expense when camping in Europe. We found the average to be about 75 cents per gallon, with the lowest rates in England and Spain and the highest in France. For our five-and-one-half-month trip we budgeted $350 for gas and found this adequate. This did not include oil changes and tune-ups.

We also wrote to the United Student Information Service, which sent us much helpful material, including lists of student service organizations in major European cities, schedules of intra-European trips and information on obtaining a Student Identification Card. If you qualify for this card, it entitles you to reduced fees in entering museums, art galleries and zoos. One other economy-minded step was to get maps from friends who had been to Europe. Maps are a very expensive but necessary item in the large cities. By taking our own, which added little weight to the luggage, we saved money as well and hours of trying to find our way around.

Additional sources of information are listed in "Summing Up." You should write these before your departure to help in planning your itinerary and to facilitate a richer travel experience.

2023 Note: Of course, now we have the wonderful assets of the internet, Google and cellphones that can take care of much of the research, even on the spot. In 1973 we had to research with handwritten or typed letters and long-distance calls.

WHAT TO TAKE

The next major concern in preparing for our trip was to choose what toys and time fillers to take for the children, aware that in order to enjoy the trip ourselves we would have to make it enjoyable for them, too. Since art activities are one of their favorite pastimes, this helped limit the range of things to bring. We also wanted things that would last, having heard that European toys and paper products are expensive.

A good idea is to make vinyl toy bags for each child, which they can carry aboard the plane and fill with all their belongings along the way. We were able to make these out of one yard of vinyl fabric, a bolt end bought at an upholstery shop for $1. The bags were waterproof and held up well. We filled them with lightweight storybooks, boxes of crayons, small blackboards and chalk, large tablets, paste sticks, construction paper and a small plastic bag of yarn and beads. There is a list of games you can play in the car and some craft activities, in "Summing Up."

We added to our toy supply in England at a London Woolworths. This marvelous five-and-ten-cent store can be found throughout England. In it we bought tiny five-and-ten-cent books, scrapbooks that we filled with pictures clipped from European magazines and small games, spending a total of about $3.50. We kept some of these items aside in a surprise bag so that when the kids were bored after a long day on the road, there was always something to "fish out." Make a small fishing pole with a paper clip as a hook, and by tossing the line into the front seat the kids can pull up a new toy.

Our next concern was wardrobe. What clothes would be most appropriate for varying weather, camping needs as well as those of more formal city dress, weight and space conditions. Because our charter flight had changed destination from Frankfurt to Luxemburg, the most important consideration became packing as lightly as possible. This would make our train trip from our arrival point to Rheda-Wiedenbrück, Germany, the location of the Volkswagen factory, easier. We set to work coordinating a lightweight, all-weather wardrobe for the four of us that would fit into two medium-sized suitcases. (See the itemized wardrobe list in "Summing Up.")

2023 UPDATE: VW Westphalia campers are no longer produced in Rheda-Wiedenbrück, Germany. Don't expect to start your trip there if you plan to buy and pick up a VW van.

Wardrobe needs can of course vary. If you are traveling for a shorter length of time your wardrobe will be smaller than ours. Or, if traveling in spring, you will not need the heavy coats that added much to our weight. One lightweight, all weather coat would suffice for late spring travel; hooded sweatshirts or windbreakers would be suitable for the kids. It is a good idea to choose sweaters of dark colors for the children to avoid frequent washing. These heavier knits will take longer to dry.

Before patting ourselves on the back at how lightly we were traveling, we had to decide on what items other than clothing would be needed, such as cosmetics, camping equipment, cookware and toys. We already had good warm sleeping bags that were easily packed into two old army duffel bags. If you do not already have your own, buy them in Europe or check in discount stores at home for good buys. In the "Summing Up" section we have listed some excellent German sporting goods stores in Gutersloh where sleeping bags can be purchased.

Camping equipment of good quality is easily found in Europe, though usually costly. Despite this, we planned to purchase our needed cookware in Germany, but did manage to slip into our duffel bags dish towels, high concentrated dish soap, Tupperware cups with lids, some assorted utensils, a flashlight and sleeping-bag liners. This latter item was a good last-minute idea, as sleeping bags can get pretty smelly after six months of use. By purchasing some inexpensive flannel sheet blankets, folding them in half, sewing up the bottom and attaching bias tape ties at the top corners to tie to corresponding ties on the sleeping bag, we had washable, handy liners that provide a cleaner sleeping bag and extra warmth as well.

One last item we made for our trip was a red canvas bag, which got constant use. It was a perfect shopping bag at the marketplace and useful for picnics and as an overnight bag when somebody invited us to spend the night indoors.

The last few days before departure were a time of rearranging our luggage to accommodate suddenly remembered items or eliminate those in the end judged to be unnecessary, all the time fighting to stay under the 44-pound weight limit allowed each airline passenger. The day of departure arrived. With goodbyes said and after six hours delay* in the flight arrival, we boarded our plane weary from fatigue and excitement.

* A benefit of our departure delay in Los Angeles was the opportunity we had to talk to fellow travelers, especially one family from Switzerland who had just ended a cross-country camping adventure in the USA. They were a delightful family and after 6 hours of talking and sharing snacks we boarded our charter flight to Europe together with an invitation from them to visit the family in Bern, Switzerland, when we got there. Their invitation proved to be a blessing towards the latter part of our journey.

SUMMING UP MAKING PLANS

SUGGESTED STEPS IN PREPARING TO LEAVE

Now that you have made the decision to go, here are a few steps you might follow in preparation for departure:

- » Order your camp mobile and make arrangements for payment. We put a $1000 deposit on our car and then paid the first six months' payments in advance so that we would not have to worry about this during our trip.
- » Initiate insurance policy, car or health, or both. (See insurance page)
- » Take care of all correspondence in advance. (Check the where-to-write section)
- » Initiate passport application at your local post office. It takes from six to nine weeks to process unless you live in a city where there is a passport office. Make sure you have a properly validated birth certificate.

» Receive any necessary vaccinations and have vaccination card stamped by the county health office in your area. (See travel documents section.)

» Start planning your wardrobe. (See clothing section.)

» Gather good-for-travel craft materials; lightweight, un-messy, versatile.

» Prepare your children for their new adventure by reading to them about children in different lands and special places you are going to see. See the children's librarian at your local library for guidance.

» Dream like mad; it may soon be a reality.

WHERE TO WRITE FOR INFORMATION

NOTE: We deleted this part of the original book as most of it was not applicable information today and any information you do need is easily attainable on the internet.

We also deleted the section about Arthur Frommer's $5-a-day club, which no longer exists. At the time, Frommer's seminal book, *Europe on 5 Dollars a Day*, changed the way Americans traveled, and foreshadowed such later budget-conscious guidebooks as *Lonely Planet* and Rick Steves' books. Arthur Frommer was generally acknowledged to be the nation's foremost travel authority. In 1975, *Europe on 10 Dollars a Day* was published, after our book came out.

Arrival and on to Scandinavia

We arrived in Luxemburg exhausted after a long but smooth flight. Happily, the children had been great, either sleeping or coloring most of the way. The train trip from Luxemburg to Rheda-Wiedenbrück where we were to pick up our VW, took about seven hours and required five train changes, an exhausting ordeal. Then there were the inevitable formalities at the office of the Volkswagen factory before the car was released to us. When at last *Miss Sunshine*, as the children named our bright and shiny yellow van, was before us, our spirits were revived. We opened her doors, made up the bed and parked in a shady spot in the camping area provided by the factory. Due to the time change in our Atlantic crossing, we were exhausted and quickly fell asleep.

Sher, Gary and kids ready to go with their new VW van,
at Westphaliawerk, Germany 1972

Plan on not scheduling too much heavy driving for the first few days, as you will find it takes your body a few days to adjust.

We spent the following morning at the Volkswagen factory, Westphaliawerk, getting our belongings organized, talking to other campers and picking up many valuable tips on campsites, how to handle German drivers (whose reputation on the road is notorious even amongst themselves) and where to find the various camping items needed. One helpful hint noted in observing experienced campers was to put a paper-towel holder into the back wall over the rear seat. Paper towels proved to be a great asset. They were used for everything from toilet tissue to wipe cloths for spilled milk.

We soon discovered that organization was the key to happy camping in a VW camp mobile. Because our living space had decreased from a three-bedroom house to a four-by-six-foot space, it took us a good two weeks and lots of petty arguments before finding the best way to organize the limited space. It was necessary to maintain an extra good sense of humor when, each night upon sliding back the rear side door, we were confronted with the "nursery" where oodles of artistic creations had been produced during the day's drive and now paper scraps, broken crayons and doll clothes decorated the floor. A small whiskbroom purchased at a German supermarket proved an invaluable tool for quickly scooping up all scraps and playthings into the toy bags. The next step in our nightly routine was to shift the suitcases stored behind the rear seat during the day to the front seat, usually set up during the meal preparation. This way the girls could climb up to their bunk and look at books while dinner was cooking, though this time was often spent running around outside discovering some new animal, meeting a new playmate or wading in a nearby stream.

We feel you should be prepared from the outset for the inevitable frustrations of adapting to a new life on wheels. Once adjusted to the small living quarters you will learn to laugh at what in the beginning upset you, like the tipping over of the potty bucket just before stopping to empty it. By the way, get one! We found it to be an absolute necessity when a turnout was nowhere in sight and the girls called out in anxious tones "I can't wait." Purchase a small plastic bucket with a lid. At a sporting goods store buy a half-gallon of concentrated toilet disinfectant. By placing a small amount of this diluted with water in the bucket, odors can be avoided.

UPDATE NOTES: We've changed the title to *Arrival* in order to include Germany where we picked up our VW camp mobile before heading to Scandinavia. The original title of this chapter, decided by our publisher, was just "Scandinavia." Rheda-Wiedenbrück is a suburb in North Rhine-Westphalia of about 21,300 residents. We also changed this as the original book just called this Wiedenbrück, which is not correct.

GÜTERSLOH

Before setting out for Scandinavia we went into Gütersloh, a small German town 15 minutes from Rheda-Wiedenbrück and found an excellent sporting goods store just off the main street. We walked out one-half hour later, 100 dollars poorer, but fully equipped for the camping venture ahead. (See "Summing Up" for the supplies you will want to purchase). We stopped for a lunch snack at a local restaurant called Rohner's Grill, suggested by a young German boy who had told us it had low to moderate prices. For us it was expensive though and suggests that if your $10-a-day maximum is serious, you settle for a stein of cold beer and lemonade for the children there. Then, after picking up some food items at a local grocery store, prepare a hearty and low-cost picnic at the local park.

Shopping at first will be a frustrating experience. After a while you learn to identify the pictures on the labels instead of trying to translate each and every word from your dictionary. We found buying fresh produce and meat was the easiest as we could just point to identify if language was a problem. Also, you begin to have favorites, which you can recognize in any store. A favorite in Germany for all of us was the canned red kraut. Along with a couple of bratwursts (fat, juicy sausages) a green salad and fruit and cheese for dessert, you have a good hearty meal that costs far less than in a restaurant.

UPDATE NOTE: There are still several excellent sporting goods stores in Gütersloh, which may or may not be relevant for you if not picking up a camper nearby. The VW factory is no longer there.

GÜTERSLOH TO HAMBURG

With full stomachs and well equipped, we left Gütersloh and took the main road to Hamburg via the road to Paderborn. By five o'clock, feeling weary from still trying to adjust to the time change that had taken place during our transit from America, we looked for the nearest campsite, **Nadermann's Tierpark**, a beautiful campground with its own zoo. What a perfect place for two little girls just beginning to get fidgety after a three-hour drive in the car. There are baby boars, coyotes, lion cubs, birds and rodents. There is also an outdoor play area equipped with swings, slides, seesaws and rocking horses. It met the girls' need to use some of the energy stored up in the car.

Tiffany and Dawn loved their front seat hammock
sleeping quarters, at least for a while!

We noticed months later that their capacity for staying in the car lengthened and they could travel for five hours without stopping.

One of the interesting aspects of our first night camping was observing the style of European campers. They see no charm in roughing it as we naïve Americans often do, but rather believe in taking all the comforts along. The usual vehicle is a caravan or, as we would call it, a trailer. When stopped, an elaborate canvas awning or whole tent is attached at one side. Tiny picket fences are put up to outline one's territory and often curtains even bedeck the plastic-paned window of the tent. Though enjoyable to observe, we concluded that our preference was for the mobility of the van, even if it was a bit cramped at times.

The next morning, we hastily left for Hamburg, arriving at eight in the evening after a midday break and a few photo taking stops (German freeways are well equipped with pull offs, often having restrooms and picnic tables, which we appreciated immensely). Tired and anxious to find a campground for the night, we learned a lesson that you should make a cardinal rule: *never wait to find a spot until after dark, especially upon your arrival in a large foreign city.* Fortunately, after some frustration we did find a place, thanks to the *American Automobile Association Camping and Caravanning Atlas.* This campground may not have been the best place in Hamburg, but it did meet our immediate needs for one night. The following morning upon viewing Hamburg we concluded that most families would not want to spend more than one night in the city anyway.

This somewhat typified our view of most of the large industrial European cities. With children they were hectic and, probably, even without children. In the cities much time was wasted trying to find our way around, leaving little time to see anything or meet anyone. The real charm and flavor of Europe exists in the small towns and villages, and in the clean open air of the countryside. However, if you do, like us, get stuck in Hamburg one night, you'll find a free city campground at Kielerstrasse 620. Consult a Hamburg map and find Kronsaalsweg; it is a right turn after that. Do not eat in a

Hamburg restaurant, for most of them are much too expensive on a $10-a-day budget. Shop in one of the many supermarkets and prepare your own meals. You'll have an opportunity to sample German cuisine in a countryside *gashouse*, a small inn or hotel, which is far cheaper.

Window shopping with Sher, Dawn and Tiffany in Germany

DENMARK

ODENSE

We left Hamburg, sunny skies still with us, and headed over flat, low green farmlands towards Kolding, Denmark, crossing a beautiful bridge to the island of Funen and the town of Odense, home of Hans Christian Andersen. The girls had been anticipating this visit ever since we had first read *The Ugly Duckling* to them and explained

30

that someday they would visit the home of its originator. It proved a wonderful visit for adults as well as children. Everywhere we went in Odense, it was as if we were in one of Andersen's fairy tales. We would recommend spending at least several days or even a week in this delightful town.

The Hans Christian Andersen Museum is located on Hans Jensensstroede. The children loved seeing the museum and surprisingly retained much about it. A later purchase of a book in English of all of Andersen's fairy tales became a favorite bedtime treat in the camp mobile, often inspiring comments on something they had seen in Odense. Across the street from the museum is a small antique shop whose owner spent much time showing us his shop and his woodworking and metal forging workshop.

After our visit to the museum we strolled the charming streets, found a Danish hot dog stand, and after buying a *polser* (an inexpensive pork hot dog) for each of us, lemonade and a delicious Danish pastry at a nearby pastry shop, we picnicked in the large city park in the center of the

Dawn and Tiffany at the door of the Hans Christian Anderson house in Copenhagen, Denmark

town. There was a play area there, which gave us a chance to read and discuss our itinerary while the girls played with some Danish children. Our enjoyable and tasty lunch had cost us about $1.75, a surprisingly low-cost meal for an otherwise expensive country. We soon learned that picnics were the most economical choice throughout Scandinavia where restaurant eating was prohibitive with our budget.

The **Funen Village** is also highly recommended. Erected in the 1940s this open-air museum depicts the life of Funen Island for the

31

past few hundred years. Typical buildings have been moved from other parts of the island, with thatched-roof cottages, mills and rural stores lining the streets. Farm livestock, including hens, geese and pigs roam in the village, and gardens and rows of hops typify a now fading rural lifestyle.

The camping in Odense is remarkably comfortable, also, being near the center of town but with a country like atmosphere. The campground, **Odensevej 102**, is on road A-9 in the direction of Svendborg. Each parking place is grassy and surrounded by large shrubberies making it quite private. There is play equipment for the children and, though not open in the fall, a large swimming pool. Also, there is a bathhouse where one can take free hot showers. We were soon to find this was a rare occurrence, for usually in European campgrounds one either has to go without or to pay for the privilege of showering. We became very adept at inner-car familial sponge baths; in fact, our typically American shower-a-day philosophy can be regarded as rather a fetish. An alternative to sponge bathing and the either dribbling or absent campground shower is the public bathhouse. In many major European cities reasonably-priced public bathhouses can be found where one can shower for little cost and with convenience and comfort. Tourist information offices will be able to direct you to these welcome sights.

We left Odense, sadly wishing we had allotted more time there, but had to keep to our schedule due to a previous commitment to visit relatives in Sweden. At this point it should be stressed how important it is not to have too confining an itinerary. Time and again you will be tempted to follow a country lane or a new friend, a flexibility you should allow yourself if adventure is what you are seeking. The rewards of such spontaneous travel will be many. Also, if you follow your and the children's moods and feelings and stop for four or five days in one place, you will not only experience more but feel better.

COPENHAGEN

From the island of Funen, we took a ferry to Sjaelland and drove from the landing across rolling green hills, past thatched-roofed houses and glistening lakes to Kobenhavn or, as we spell it, Copenhagen. It is important to know the foreign spellings when watching for signpost along a speeding autoroute. It can be most distressing if one is looking for the names in English, for they are nowhere to be found. Upon arrival in the city we decided to try and spend the night indoors as light showers were threatening. Luckily, we had read about **Kiosk P** located in the Central Train Station where one can go in search of fairly inexpensive lodging, often in the home of a Danish family. Be prepared to stand in a line and also be specific about your financial limitations. The reservations clerks all speak English beautifully, so communication is not a barrier. However, we did meet several couples that, much to their chagrin, were put up in rather expensive, shabby city hotels. We were lucky and stayed at a wonderful Danish home we highly recommend, in spite of its slightly out-of-the-way location. It was the suburban home of the Eric Leisner family. The atmosphere there was marvelous for the children, and the Leisners quickly accepted the role of much-missed grandparents. The accommodations were also far better than many we heard about, for we had private quarters: a tiny garden cottage with a small kitchen and our own bathroom complete with large bathtub. Nearly luxury accommodation for only $5 per night. The kitchen was truly a budget saver, allowing us to stretch our money and stay longer.

There are many things to do in Copenhagen and of course the famed **Tivoli Gardens** was first on our list. Regretfully, we found it expensive and tiring, and much like Disneyland, which we could see at home. The **Copenhagen Zoo,** on the other hand, was one of the best we saw in Europe, with a special little children's zoo where the girls could pet the goats and other animals. After our visit to the zoo, we stopped at a small restaurant across the street and had a *smorrebrød* (an open-faced sandwich). Though we enjoyed them, the kids preferred the camp mobile cuisine, another reason for avoiding the expense of too much dining out.

Another recommended visit is to the **Carlsberg Brewery** where all of us were fascinated with watching the brewing of beer. The free tour lasts about one and a half hours and ends in the tasting room where beer is served to the adults and soft drinks to the children.

Sher with Dawn and Tiffany in front of Elephant Sculpture at Carlsberg Brewery, Copenhagen, Denmark

Being interested in the crafts of each country, we were happy to learn about Mrs. Godrun Harder who conducts small tours through the studios of local craftsmen (see **Summing Up**). The number of people allowed on each tour is six, and visits are made to two or three studios during an afternoon between two and six o'clock, except Saturday and Sunday. Though the fee is a bit high, $6 per person if there are only one or two visitors, $5 if there are three or four, and $4.50 with five or six, it proved worth it. This is something you may want to do individually if one of you has a particular interest in handicrafts.

We often found the best way to see special things more to the tastes of an adult was for one of us to volunteer to take the children for two or three hours while the other could see something he or she wished. There is also always the possibility of getting a babysitter if you have been particularly good with your budget. In Copenhagen, call Babysitters-Studenternes. These are student babysitters and reputed to be most reliable. Their fees are a bit higher that those normally paid in the United States, 75 cents to $1.25 per hour, so you will have to consider this a big splurge. But you just may be ready for an hour or two away from the children.

2023 Note: Our attitude in 1972 regarding fees for babysitters shocked us when re-reading our book. We are believers of "fair wages." For the times, I guess, 50 cents to 75 cents an hour for babysitters was considered fair.

HELSINGÖR

It was soon time to head north to Helsingör and Hamlet's Castle, one of the most enjoyable castles to visit with the children. After your visit, picnic on the beautiful beach outside the castle and enjoy the view of the channel, which separates Denmark from Sweden. That night after crossing the channel by ferry, we camped outside Helsingborg, Sweden, at a seaside campground. It was a pleasure to drive on the Swedish highways the next morning, after having driven on those in Germany. The Swedes have a tightly controlled highway system with a maximum speed limit of 90 kilometers per hour. Swedish drivers were far more considerate and less erratic than we had found German drivers to be.

SWEDEN

MALMÖ

Our next few days were joyfully spent at the home of Swedish relatives in Malmö. One really begins to learn about a foreign culture when he or she can visit private homes. If you do not already have contacts in some of the European countries, we highly suggest you go out of your way to foster friendships with Europeans while traveling. You will learn much about a country's customs and cuisine this way. In some of the countries there are special programs that arrange visits in the home of a national, such as Kiosk P in Copenhagen. Ask about these kinds of programs at the local tourist offices.

Highlights in the city of Malmö are the old sector of the town with its brick and half-timbered buildings, the Malmö Museum and the parks. It was in the old sector that we found the interesting art shops, such as **Art Form**, which specializes in the beautiful contemporary Scandinavian designs in glassware, textiles, pottery and wood. While in this section also visit **Charlotte Weibull's Doll Shop**, a famous shop where one can not only delight in hundreds of handmade dolls, but also in miniature doll furniture and fully decorated doll houses. The girls found a doll representing Pippi Longstockings, the famous storybook character of Scandinavia created by Swedish writer Astrid Lindgren. This prompted the idea of buying one storybook in each country we visited, which was not only an education, but also an added time filler for the road. Even if we could not always get them in English, the girls enjoyed spending the hours going over the pictures in a new book. Reading the adventures of Pippi Longstockings filled many an hour as we sped along the beautiful Swedish highways.

FALSTERBO

If you have time to visit the southwest region of Sweden, we suggest you drive to the beautiful seaside village of Falsterbo. This town typifies the region called Skåne (pronounced *scone-eh*). The sand there is white and the tiny-whitewashed village houses suggest the provincial atmosphere of old Sweden. The beach is an ideal play area for the children and provides a good chance to release some of the stored energy from being in the camp mobile. You might start a seashell collection here and add to it as you visit other European beaches. Children love to collect things and can also use small shells, along with their tube of glue and construction paper, to construct collages.

You might even let them gather a small container of sand that you can color with food coloring and sprinkle onto the collages like glitter. It was also in this village that we decided to collect wildflowers from each country, press them between the pages of our journal and bring them home to make a collage representing our adventures. The girls delighted in finding the most unusual flowers for the collection in each country. Things we noted in this region are the very stylized architecture of the old churches and the tombstones in the church graveyards dating back to the 10ᵗʰ century. The symbols of the region are the goose and the willow tree, and everywhere one sees both.

On our way north to Norway we made two major stops of interest: one to visit **Gothenburg** and the other to see the **Viking rock drawings.** The latter is something one could easily miss without good directions. Taking the coastal Route E-6 north, watch for the blue and white signs saying *Mineva* (meaning National Historical Monument) marking the spot of many Viking burial areas and the rock drawings near Tanum. To reach Tanum you must go about 60 kilometers north of the town of Uddevalla. Once in Tanum take the little road just beyond the church and to the left of the main road. The rock carvings are marvelous, typically Scandinavian in design, suggesting the simplicity of line so characteristic of contemporary art forms, though done hundreds of years ago. The kids also enjoyed climbing among the huge rocks.

GOTHENBURG

Gothenburg is a large seaport city and home of one of the grandest children's parks we were to visit in all of Europe, **Slottsskogen Park.** In the center of this verdant city park is a play place and a children's zoo. We spent a whole day in the park and the kids thoroughly enjoyed it. There is also a small city-operated recreation building where children can do nature crafts. At the other side of the park is the **Natural History Museum,** full of items interesting both to children and adults. There is a huge whale carcass in one room and rooms and rooms of stuffed animals. Be sure and allow enough time for a tour of the museum; get there before two o'clock, at least, as it closes at four.

Tiffany makes a new Swedish friend at the park in Gothenburg

A good place to go upon arriving in Gothenburg is the old **Dickson Palace**, which houses the *Västkustens Turistrafikförbund* (the West Coast Tourist Traffic Association), where you can obtain general information and learn of weekly events. For example, while we were in Gothenburg, we were able to visit a home craft show featuring the crafts of every region of Sweden, an annual event. If interested, you can write the Tourist Traffic Office to find out in which Swedish city this event will be held when you are there and perhaps fit it into your itinerary.

Sightseeing attractions in Gothenburg are many. Besides the wonderful Slottsskogen Park, we found the following to be most interesting for the children as well as adults: **The Ethnographical, Historical and Archaeological Museum,** housed in what used to be the premises of the Old East India Company that once sent pilgrims to America; **Paddan** for tours of the canals and harbors; the **Liseberg Amusement**

Park, reputed to be the loveliest in Europe with its beautiful flowerbeds; the **Lilla Bommen**, where a four-masted Viking ship, now a sea cadet training school, lies berthed; and the **Maritime Museum and Aquarium** with its lofty campanile erected in memory of the seamen who lost their lives in the First World War. Also of interest is the fish quay where fish are auctioned every morning at 7 am. If you arise early, this is a good place to pick up seafood for an economical meal. We found cod to be very good and easily prepared by frying it in butter.

Gothenburg taught us much about Swedish cities, especially how very uneconomical they can be. Parking for one thing is expensive. In the case of Gothenburg, it is best to park outside the town center in the areas known as the Sten Sturegatan or Gamla Ullevi. It is only a 10- or 15-minute walk from these to the town center, good exercise and good on the budget. When putting coins in the meters, be careful to use the right slot. In the following areas the rate is about 19 cents for a full day: Pilgatan, Friggagatan at Svingeln, Gamla Ullevi, and the major parts of the parking area east of Sten Sturegatan.

Some additional things should be mentioned before we move on to Norway. For those who love exploring nature and the outdoor life of fishing, hiking and camping, consider visiting one of Sweden's many beautiful national parks. For a handy map of where they are located and detailed information about each one, write to the Swedish Forest Service. You might want to check with them before planning your itinerary for Sweden. There are also a couple of items we found in this country's supermarkets that were most helpful. The Swedish have packaged handy disposable washcloths, which we found a great help in wiping up messes as well as kids' faces. A food item that is available and very good is the packaged rosehip soup, which makes a delicious and nutritious prepared dessert.

We were lucky to have family friends in Gothenburg with two little boys the same age as our daughters. They had a great time playing together at the Slottsskogen Park.

Playing with family friend's kids in Slottsskogen Park,
in Gothenburg, Sweden

NORWAY

FREDRIKSTAD

Our first stop in Norway was just beyond the Swedish-Norwegian border, Fredrikstad, where the **Plus Colony** of artists and craftsmen is located. We arrived in this craftsmen's town in the morning and spent the day browsing in the tiny shops and watching a few of the artisans at work in the old sector just off the square. A small stretch of ground down at the water's edge makes a good picnic spot, and across the street from this is a small fish market and grocery where we made our first purchase of whale meat for that night's dinner. Watch closely for the market as it is easily missed, being in a cellar, down a few steps from the sidewalk. The word for whale meat is "val" and it tastes much like beef with a bit of a wild flavor that is not at all fishy. It made an economical stew. Whale meat, along with the great variety of fish in the markets, became our mainstay while in Norway.

OSLO

After a three-hour drive, we arrived in Oslo and drove to **Bogstad Camping,** located on a hill overlooking the city. The campground is easy to find, being well indicated with signs all along the road. This was one of the best campgrounds we had stayed in so far, in terms of cleanliness, environmental beauty and conveniences.

Looking back, we feel Oslo was one of the few large cities we did enjoy in Europe. It was easy to get around and filled with natural beauty, plus many interesting things to see and do for the whole family. That first morning we headed for **Bygdöy Peninsula,** a 15-minute drive from the Bogstad campground, to visit the **Norwegian Folk Museum** and other sights. We arrived just in time to see a large group of children brightly dressed in Norwegian costumes entering the museum. This was a special festival day during which the children would be performing Norwegian folk dances in the outdoor theater, a special treat for all of us. Later we first watched an exhibition of antique bicycles being ridden by people costumed in outfits of the age, and then walked through buildings filled with Norwegian artifacts. The most interesting building for us was the one flank-ing the courtyard in which there was a room of old dolls, doll houses, rocking horses, children's furni-ture and clothing. Walking around the folk museum is like visiting lovely woods in a wild park; in fact, much of the museum is wooded walkways along which have been placed reconstructed buildings, houses and stave churches from various re-gions of Norway.

An exhibition of antique bicycles at the Norwegian Folk Museum

41

We loved visiting the Folk Museum, where we saw Norwegian folk dancers perform in the outdoor theater

From the Norwegian Folk Museum, it is only a few short blocks to the **Viking Ship Hall** with its display of Viking ships. The children enjoyed seeing the ships but were quickly bored by the many displays of ancient tools and implements. You might plan on letting the children play in the park of the Norwegian Folk Museum while you take turns visiting the museum.

If you don't feel like cooking, try one of the many low-cost, cafeteria-type restaurants located in the center of Oslo. At the **Kaffistova** at Stortorvet 8 we had a hearty meal for about $5 for four. It is not fancy, but a perfect place for children with a good selection of meat and potato entrees.

On the way back to the campground, stop at the **Frogner Park** to see the **Vigeland sculptures.** At the turn of the century, Gustav Vigeland proposed to the city of Oslo that if they would support him during his lifetime, he would fill a city park with sculptures showing man in all his triumph and anguish. The offer was accepted and Vigeland more than fulfilled his promise. This park is something one should not miss while in Oslo. There are several

**At Frogner Park, playing on the steps of
Vigeland Sculptures, Oslo, Norway**

children's play areas throughout the park and it's a pleasant place
for a picnic, too.

The outdoor market on the wharf in Oslo is the most economical
and a fun place to shop. The children were fascinated with the many
different types of fish on display. After shopping you might buy a
bag of shrimp on the quay in front of the Town Hall and seat yourself along the wharf with the Norwegians, relishing the taste of the
freshly cooked shellfish. Our children soon mastered the technique
of snapping off the shells and eating the shrimp, too, while dangling
their feet over the wharf and watching the boats.

Don't miss the **Edvard Munch Museum** while in Oslo. It contains
almost the complete life work of Munch, Norway's best-known
contemporary artist, housed in a beautiful building at Töyengate 53.
The collection, though, will probably quickly bore the children, so
take turns visiting it. There is also a nursery held there each Monday
from 10 am when the museum is closed. This is a good place to leave
the children to play with other children for a couple of hours while
you go off sightseeing in the area.

BERGEN

The trip from Oslo to Bergen is spectacular. The first night on this drive through the beautiful Norwegian mountains to Bergen we camped outside the small town of Gol in a wooded area next to a rushing river. After building a campfire and hanging out our wash on a tree it felt like we were back in California on a summer camping trip. The rest of the three-day journey was full of dramatic scenery, from gorgeous waterfalls that fall straight into crystal-clear fjords to rolling hills covered with first snows. Meeting sheep on the windy mountain roads is not unheard of, and one learns to be patient and wait until they clear out of the way.

Sheep blocked our way on the road to Bergan. Gary and the girls enjoyed watching them.

Once in Bergen we found a beautiful camping spot right on a fjord, **Grimen at Helldal** just 15 kilometers from the city center. Similar to many of the campgrounds in Europe, one can also rent small huts with accommodations for two to six persons. This does offer an alternative if the camp mobile is getting tight and kids and parents need a break for a day or two. The cabins are not elaborate and thus, reasonably priced.

Camping near Bergen, Norway

While in Bergen, we took a ride on the funicular to the top of **Mount Floien** and walked along lovely wooded paths enjoying the view of the city. An afternoon visit to the Bergen Aquarium, filled with fascinating marine life, was fun, too, though not a must unless you have time and feel the budget will withstand the rather high admission fee.

One evening we decided to splurge on a big, typical Norwegian dinner at the local **Bristol Hotel**. Though savory, it turned out to be a drastic mistake. We relished the buffet of a variety of interesting foods including pickled raw herring, pickled pigs' feet, delicious cream-filled pastries and rich sauces, but our stomachs reacted violently to these new delicacies. All we can say for this experience is that it is another reason to save your money and fix meals in the car. That way your stomachs do not have to readjust to such sudden changes in diet and the whole trip becomes more pleasant.

In Oslo we stopped at the American Express office to check the cost of taking a ferry from Bergen to Newcastle, England. We made reservations and paid $110 for four plus the car, which included a second-class cabin. Deck chairs would have been less, but they were sold out. Later we were happy we had the cabin, for sitting up all night with the children in a deck chair would have been very uncomfortable. Our well-equipped cabin was worth the extra $20 it cost us, an extravagance we made up for with a few very budget-conscious days in England where food costs are much lower than in Scandinavia.

Dawn and Tiffany had fun rolling down a hill in Bergan, Norway and then picking a bouquet of wildflowers for Miss Sunshine.

SUMMING UP SCANDINAVIA

When giving admission charges for the Scandinavian countries where there are not individual listings for adults and children, the figure given is total for our family of four. For Denmark, prices are given computed at the exchange rate of 7.45 kroner to $1. In the Swedish section, prices are computed at 5.18 kroner to $1. Prices in Norway are computed at the exchange rate of 7.15 kroner to $1.

DENMARK

ODENSE, FUNEN

Camping

Odensevej 102, Route A9 in the direction of Swendborg. Play equipment, hot showers, swimming pool. Admission: $1.50 for one night.

Tourist Information Office, Located in the Town Hall, at Flakhaven in the center of town; telephone (09) 12-75-20. Hours during tourist season; daily 9 am to 9 pm, Sunday 10 am–noon and 5:30 pm–9 pm. Off-season hours: weekdays 9 am to 5 pm, Sunday 9 am–noon

Post Office Lille Grabrødrestroede 1; telephone (09) 12-04-83

Launderettes

Økembråten vasketeria, Nordalveien 79: telephone 22-55-90.
Kladbakken Vasketeria, Kaldbakkstubben 11; telephone 25-22-76
Tokerud Vasketeria, Tante Ulrikkes vei 32D; telephone 25-36-76

Hans Christian Anderson's Childhood Home, Munkemø Llestroede 3-5, Open April–September, 10 am–5 pm, October–March, noon–3 pm. Admission: $1.50

Hans Christian Anderson Museum, Hans Jensensstroede 39-43. Open April–May, 10 am to 5:30 pm; May 15–May 31, 9 am–5 pm; June, July and August, 9 am to 9 pm; September 1–September 15, 9 am to 8 pm; September 16–September 30, 10 am to 5 pm; rest of the year, 10 am to 3 pm. Admission: 68 cents.

The Funen Village, Sejerskovvej (bus line No. 2). Open April 10 am–5:30 pm; May, 10 am–7:30 pm; June–July, 10 am–8:30 pm; August 1–August 15, 10 am–7:30 pm; August 16–August 31, 10 am–6:30 pm; September, 10 am–5:30 pm; October, 10 am–4:30 pm and November–March on holidays only.

Odense Zoo, Sadr. Boulevard 320 (bus line 3). Open all year 9 am–sunset.

Cruising on the Odense River. Services available May 1–September 15. Daily departures Munke Mose to Zoo/Tivoli and Funen Village. Detailed information available at the tourist bureau office or telephone 13-03-83 from 10 am–8pm.

Stokkebyes Tobacco Museum, Overgade 20; telephone (09)12-0051. Open 8 am–4:30pm; closed Saturday. Conducted tours given May–September, Monday–Friday at 2 pm. At other times by special appointment only.

Open-Air Swimming, Elsesmindevej 5; telephone (09) 11-42-90

Indoor Swimming, Klosterbakken 5; telephone (09) 11-90-90

Odense Tennis Club, Aadalen, Sadr. Boulevard 172; telephone (09) 12-17-03

Odense Rowing Club, Lamalvej 160; telephone (09) 12-28-01

Odense Sailing Club, Østre Kanalvej 10; telephone (09) 12-04-23

Shopping Den Røde Butch-H. Daniel Hansen, across from the Hans Christian Andersen Museum, for woodcarving and copper work.

The Hans Christian Andersen Festival held every year from July 5–August 9. Live performances of Andersen's fairy tales. For more information and reservations write to the Tourist Bureau, Town Hall, Odense.

Special Expenses Ferry from Funen to Sjaelland $7 for camp mobile, two adults and two children.

COPENHAGEN

Camping Information Danish Camping Union, Gammel Kongevej 74; telephone (01) 21-06-00

Camping

Absalon, nine kilometers from city center off E66 to Roskilde at Rodovre. Open all year. Admission: Adults 55 cents, no charge for car.

Naerum, Ravnebakken, on Copenhagen-Helsingör road, 13 kilometers from Copenhagen. Open May 1–September 1. Admission: Adults 55 cents, no charge for car.

Staying with a Danish Family Go to Kiosk P in the Central Station on Vesterbrogade. There is a small booking fee.

Tourist Information Office at Banegardspladsen 7, in the Central Station; telephone 11-14-15. Open May–September 9 am–6 pm, closed Sunday; January–April, 9 am–5 pm, Saturday 9 am–noon, closed Sunday.

Post Office in Central Station. Open 8 am–11 pm daily, except Friday and Sunday, 8 am–9 pm.

Supermarkets, The Irma chain

Launderettes

Quick-Vask, 45 Istedgade, at the side of the Central Station. Seventy cents for a six-kilo machine load. Attendant until 6 pm on weekdays, 1 pm on Saturday.

Vasketeria, 2 Borgergade, in vicinity of Kongens Nytorv. Eighty-five cents for nine kilos of wash. Open 24 hours.

Babysitting Babysitters-Studenternes, Martensens Alle 5A; telephone 22-30-38, 22-24-36 or 22-38-48. Open daily from 8 am–9 pm.

Renting a Bike Cycling is fun in Copenhagen where for so many of the Danes this is the major means of transportation. Kobenhavn's Cykle-bors at 157 Gothersgade near the parade grounds of Rosenborg Castle is the cheapest. Rental fees for regular bikes are 70 cents per day, $1.10 for a weekend and $2.05 for a week. A deposit of $2.75 is required.

The Stroget (pronounced *stro-yet*) is Copenhagen's mile-long shopping street maintained for pedestrians only. Be sure to watch for the vendor (pushing an antique baby carriage) of the children's magazine "Strawberry Fizz."

Tivoli Gardens The amusement park, between the Central Station and Town Hall Square. Admission before 2 pm is 14 cents; after 2 pm, 27 cents on weekdays and 39 cents on Saturday and Sunday. Open from May 1–mid September.

Evening Entertainment at Tivoli:
7:40 Pantomime on the Peacock Stage to the left of the main entrance: free.
9:45 Modern ballet on Peacock Stage: free.
Midnight Fireworks three times a week, on Wednesday, Saturday and Sunday. A bit late for the kids.

Breweries
Carlsberg, 40 Ny Carlsbergvej (tram No. 10 or S-train to Enghave Station). Weekday tours only from 11 am–2:30 pm; free.

Tuborg, 54 Strandvej (bus No.1 from center of town or bus No.21). Weekday tours only from 8:30 am–2:30 pm; free.

The Little Mermaid Stroll along the harbor and see Hans Christian Andersen's Little Mermaid sculpture and the old harbor shops and historic houses. Summers only, take the "Mermaid Bus" (one-way fare, 16 cents) leaving from the bus port on Hans Christian Andersen Boulevard (corner of Studiestraede, one block from Town Hall Square). First bus leaves at 9:30 am and then at half-hour intervals until 8:30 pm. Bus marked "Langeline."

Ny Carlsberg Glyptotek Primarily a museum of modern art and sculpture, the Glyptotek also houses an impressive collection of ancient art. It is located on Dantes Plades off Hans Christian Andersen Boulevard across the street from the back entrance of Tivoli. Open daily May–October, 10 am–5 pm; November–April weekdays, 1–3 pm and Sunday, 10 am–4 pm. Admission is 48 cents; free on Wednesday and Sunday.

Copenhagen Zoo Located at Roskildevej 32. From Carlsberg Brewery walk up Vesterfaelledvej to Verterbrogade, turn left and go straight crossing Pile Alle. You will find the entrance to the zoo on your right. Take Bus No. 28 or No. 41 via Kongens Nytorv and Town Hall Square daily until 9 pm.

The Cirkus Shumann (Circus), on Axeltorv, one block from Town Hall Square. Matinees on Wednesday, Saturday and Sunday at 4 pm; evenings at 8 pm. Prices range from $1.25 to $3.80.

Shopping There's no charge for looking (window shopping is the best buy here). Follow the Stroget that runs from Town Hall Square to Kongens Nytorv and look for the following shops: Georg Jensen (silversmith), Royal Copenhagen (porcelain) and Illum's Bolighus (department store). *Den Permanente* (The Permanent Exhibition) is two blocks from the airline terminal on Vesterbrogade. An exhibition of art and craft items from all of Denmark, chosen for their craftsmanship by a special committee and offered for sale.

Meet the Danish Artist Tours Contact Gudrun E. Harder, 6 Annettevej, Charlottenlund 2920; telephone OR 8317.

CHILDREN'S VACATIONS IN DENMARK

If you want to "park your children" and have the budget to do it, Denmark is the country. You may want to see some of the many sites we discussed on your own and then rejoin the family for the remainder of the trip. In the meantime, the kids can have their own separate adventure.

Note: times are different now. We would not think of "parking our children" now, nor leaving them with babysitting services.

Camp for three to six weeks Camp Viking for boys and girls 8 to 15 years old is situated at Asserbo, Frederiksvaerk, 60 kilometers north of Copenhagen in the heart of Danish vacationland. The first period is from June 30 to July 19; the second from July 21 to August 7. There is an American director, Mrs. Sigrid B. Ott. The camp fee is $220 per period, with each additional period costing $210. For further information write Camp Viking, Asserbo, Frederiksvaerk, Denmark.

A one-week children's vacation on horseback The Jutland Riding Institute at Vejle offers summer-camp riding courses for children. The participants live and eat at the Athletic School of Jutland. Half an hour away is a real wild-west vacation center for children from age 7 to 16 years on a 70-acre farm. It is open from June 1 to August 31 and the participants of the camps change every Sunday. Arrive Sunday at noon; depart the following Sunday morning. Price is $57 per week, all-inclusive. For further information write Jydsk Rideinstitut, Box 55, DK-7100 Vehke Denmark, or Wild West Center, The Sherriff's Office, DK-6623 Vorbasse, Denmark.

One week on a Danish Farm at Aarhus, on the Peninsula of Jutland. The price is $5 a day, including full board. English is spoken on the farm. For further information write Aarhus Tourist Office, Raddhuset, Aarhus, Denmark.

Special Sites for Children

Legoland, located at Billund, Jutland, 20 kilometers west of Vejle and 75 kilometers from the thousand-year-old town of Ribe. This new playland for children covers about 10 acres of land laid out as a park with lakes and watercourses, all illuminated in the evenings. The center of Legoland is an area of towns, villages, railways and harbors constructed in miniature, giving children the feeling of being in a toy land as they walk in the streets. The outer area has a road system where children drive electric cars on realistic roads in correct traffic surroundings and may obtain a Lego land driver's license as proof of their ability. Moreover, the park has playgrounds, both indoor and outdoor, with and without supervision, where children may find an outlet for their imagination and need for activity. An exhibition hall shows changing collections of models built of Lego toys and big panoramas illustrate some of Hans Christian Andersen's best-know fairy tales. Another of the many highlights is the antique doll collection consisting of more than 300 dolls in doll-size interiors from the 16th to the 19th centuries. In a separate section there is a Lego land theater, with about 200 seats for plays, ballet, films, music and marionette shows. Legoland is truly a must for children and parents alike when visiting Denmark.

Lion Reserve

Veale Zoo at Risked Beyond Lego land on Highway A18 between Veale and Branded. This is an extraordinary natural setting for keeping wild animals in confinement yet at the same time somewhat free. Built in 1969, the reserve stands on 272 acres of land on the Jutland Ridge. The ground is a heather-covered inland dune with scattered spruce and fir. The terrain is varied and of great scenic beauty. A three-kilometer road winds its way through three sections of the reserve. Visitors enter through a lock system of double gates from where they are escorted by a patrol car on a drive taking approximately a half hour. As of spring, 1971, a new section of large enclosures was added to the reserve with other kinds of animals, including four full-grown elephants, yaks, camels, water buffaloes, zebra and reindeer. After a visit to the Lion Reserve, park the car and wander through the mini farm of baby animals for the children to see and pet. Tickets are available for the reserve just before coming to the double-gate entrance. For prices and other information write Vejle Zoo's Løvepark, Givskud, 7300 Jelling, Denmark.

RIBE

From Vejle you can proceed to Ribe, a medieval cathedral town founded in 948. Its unusual, ancient houses and courtyards line picturesque lanes. Ribe is known as the town of storks because of the stork nests on the rooftops.

Cathedral, built in the 12th century, a combination Romanesque and Gothic architecture.

Black Friars' Abbey, a 13th century Dominican monastery considered the most beautiful and best preserved in Denmark.

Hans Tavsen's House, the oldest remaining bishop's palace in Denmark.

Ribe Art Kunstmuseum, St. Nikolaigade, housing a collection of Danish art from the 18th to the 20th century.

Campgrounds near Aarhus

Camping Blommehaven, six kilometers south of Aarhus. Admission: Adults 48 cents, car 35 cents.

Aarhus Nord, on Aarhus-Randers road, nine kilometers from Aarhus at Lisbjerb. Open all year. Admission: Adults are 35 cents each.

Campgrounds near Vejle

Graerup Strand, FDM Camping. Open May–September
Frederika, Bommunens Lejrplads. Open May–September.

DANISH FOOD SPECIALTIES

Smørrebrød, literally meaning butter and bread, these delicate open-faced sandwiches are made with a variety of ingredients dressing a slice of buttered bread. It may be a piece of cheese or a more elaborate topping of tiny fresh shrimp, salmon or raw beef served with a raw egg yolk. A particularly popular smorrebrød is *leverposte* (liver paste) and pickled cucumbers. These sandwiches are always eaten with a knife and fork rather than in the hand.

Wienerbrød, Danish cream-filled pastries

Pølser, Danish hot dog available at mobile stands

SWEDEN
CATCHING FERRY TO MALMÖ

Boats leave and tickets are sold from the Oresund company pier on Havnegade, just at the end of Nyhavn, Copenhagen's Greenwich Village. Departures are almost hourly during the summer; less frequent in fall and winter. The trip takes one and a half hours each way at a cost of 88 cents for each adult plus a small fare for the car. The alternative is to do as we did and drive up to Helsingör to see Hamlet's Castle and then take the ferry which runs frequently from there to Helsingborg, Sweden. It cost $4.30.

MALMÖ

Camping
Sibbarp, five kilometers southwest of town center on Strandgatan. Open May 15–September15; hot and cold showers, swimming in the sea. Admission: Adults 20 cents, car 40 cents.

Malmö-Ribersborg Hylliekrokens, two kilometers southwest of town center on Linham road. Open May 15–September 15.

Tourist Information Office Skeppsbron 2; telephone 040/22202

Launderette
Called *kilowash*, there are many of these establishments located throughout Malmö. Most charge about 98 cents per kilo.

Babysitting
In most of the supermarkets you can leave your children free of charge while you shop. The most well-known market offering this

service is Mobilia. In the town hall, there is a children's center, which charges about 20 cents per hour for childcare.

Charlotte Weibull's Doll Shop, Lilla Torg, 203 11. Open daily.

Malmö Museum (Mälmohusvägen) Open weekdays noon–4 Sunday 11 am–4 pm. Admission: Adults 10 cents, children 5 cents. Restaurant in museum open Sunday–Friday.

Frostavallens Djurpark About 50 kilometers from Malmö, an animal park where the animals roam free.

GOTHENBURG

Camping

Askim, 10 kilometers south of town center via Road 158, Open June 1–September 1; grassy, shaded, swimming, small store.

Tourist Information Office Västlistems Turisttrafikförbund (The West Coast Tourist Traffic Association) in the old Dickson Palace on Parkgatan across from the Kungpaken.

Launderette

Tvättbaren, Linnegatan 59; telephone 120381, open Monday–Friday 8 am–8 pm; Saturday 8 am–1 pm. About $1.10 for a six-kilo load.

Dry Cleaning Self-Service Shops

Vic Kem. Tvätt, Sondravägen 32.

Vic Kem. Tvätt, Nord erskioldsg 22 around the corner from the launderette. Open Monday–Friday 8 am–6 pm; closed Saturday and Sunday. Four kilo load $2.70; two kilo load $1.50

Babysitting Call the city employment agency, Abetsförmedling telephone 80-16-20, and request a temporary babysitter.

Slottskogen Park An excellent play area for children with children's zoo. Open May–September

Museum of Natural History in Slottsskogen Park. A good rainy-day activity.

Trägårds Forenigens Park in the middle of the city overlooking the canal, with a coffee shop and children's play area completely surrounded by a fence.

Tour of the Canals and Harbor Make arrangements at the tourist office.

Botanical Gardens in Kungsparken just across from the tourist office.

Ethnographical, Historical and Archaeological Museums, all located in the same building at Norra Hamngatan 12. Fascinating, but a bit dry for the kids.

Liseberg Amusement Park, at Sodrävagen and Ørgrytevägen. The Tivoli Gardens of Gothenburg.

Maritime Museum and Aquarium, located down near the canal on Andreegatan.

Shopping

Nordiska Kompaniet, Øttamngatan 42: A huge department store with restaurant, beauty salon, travel agency, shipping office, nursery, changing rooms with showers, restrooms and a supermarket. Open in the summer Monday–Friday, 9:30 am–6 pm; Saturday, 9 am–2 pm/ supermarket until 10 pm.

Domus, Kungsportsavenyen 26-28: A large store with supermarket and a nicely decorated cafeteria offering meals at reasonable prices. Hours of operation same as at Nordiska Kompaniet.

FOLLOWING THE BALTIC ROUTE

Suggested alternative itinerary along the east coast for those going toward Stockholm rather than Norway; the Baltic Coast Route, Swedish

Highway 15, goes through three provinces in Sweden's sunny south and within short ferry range of Gotland and Oland. There are many excellent campgrounds along the way. If traveling in the summer, the swimming is good and within easy reach of the highway; long sandy crescents, steep cliffs, Nordic island clusters, skerries worn smooth by the waves, tree-lined inlets and everywhere crystal-clear saltwater.

SKÅNE

A province known for its verdant beech forests, small farming villages and old churches, Skåne was once the scene of Danish Swedish feuding.

Lund A town in the region known as an ancient seat of learning and site of Dalby, oldest remaining stone church in Scandinavia.

Glimmingehus Medival fortress in its original state.

Dag Hammarskjöld Retreat "**Backakra**" Located between Ystad and Simrishamn, now a memorial museum.

Blekinge A province known as "The Flower Garden of Sweden."

Sölvesborg Smallest and oldest village in the province, containing castle ruins and an interesting medieval church.

Karlshamn Idyllic merchant houses from the 18th century trading boom are the highlight of this village.

Ronneby has a health and bathing spa with an interesting ancient church.

Karlskona is an ancient naval port with a naval museum and the largest wood church in Scandinavia.

SMÅLAND COAST

Kalmar Prominent town of the province and location of Kalmar Castle, once called "The Key to Sweden." Cabins available at the small towns of Mönsterås, Oskarshamn, Virserum and **Västervik** along the north coast.

Oskarhamn Village that is the home of noted woodcarver "Döderhultary" Axel Pettersson.

Västervik Noted for its idyllic old fishing harbor.

Oland A 90-mile-long island, easily reached by car ferries, has many campsites and is famous for its profusion of wildflowers in early summer. There is a well-known bird sanctuary in the south, plus many windmills, prehistoric forts and burial grounds.

Gotland Island also easily reached by car ferry. Look for Visby, known as "the city of ruins and roses." It is one of the most remarkable walled cities in Europe.

SWEDISH FOOD SPECIALTIES

Sill, pickled herring
Röktål, smoked eel
Kaffee och kakor, coffee and cookies or cake

NORWAY

FREDRIKSTAD

Camping
Nearest campsite is at Holen, 40 kilometers south of Oslo.

Tourist Information Rosiggården.

Plus Colony of Craftsmen Conducted tours from Rosiggården are available weekdays 9 am–3 pm; Saturday 9 am–noon. Tour takes approximately one hour and 15 minutes. Following workshops are visited: textile-printing studio, silversmith, weaver's studio, pottery workshop, glass house, bookbinder's studio. Admission fee: Adults 70 cents; children under 16, 35 cents; children below school-age, free.

OSLO

Camping

Bogstad Camping, reached by turning right off E-18 (Oslo-Drammen road); site at Bogstad Lake. Open May 1–September 15; showers, laundry room, dishwashing facilities, well-equipped camp store, tourist information, bus services. Admission: Adults 64 cents, car 21 cents, tent 14 cents.

Post Office The main office is on the corner of Prinsensgate and Dronninggers.

Tourist Information Osloterrassen, Rosenkrantz Gate 28; telephone 42-17-70. Open daily except Sunday and holidays, weekdays 9 am–4 pm, Saturday 9 am–noon; summer season from June 1–August 31, weekdays 9 am–7 pm, Saturday 9 am–6 pm, Sunday 9 am–1 pm. Check here for hours on Oslo sights.

Launderette

Okernbråten Vasketeria Follow Route E-6 (Trondheimsveien). Turn right at Refstadveien, right at Brobekkveien (the fifth street), and right again at Nordalveien. Here you will find it, near the corner.

Kaldbakken Vasketeria Follow Route E-6 to Kaldbakken, turn right then left at the first street, then left again.

Tokerud Vasketeria Turn right on Fossumveien, right at Fjellstuon, left on Tante Ulrikkesvei and right on the first street.

BYGDØY-PENINSULA

If you leave your car back in town, the following museums may be reached by bus No. 30 or in the summer go by ferry from Rådhus-plassen, Pier C.

Museumsveien (Norwegian Folk Museum) This fantastic outdoor museum has a collection of Norwegian wooden buildings, among which are many of Norway's unique stave churches dating from the 12th century. The indoor collections, in three centrally located museums, house examples of Norwegian rural and urban culture including ancient Norwegian farm implements, antique children's toys, old bicycles and a fascinating collection from Lapland. In the summer there is folk dancing in the outdoor theater; in the winter months lectures are held every Sunday. Admission: Adults 42 cents, children 14 cents.

The Viking Ships and Archaeological Finds, Huk Avery 35, contains relics of the Viking Age; the Oseberg ship, the Gokstad ship and the Tune ship, all found near the Oslo Fjord. Admission: Adults 21 cents; children accompanied by adults, free, unaccompanied 7 cents.

The Kon-Tiki Museum, built in 1957, houses the raft on which Thor Heyerdahl and five companions drifted close to 5000 miles across the Pacific Ocean from Callao, Peru, to Rarotonga Island in Polynesia. Admission: Adults 21 cents, children 7 cents.

The Polar Exploration Ship "Fram" Here one can see the ship built for Hansen's polar expedition, 1893–1902. May be a bit boring for preschoolers. Admission: Adults 21 cents, children 7 cents.

CENTER OF OSLO

Rådhus (Oslo City Hall) is a magnificent building richly decorated with paintings and sculptures by Norway's leading artists. The children will probably become bored here though, and we suggest one adult stay with them in the tiny park beside the City Hall. You might also wander down to the harbor just in front of the Rådhus and watch for the shrimp boats. Free admission.

OSLO EAST

The Munch Museum: Located at Tøyengaten 53, this museum contains all the paintings bequeathed to the city of Oslo by one of

Norway's best-known painters, Edward Munch. To get there take the underground east to Tøyen Station, bus No. 20, Frogner Plass Galgeberg, bus No. 29, Rådhusplassen-Hasle. Open daily except Monday, 11 am–7 pm, Sunday noon–7 pm. Free admission.

The Norwegian Museum of Science and Industry: Located at Fyrstikkaleen 1, Etterstad, this museum illustrates technical development in Norway, from the Industrial Revolution to the present day. Extensive model railway and antique automatic musical instruments on display. Admission: Adults 42 cents, children 21 cents. Transportation: Take the Underground east "T" to Helsfy station.

OSLO WEST

The Vigeland Sculptures in Frogner Park. This should interest the kids for they can romp in the park and the children's play areas while you look at the sculptures, a world of people and animals carved in granite, cast in iron and bronze. Also, in the park are a modern open-air swimming pool, cafeteria, sports arena, tennis courts and two restaurants. The park is open all year round with no admission charge. For transportation take tram No. 2 to Frogner Park.

The Vigeland Museum, located at Nobels Gate 32, outside the Frogner Park is the former residence and studio of Gustave Vigeland. A visit is recommended for those who desire a more intense view of the work of this prolific artist. We suggest you take turns with one adult staying outside in the park with the children while the other visits the museum. The kids will enjoy the swings more than the sculptures. A great park for picnics in the spring and summer. Open daily except Monday 1 pm–7 pm. Free admission.

The Sonja Henie-Niels Onstad Arts Center Located at Hovikodden, 13 kilometers from Oslo (can be reached by taking bus No. 32, 36 or 37 to Hovikodden), this art center, opened in 1968, houses a fine collection of 20th century art donated by Sonja Henie and her husband,

Niels Onsad. Changing exhibitions and other events are held to illustrate current trends in dance, literature, architecture, music and applied art. For a schedule of current exhibits and activities see the small pamphlet "Oslo This Week," available at newsstands. There is a restaurant and cafeteria at the center. Guided tours are available upon request. Parking available. Open daily 11 am–10 pm. **Admission: Adults 70 cents, children and young people 35 cents.**

Restaurant Suggestion in Oslo

Kaffistova, Stortorvet 8 (alternate back entrance at 13 Karl Johans Gate). The Kaffistova chain has the nicest, basic restaurants in Oslo, offering one of the lowest-priced good meals in town.

SUGGESTED ROUTES FROM OSLO TO BERGEN

Highway 10 and 20 to Sandvika; Route 20 to Honhefoss, Gol and Ustaoset to Eidfjord and go along the fjord wall to Kinsarvik. From there, take a ferry to Kvanndal and continue by road to Bergen.

From Oslo, pass Oslo Fjord and woods of Skaret, stop to see view over Tyrifjord and Fingerike with Norefjell in the background. At Sundvolka you can ride a chair lift to the summit of Krokkleiva. Then drive to Honnetoss where a large waterfall runs through the middle of town. Around Lake Kroderen, hill country and little farms push down to the wooded shores of the lake. At Nesbyen stop for a visit to the **Museum of Valley Folk Art**. Beyond Gol go 15 kilometers to Torpo to see a stave church of the 12th century. The main road continues to Geilo and Ustaoset. Near Haugastøl you enter the Hardanger Mountain plateau. Hardanger Jøklen is a blue, glassy-looking glacier and the highest point of the trip after a 200-mile climb. From there you will continue to the 530-foot Voringsfossen Waterfall. At Eidfjord you should stop to see the 900-year-old church. Continue on to Kinsarvik where you take a ferry to Kvanndal and drive the remaining 133 kilometers to Bergen.

The Myrdal-Flåm Line Train on the Flåm Line

This is a dramatic journey of just 21 kilometers through a steep, narrow valley. Take the turnoff at Haugastol toward Finse, then Myrdal. From the Myrdal Station, altitude 2,845 feet, the train takes you down to Flåm Station, on the Aurland Fjord, an arm of the Gognefjord, Norway's longest. On the trip you will pass through 20 tunnels, 5 ½ kilometers, and much magnificent scenery. Over the most scenic sections, the train proceeds slowly or stops to let passengers take pictures of the many waterfalls, cliffs, fjords and other creations of nature. You can make reservations for this trip at the Oslo tourist office and stop on your way to Bergen. From Myrdal take the road (via Mjolfjell and Raundal) to Voss and then on to Ulvik, at the head of the Ulvik Fjord, one of the innermost arms of the Hardanger Fjord. There you will have a choice of accommodations between the campground (open from May 1 to October 1) located about one kilometer west of the center of Brakanes, 400 meters from the ferry stop, and the Brakanes Hotel, a famous Norwegian inn. Your decision will rest on your budget. The hotel stands at the water's edge with a breathtaking view down the fjord and over the surrounding hills. The setting and the accommodations are luxurious. For more information write to Brakanes Hotel, Ulvik in Hardanger, Norway.

Suggested Campsites on the Road from Olso to Bergen

Honefoss at Ringeriksgarten 20. Open May 15–September 15; swimming pool, shaded grassy area, hot and cold showers. Admission: Adults 21 cents, car $1.05, caravan $1.20, tent 28 cents.

Gol at Fossheim, three kilometers west of Gol near main road to Bergen (Road 7). Open June 1–October 1; shaded grassy area, hot and cold showers, bungalows for rent, swimming in a river. Admission: Adults 14 cents, car 65 cents, caravan 14 cents, tent 14 cents.

Kinsarvik at Harding Hagekafe, by River Kinso, about 250 meters from Kinsavik ferry. Open May 20–September 1; grass area, hot and cold showers, swimming in a pool or sea.

Nesbyen at Roløkken, four kilometers south of Nesbyen by Road 7. Open June 1–September 1; shaded grassy area, hot and cold showers, bungalows for rent, swimming in a lake or river. Admission: Comprehensive campsite for one 70 cents, one additional adult 14 cents.

BERGEN

Camping

At **Helldal, Grimen**, by E 68/7, 12 kilometers from center of Bergen. Open May–October: hot and cold showers, shaded grassy area at edge of lake, camping gas available, bungalows for rent, swimming in lake.

Post Office Main post office is on the corner of Christiesgate and Stradgaten.

Tourist Information Office Torgalmenning; telephone 11 487, 19 026. Open January 5–May 1, daily 10 am–3:30 pm, May 2 –September 30, weekdays 8:30 am–11:30 pm, Sunday 10 am–11 pm; October 1–December 20, daily 10 am–3:30 pm.

Fish Market, down by the wharf, open every day except Sunday, 8 am–3 pm. A great place to buy your daily fish, which we found to be the most economical food fare while in Scandinavia.

Mt. Floen: For a magnificent view of Bergen and a good picnic spot, take the funicular to the top of Mt. Floien. Numerous paths offer easy walks through beautiful wooded terrain.

Bryggen—The Waterfront Buildings: Take a walk along the waterfront and look at the old buildings with characteristic pointed gables facing the harbor, a unique example of Norwegian medieval architecture. Also, if interested in antiques, this is a good place to find shops carrying such items as old ship lanterns, captain's chairs and so on. Bryggen today is also a center for arts and crafts, where painters, weavers and craftsmen have their workshops.

The City Park This is a beautiful park for strolling. Stop and look at the magnificent fountain in the center of the park. Also, brass bands play most evenings during the summer season.

Bergen Indoor Swimming Pool, 9 Teatergaten. Stop and take a break from the camping in one of the two heated, salt-water pool; then experience the relaxation of a thermal bath so popular throughout Scandinavia. Hours: Swimming pools, Monday–Friday, 8 am–6:30 pm; Saturday, 8 am–3 pm, other days, 11 am–5 pm. Closed Sunday and the month of July. Admission: Adults 42 cents, children 18 cents.

Bergen Aquarium The aquarium is situated on the Nordnes peninsula. It is a 10-minute walk from central Bergen or can be reached by bus No.6. Fascinating marine display for adults and children. Open daily May 1–September 20 from 9 am–8 pm. Admission: Adults 79 cents, children 35 cents.

Museum of Arts and Crafts (Vestlandske Kunstindustumuseum) Collections of old European and Chinese arts and crafts and examples of contemporary Norwegian and foreign ceramics, glass, textiles, furniture and metal work.

SIDE TRIPS FROM BERGEN

Old Bergen, Elsesro, Sandvihen. A charming collection of characteristic wooden buildings of the 19-century, an old town complete with streets, marketplace and alleys. Open May 10–September 20 daily, with guided tours every hour from 10 am–7 pm. Transportation: Bus No. 9 or 10 from the fish market via Bergen Aquarium every hour 10 am–5 pm.

Trolhaugen, Hop: This was the home of Norway's famous composer Edward Grieg. It is beautifully situated by the peaceful Nora's Lake, and we suggest a visit there if only to enjoy the idyllic setting (the admission to the house is high and we do feel this is a bit of a tourist trap). Open May2–October 1, daily 11 am–2 pm and 3 pm–6 pm.

The park around the house is open to the pubic all year. Take the bus from Bergen to Hop from there it is a 15-minute walk to the house.

A Norwegian Country Festival Each year from May 20–August 31 on Monday, Tuesday, Thursday and Friday you can take a bus at 7 pm from Fesplassen and to the beautiful district of Fana. For four hours you will experience an evening spent in true Norwegian tradition with old farm customs, lively dances and folk music as well as traditional Norwegian foods. The cost is about $5 per person. You must make reservations in advance for the festival at the tourist office.

Fantoft Stave Church This typical example of the Norwegian stave church was built in the 12th century and can be reached by a 12-minute bus ride to Paradis and a 10-minute walk to the church. Open May 15–September 15 on Sunday, Tuesday, Thursday and Saturday, 10 am–1 pm, every day from 3–6 pm; during the month of July every day from 10 am–1pm.

Independent sightseeing trips to the fjords via bus, ferry and your own car can be planned at Fylkesbaatane, a97 Strandgate (telephone 17 690) where you can also make reservations and pick up schedules of daily departures.

Town Buses

The bus system in Bergen is very good. Each bus bears signs showing the route number and its destination. The fare is about 18 cents. Special tickets for $1.40 are available to tourists at the tourist office for unlimited travel within 48 hours. We suggest you leave your camper at the campground and take advantage of this good system. Central Station is at 8 Sromgaten.

Shopping hours in Bergen

Monday, Tuesday, Wednesday and Friday 8:30 am–7:30 pm; Thursday 8:30 am– 7 pm; Saturday 8:30 am–3 pm. In July and August most shops close a half hour earlier except Thursday when they stay open until 7 pm.

Shopping Hints

A good general department store: Wallendahl's.

For Norwegian sweaters: go to Nilssen's at 2 Bryggen.

For silver, gold and enamel work: A. David-Andersen A. S., at 1-Towalm (entrance from Rådhusgaten).

For food: the grocery store across the street from the Fish Market, on the corner of Strandkaren and Torgaten. **Look for the free booklet, "This Fortnight in Bergen,"** listing events in Bergen.

We took the Ferry from Bergen to Newcastle, England. Here's Sher and Tiffany enjoying the shipside view.

England

NEWCASTLE TO THE LAKE DISTRICT

Our arrival in Newcastle early the next morning was not exactly the greeting one would wish for when first entering a new country. As the sun made its initial appearance of the day, we gazed at it through a heavy blanket of smutty, red smog, which had settled itself over this industrial city of northern England. This was a good prelude to other British industrial cities, which we deliberately avoided thereafter.

On a windy country road about a half hour out of the city there is a sign scrawled in white chalk on an old board: "Farm Meals—Welcome." Following a curving dirt lane that the sign had directed us to, we arrived at a modest farmhouse where sunflowers, geraniums and vegetables grew in the front yard, dogs barked, and geese honked.

A lady named Mrs. Bowman greeted us and seated us beside a small fireplace at a charming old wood table with a bushel of flowers in the center and set with old English china. We ordered roast lamb from a well-worn menu and anxiously awaited our first English meal. Delicious aromas wafted out from the tiny back kitchen, but the meal was a letdown in terms of cookery. Our plates were filled mostly with mutton bones and bland potatoes and vegetables;

Sher and Dawn at Mrs. Bowman's house outside of Newcastle

however, the homemade biscuits, farm butter and mincemeat pie with whipped cream saved the day. As the sun went down and darkness came, Mrs. Bowman made another appearance with old-fashioned kerosene lanterns, which she set about the room. At this point we realized the farmhouse had no electricity and our meal had been cooked on a wood stove. We highly recommend Mrs. Bowman's to any wayfarers on road A69 from Newcastle to the Lake District. You might also consider spending a night at one of the many reasonably priced "bed and breakfast" establishments found throughout England.

First good camp breakfast at Mr. Craddock's

Mrs. Bowman also directed us to a nearby campsite not listed in our directory. We followed the same road we had come in on until the next small village where we found Mr. Craddock's campground, **The Poplars.** He

Tiffany and Dawn enjoyed playing with the kitties
at the campground.

greeted us with a friendly hello in spite of the hour, directed us to a
parking spot and proceeded to ask how many bottles of fresh farm
milk and how many eggs we would like in the morning for breakfast. This turned out to be a welcome surprise, having accustomed
ourselves to the small, continental breakfast. The following morning
the eggs and milk were on the ground outside our camper door, and
while the children played on the old swing and teeter-totter in the
campground, we prepared a big English-style breakfast with eggs,
crumpets and jam, milk and fruit. Mr. Craddock is also a good
source of information about this interesting region.

On our way to Hadrian's Wall we stopped at the town of **Hexham**
and did our grocery shopping for the day, being delightfully shocked
at the low cost of food compared to expensive Scandinavia. For little
money, we were able to buy fresh produce, dairy products and meat,
usually mutton, which always tasted a bit bland when eaten out but
great in one of our camp mobile-made concoctions. England is notorious for its unimaginative cuisine, so it is both economical and wise

to prepare your own meals in the country without missing much, and splurge occasionally on a crumpet at teatime or an evening out at an Indian restaurant. We did find the packaged cookies (biscuits) to be very good, and the packaged mixes such as for Stroganoff dinner proved convenient. Though we usually tried to avoid these kinds of things for dietary and budget reasons, they are easy to stock up on for later days in France where food is considerably more costly. Another of our favorite packaged items was the crepe mixes that are easy to prepare and make a delicious breakfast with canned English maple syrup. Dehydrated soups are also a good buy, and for the juice the syrup concentrates are best. An especially important thing to remember when traveling in England is the existence of the "early closing day." Each town closes it shops for one afternoon every week. The problem for the traveling shopper is usually not knowing the early closing day prior to his arrival. The best way to avoid arriving in a town with the expectation of doing your daily grocery shopping only to find the stores closed is to do your shopping in the mornings.

Shopping over, we headed for **Housesteads Fort** in Northumberland, one of the forts along **Hadrian's Wall**, which was built across

Sher and the girls exploring Hadrian's Wall in Northern England—
fun to climb!

England by the Romans to protect against the invading Scots. Once there we found ourselves amidst ruins more than 1700 years old. The district of Northumberland is famous for its historical monuments and brochures listing details on these and other districts are available from the Department of the Environment in London. (See "Summing Up" for address.)

LAKE DISTRICT

From Housesteads Fort we drove to Carlisle, Penrith and then to Ullswater Lake in the heart of the famous Lake District where so many English families take their yearly holiday. One can easily understand why they do so, for the whole region is green and lush with tiny lakes scattered everywhere and picturesque views reminiscent of old English prints.

The next three days spent in the Lake Districts of Cumberland and West moorland were some of our most memorable in England. While at Ullswater we visited an **Outward-Bound School**. There is also one in Eskdale. For those of you not familiar with this program, a brief explanation is in order. Outward Bound is a program, which originated in England during World War II as a survival training curriculum for young people from the ages of 16 to 22. The schools in England are quite impressive, often housed in huge, old castle-type buildings in wilderness settings equipped with obstacle-course training grounds for the students.

The route from Ullswater to Eskdale is very exciting—30 mile over hills and through valleys on roads sometimes of one-car width with frequent turns. As often as not we'd meet a meandering cow in the road just as we rounded a curve. On Kirkston Pass is the **Kirkston Inn,** said to be the highest inn in England. Beyond is the quaint and interesting town of **Ambleside,** a good lunch stop, with many little shops. From Ambleside, the drive continues to Little Langdale, over Wrynos Pass and via Hardknott to Boot just 15 minutes from Eskdale.

Picnic by Windemere Lake in the Lake District of
Northwestern England

In Boot, we spent the night at **Pitt Farm,** an old farm where the
campers are put out to pasture but have access to a not so modern
but perfectly adequate outhouse and cold running water. Over the
fence the cows moo and horses whinny and it is all very pastoral.
The children had a good time running in the tall grass and peering
at the cows and baby calves.

The campground is just a few hundred yards from the railroad
station where you catch **The Ratty,** a miniature steam train used to
haul rock to the coast. Before the one o'clock departure we picnicked
next to a little stream behind the station. On the ride to Ravenglass
the train whisks by small farms and then through verdant forests to
the coast. Ravenglass is a seaside town, rather shabby and not too
picturesque. During the hour's wait before our return train trip, we
explored the beach, which is full of treasure finds. We even discovered
a railroad lantern poking its nose up from the sand.

CHESTER

We drove into Chester and pulled off on a side street just before entering the city, finding ourselves on a cul-de-sac, which ended at a tiny

400-year-old country church. It turned out to be a perfect spot for the night, quiet, peaceful, private and free. It was after this experience and our becoming more adept at using the potty bucket and sponge bathing in the car that we more often found out-of-the-way, free camping areas, saving money and also having more adventures. It is best though, to always try to ask the owner first if you plan to pull into a field.

Chester is a medieval city where the original city wall has been well preserved and ancient half-timbered buildings line the streets. It is one of the most historically interesting and picturesque cities we saw in England. The most delightful thing for the children was our visits to **Galts** on bridge Street, the famous English toy store similar to Creative Playthings in the United States with a comparable price structure.

PORT MADOC, WALES

On the way to Port Madoc we stopped at one of the many **Welsh wool mills** along the road. This was an educational and artistic experience for all of us. The girls were fascinated with the big looms and even gathered some scrap yarn for future art projects.

Portmeirion was our reason for coming to Port Madoc. It is an Italian villa built by an Englishman who was much enamored with Portofino, Italy, and wished to reconstruct that town as accurately as possible. From our viewpoint, he succeeded. The surroundings are those of Renaissance Italy, with buildings of blue and pink, Italian gardens bedecked in sculpture, iron balustrades on balconies overlooking the sea, all in the beautiful setting of a natural rhododendron forest.

COVENTRY

Coventry is a large industrial center, but the cathedral there merits a few hours stop in the city. Coventry Cathedral is one of the most interesting of Europe, a combination of the new and the old. Bombs gutted the original Gothic cathedral during the war, leaving only a shell in which has been placed beautiful sculptures from all over the world. Attached to this ancient skeleton is the new, very contemporary cathedral with huge, dramatic stained-glass windows, a magnificent 70-foot-high tapestry created by French weavers crowning the nave and altar pieces and sculpture from many nations.

When in England you should try to see not only Coventry but also the cathedrals at Chester and Canterbury. We were careful, though, throughout our trip not to take in too many cathedrals and museums so that the ones visited would leave a lasting impression rather than being dulled by the rest. Also, cathedrals proved rather boring for the children after the first two.

From Coventry a three-hour drive brought us to London.

LONDON

In London there are camping facilities at **Crystal Palace,** a suburb about half an hour outside of the city. The camp itself is like a suburb, being quite large and fully equipped with showers, restrooms,

Tiffany at Trafalgar Square in London, England

76

washing rooms, and a small variety and grocery store. Buses into London run regularly from the stop across the street from the campground, and we soon learned that this was the best way to get around for traffic is very hectic, as in most big cities of the world, with the added problem of left-hand driving. We soon learned, however, not to return too late in the evening to the campground. Our first night in London we went to the movies and arrived at the bus stop about 11:15 to find that the last bus to Crystal Palace had left. Tired, crabby and cold, we finally made our way to the campground thanks to a generous cab driver that picked us up in spite of his regulations. In London there are both taxis and cabs. The former can be flagged down on any London street and charge exorbitant prices; the latter can only pick you up if you call into a central station. At any rate, keeping your budget in mind, you should avoid both and take in an early show if you have to come into London by bus.

One of the first things you should do upon arriving in the city is pick up a copy of "This is London," a small schedule of events and things to see, published weekly and available at newsstands. Of course, traveling with the children does put some limitations on going out at night, but if you economized while in the countryside, you can afford a babysitter and a highly recommended one at that. We called **Babyminder's Ltd.** and were given the name of a young nurse who cared for the children at her flat. She not only took care of the kids, but bathed them, fed them a healthy dinner and read to them. The charge was 75 cents an hour with a minimum of four hours. Meanwhile we enjoyed a very reasonable dinner at an unpretentious but authentic Chinese restaurant, the **Golden Bamboo** at 41 Wardour Street, just 10 yards off Shaftesbury Avenue in the theater district, and then went to see a play. The cost of legitimate theater is reasonable in London, and since performances are offered as often as three times a day on some matinee days, there is even the possibility of finding a play appropriate for the children and taking in a matinee or early-evening performance.

London taught us an important lesson: when in a large European city one of the first things you must do is make choices, unless you have an unlimited schedule and budget. Pick the highlights with special consideration for those that will most interest the children. Secondly, you must not try to see everything in one day. See one major sight and spend the rest of the day picnicking in the park where the children can play or stroll along the streets at a leisurely pace. This will be just as enlightening and entertaining as sightseeing, for you will have lots of opportunity to engage in the interesting and amusing pastime of people watching. Our list highlights for London were **Madame Tussaud's Wax Museum,** the **British Museum, Buckingham Palace, St. James Park** (for the kids), the **Tate Gallery** and the **National Gallery.** Please do not waste your time with the much-overrated **Old Curiosity Shop.** We walked 12 blocks to see it one cold day and were terribly disappointed. What one would expect to be a quaint old shop recalling the day of Dickens turned out to be a tourist trap. The British Museum is a bit too heavy for the kids, though they might enjoy a half hour in the Egyptian section. The best plan is to trade days with this sight. While one sees the museum, the other takes the kids to St. James Park where there is an extensive play area. On the next day, switch. After two days at the park, the kids will be ready to put up with either more sightseeing or perhaps just a walk along the Thames, making the Tower Bridge your destination.

If your stay in London allows it, you might want to take in the **London Zoo** or a more unusual event, the greyhound races that usually run on Wednesday and Friday in the fall at Wimbledon Stadium. Another choice would be the dolphin show at the **London Dolphinarium.**

One rather interesting excursion for all of us was an afternoon of visiting neighborhood recreation areas. In Notting Hill, we went to the Adventure Playground, a place built by ghetto children themselves. The playground brochure states that here "children are free to do things that they cannot easily do elsewhere in a crowded city.

They can build houses, have dens, or bonfires, garden, cook in the open and work freely with earth, clay, tools and timber. The atmosphere is permissive and attractive to children whose lives lack freedom both at home and at school and who do not have the space or opportunity to do, in their homes, all the things that should be a child's birthright."

SUMMING UP ENGLAND

For England and Wales prices shown are in dollars, computed at an exchange rate of one pound equaling $2.50. For information on all of Great Britain that will be helpful in planning your itinerary, check the Where to Write for Information section in Chapter 1.

NEWCASTLE

We do not suggest you make an extended visit to this northern city; it is dirty, crowded and unpleasant. However, if it is your port of entry into England, as it was for us, we suggest a campsite near Hexham. Take A69, Newcastle-Carlisle road, to Hayden Bridge. Then take A686 for three miles. The campground is open all year.

VICINITY OF NORTHUMBERLAND

The area between England and what now is Scotland was once the northern limit of the Roman Empire. To protect the lands to the south, Emperor Hadrian instructed the governor to build a wall between Newcastle and the Solway Firth. Forts were also erected as protection against warring tribes. Today, these can be visited and give one a remarkable insight into the past.

Housesteads Fort Located eight and a half miles west of Chollerford on the North Tyne and six miles northeast of Haltwhistle on the South

Tyne. The fort is half a mile north of the road connecting these places. The nearest railway station is Barden Mill, on the Newcastle to Carlisle line, and there are buses along the roads from Hexham and Newcastle. Hours of Admission: March–April, weekdays 9:30 am –5:30 pm, Sunday 2–5:30 pm; May–September, weekdays 9:30 am–7 pm, Sunday 9:30 am–7 pm; October, weekdays 9:30 am–5:30 pm, Sunday 2–5:30 pm; November–February, weekdays 10 am–4:30 pm, Sunday 2–4:30 pm. Admission: Adults 19 cents, children under 15, 10 cents.

Corbridge Located on the main roads from Newcastle upon Tyne to Hexham (A69) and from Darlington to Scotland by Carter Bar (A68). There is bus and train service from Newcastle and Hexham. The Roman Stations lies a half-mile northwest of the modern town. Hours same as Housesteads Fort.

Chester's Roman Fort Located on the west bank of the North Tyne, south of the Chollerton-Walwick, road (B6318), and five miles northwest of Hexham. The East Bridge abutment is on the opposite bank of the river, half a mile southwest of Chollerford, and is reached by a footpath along the west side of the former railway line. Open March–April, weekdays 9 am–5 pm, Sunday 2–4:30 pm; May–September, weekdays 10:00 am–4:30 pm, Sunday 2–4:30 pm. Admission: Adults 19 cents, children under 15, 10 cents.

Castles and Churches
Finchale Prior On the banks of the River Weare, five and a half miles north of Durham. Entrance after 9:30 on Sunday mornings and at standard hours following.

Barnard Castle In the town of Barnard Castle.

Lindistarn Priory Located at Holy Island.

Hylton Castle About four miles west of Sunderland.

Dunstanburgh Castle North of Craster, about eight miles northeast of Alnwick. Access is by footpath across fields.

Warkwork Castle on the River Coquet, seven and a half miles south east of Alnwick.

Tynemouth Castle and Priory on a promontory bounded by the north by Tynemouth Bay, on the south by the River Tyne, eight miles east of Newcastle.

Brinkburn Priory on the River Coquet about five miles east of Rothbury off B6344.

Norham Castle on the River Tweed eight miles west of Berwick. Open from noon–8 pm.

Standard hours of admission for the above monuments: March, April and October, weekdays 9:30–5:30 pm, Sunday 2–5:30 pm; May–September, weekdays 9:30 am–7 pm, Sunday 2–4 pm; November–February, weekdays 9:30 am–4 pm, Sunday 2–4 pm.

CARLISLE (CUMBERLAND)

This ancient border town, eight miles south of Scotland, was the scene of many border skirmishes between the English and Scots. Today it is a growing industrial town. We did not find it of any special tourist interest but a convenient stopping spot to camp and do a laundry.

Camping

Cottage Caravan Par, Port Carlisle, near Carlisle. Between Birchby-Sands and Bowness, turn left half a mile east of Port Carlisle. Open all year.

Launderette

Take road to Penrith. Just outside Carlisle on the left-hand side of the road is a large modern apartment complex. The launderette there is open for public use and quite reasonable compared to those in Scandinavia.

ULLSWATER (WESTMORLAND)

Camping

Hill Croft Caravan Site, Pooley Bridge, Penrith; telephone Pooley Bridge 363. Take Howtown Road at Pooley Bridge (on A592), follow "Roe Head" sign. Open March–October. Admission: Camper or caravan each 93 cents per night, tent 62 cents.

Park Foot Caravan and Camping Site, Howtown Road, Pooley Bridge, Penrith; telephone Pooley Bridge 309. Take A592 Penrith-Pooley Bridge, and turn left for Howtown. Open March–October. Admission: Camper and caravan each 93 cents, tent 75 cents.

Waterfoot Estate, Pooley Bridge, Ullswater (in village); telephone Pooley bridge 302. Open March–October. Admission: Camper and caravan each $1.25.

All three of these campgrounds come equipped with showers, laundry facilities (except for Park Foot), shopping facilities, restaurants, boating, tennis, water skiing, fishing and a place to buy camping gas. Busiest months are July and August. If there at that time, you may want to call ahead to be sure there is space available.

Sightseeing

We suggest a visit to the **Outward Bound School** at Ullswater. A walk around the beautiful grounds gives the children a chance for exercise and a look at some of the natural environment of the Lake District. The region is also quite famous for its history of Viking invasion.

WINDERMERE

One of the most famous lake towns, Windermere, is a center of tourism and holiday resorts. The lake is the largest in the English Lake District and the view of it from the town is superb. Bowness, where most of the resorts are located, is next to Windermere but the latter name has come to indicate both towns.

Camping

Windermere Camping, Limefitt Park, Windermere, on A591 between Windermere and Ambleside; telephone Ambleside 2300. Open April–September. Admission: Camper and caravan each $1.50, tent $1.

Brockbank Park Cliffe Farm, tent and caravan site, Tower Wood, Windermere. Take A 592, five miles south of Windermere; telephone Newby Bridge 344. Open March–October. Admission: Camper and caravan each 75 cents, tent 19 cents.

Fallbarrow Caravan and Boat Club, on lake adjoining north side of Bownes Bay, Lake Windermere; telephone Windermere 2206. Open March–October. Admission: Camper and caravan each $1.55–$2.50

White Cross Bay Caravan Park, Windermere, on A591 between Windermere and Ambleside; telephone Ambleside 2300. Open March–October. Admission: Camper and caravan each $1.25.

All of the above campsites have facilities for laundry (except Brockbank), buying camping gas, shopping, showers, fishing, swimming, water skiing, boating, sailing and tennis.

AN ADVENTURESOME ROUTE FROM ULLSWATER TO ESKDALE

Go from Ullswater to **Kirkston Pass** via **Padderdale**, pass the **Kirkston Inn**, then to the quaint town of **Ambleside**, Little Langdale, Wrynos Pass and via **Hardnott** to **Boot**, just 15 minutes from Eskdale. The natural scenery along this route is remarkable. Farmland, hills and dells, miniature birch forests and magnificent stonewalls erected without mortar by the farmers for hundreds of years—a dying art now.

Camping

Ambleside, Langdale Estate, near Ambleside. Turn north off A 593 at Skelwith Bridge, one and a half miles on left. Open March–October. Admission: Camper and caravan each $1.25.

Pitt Farm, at Boot. Grassy spot for camping, one outhouse, no showers; very primitive but adequate. Admission 75 cents per night.

ESKDALE

Outward Bound School This school is situated in magnificent forested grounds in one of the most beautiful and least frequented valleys of the Lake District. See the warden's office for permission to visit the school and grounds, or a more thoughtful gesture would be to write ahead asking about the possibility of visiting the school. Write Outward Bound Mountain School, Eskdale Green, Holmrook, Cumberland, England.

The Ratty is a railway that dates back nearly a century, operated for a long while on three-foot gauge, revived and existing today on 15-inch gauge tracks and running from the Lake District Mountains to the Cumberland coast. It leaves from Eskdale Green Station and goes to the town of Ravenglass on the coast. Check at the station for a current timetable. Cost of the trip for a family of two adults and two children is about $2.50

Wastwater Lake Take road to Wasdale; turn right at junction to Wastwater. Dramatic scenery.

CHESTER (CHESHIRE)

Chester on the River Dee, 18 miles south of Liverpool, has a unique medieval atmosphere visible in its half-timbered houses, rows of ancient arcades, cathedral and Town Hall. It is also one of the few remaining walled cities where you can actually walk along the top of the walls around the city.

Camping
Little Roodee, Castle Drive, Chester, in the center of the city. Open all year; restaurant, fishing, boating, riding, tennis. Admission: Caravan 15 cents

By River Dee, at the truck stop. Open all year; restrooms available. Free.

Shopping

Be sure and browse in the many beautiful shops along the "Rows", the arcaded galleries on two levels, in the heart of Chester's shopping district. The most interesting shop for kids will be Galts. (Ask for directions from a local passerby.)

Chester Cathedral Famous for its elaborate woodcarvings and cloisters. Open daily.

Town Hall Fascinating architecture. Ground floor is center of frequent special exhibitions.

Grosvenor Museum, Grosvenor Street. Collections illustrate the archaeology and natural history of Chester and the surrounding district. Special prominence is given to the display of exhibits of the Roman period. Open weekdays 10 am–5 pm, Sunday 2–5 pm. Admission Free

King Charles Tower Civil War exhibition. Open May–September, Monday–Friday 10 am–6:30 pm; Saturday 10 am–6:30 pm. Admission: Adults 13 cents; children 8 cents.

Water Tower Medieval Chester exhibition. Open from May–September, Monday–Friday 10 am–6:30 pm, Saturday 10 am–7 pm, Sunday 2:30–6:30 pm. Admission: Adults 13 cents, children 8 cents.

Chester Zoo, at Upton, two miles from the Chester Town Hall. Frequent buses to zoo depart from Odeon Cinema. Restaurant, cafes, boating lake. Open daily throughout the year, 9 am–dusk.

Children's Story Hour, at the Central Library, St. John Street. On Wednesday 10:30 am, Friday 2:30–3 pm. This might be just the break the kids will need from sightseeing.

WALES

From Chester take A483 to Wrexham, Ruabon, then to Llangollen and along A5 to Snowdon via Corwen, Cerrig-y-Drudion, Bettus-y-Coed, and Capel Curig.

LLANGOLLEN

This lovely town of northern Wales on the River Dee is the home of the International Musical Eisteddfod, held annually in July.

Camping

Wern Isaf Farm, Llangollen. Take A539 road, turn right at Bridge End Hotel, half a mile. Open April–October. Admission: Camper and caravan each 75 cents, tent 19 cents.

PORT MADOC

From Snowdon, where you will enjoy the dramatic scenery, continue to Caernarvon (A4086), then to Port Madoc via A 487.

Camping

Cardigan View Caravan Park, Morfa Bycan, Port Madoc.

Take Port Madoc-Morfa Bychan road; turn left at the post office. Open March–October; showers, laundry facilities, shopping, restaurant, boating, fishing, sailing, tennis, water skiing. Admission: Camper and caravan each $1.25.

Camp free at the beach, Blackrock Sands. Watch for sign to your right shortly after you arrive in Port Madoc.

Portmeirion is the major sight of interest here. It is an Italian village modeled after Portofino, Italy. West of Port Madoc; half a mile after toll gate turn right. Toll gate fee is 12 cents; admission to Portmeirion is $1.20. We felt it was well worth the entrance fee, which covered all of the car and us.

Launderette

In Port Madoc, just off the main street behind a pub. Ask someone for specific directions when in the center of town. It is not difficult to find. For about $1.15 we did two wash loads and one dryer load.

Take A487 from Port Madoc to Dogellau, Machynlleth, A4984 to Mallwyd, then A458 to Shrewsbury and A5 to Coventry.

DOLGELLAU

An ancient market town at the foot of the famous Cader Idris (2,927 feet high). Nearby are **Cymmer Abbey**, a 12th century Cistercian monastery, and the Precipice Walk and Torrent Walk for hikes.

Camping

Tanyfron, Arran Road, Dolgellau. Take A487 Dolgellau-Machynlleth road for a quarter of a mile. Open April–October; showers, camping gas, laundry facilities, restaurant, shopping swimming, boating, fishing, riding, tennis.

Admission: Camper and caravan each 45 cents, tent 25 cents.

MACHYNLLETH

A small town 16 miles from Dolgellau. Dovey Forest, 17,000 acres of woodland, lies just north of the town, making a wonderful backdrop for the local scene as well as a great place to hike and picnic.

COVENTRY (WARWICKSHIRE)

Primarily an industrial center, Coventry is known for the legend of Lady Godiva whose statue stands in the city's modern shopping district. Its most famous site today is the modern Coventry Cathedral standing next to the ruins of the old one, razed by the heavy blitzing during the war.

Camping

Kilworth Caravan Park, North Kilworth House, near Rugby. About 12 miles southeast of Coventry along A428; campgrounds located on A4114 three miles east of Lutterworth. Open all year; showers, camping gas. Admission: Camper, caravan and test are each 64 cents.

STRATFORD-UPON-AVON

This is a typically Tudor town, wonderfully preserved as a shrine to England's greatest poet. Nearby are the Severn Valley and the beautiful Warwick region.

Camping

The Elms Camp, Teddington, Stratford on Avon. Take B4086 from Stratford. Open April–September; showers, shopping restaurant, riding, boating, golf, tennis, camping gas. Admission: Camper and caravan each 88 cents, tent 75 cents.

The Shakespeare Memorial Theater, built on the Avon Meadows, has performances of the bard's works, April–November.

Ann Hathaway's Cottage, at Shottery, one and a half miles west of Stratford.

Grammer School, where the bard was educated.

Holy Trinity Church, containing Shakespeare's grave and monument.

Memorial Museum

OXFORD (OSFORDSHIRE)

This picturesque and ancient University City is on the Cherwell and Thames rivers. Visiting the many old colleges throughout the town, the oldest begun in 1299, is the main attraction: a bit boring for kids however.

LONDON

Camping

The Caravan Harbor, Crystal Palace Parade, S.S. 19. Take South Circular Road to Dulwick Common, follow sign to Crystal Palace. Open all year; showers, small store, laundry room, camping gas; supermarket and launderette nearby. Admission: Camper, caravan and tent each 50 cents.

Abby Wood, Co-operative Woods, Camping and Caravan Site, Federation Road, Abbey Wood, London S.E.2. In London take North Circular Road to Blackwell Tunnel, then A 206. Open all year; showers, shopping, laundry facilities, camping gas. Admission: Camper and caravan each 86 cents, tent 50 cents.

Launderettes

If staying at Crystal Palace there is a launderette on the main street, just three blocks up from the campground.

Near Paddington Station, McClary Self-Service Laundry, at No. 14 Craven Road, open every day.

Near Russell Square, Red and White Laundries, 78 Marchmont Street, open daily 8 am–10 pm.

Near Marble Arch, Bendix Self-Service Launderette, 27 Edgeware Road.

Post Office

The easiest one to find is in the big central Charing Cross Station across the Street from Trafalgar Square.

Tourist Information

American Express Office, Haymarket Street, one block off Trafalgar Square. Buy a "What's On In London" at any newsstand or pick up a "This is London."

British Travel's Tourist Information Centre, 64 St. James Street, S.W. 1. Be sure and purchase the helpful British Travels booklet, "This Month in London," about 30 cents.

For travel enquires, including times of Green Line Coaches and bus services, write to the Public Relations Officer, London Transport, 55 Broadway, S.W.1 or call 01-222-1234

Babysitters

Babyminders, 32 James Street, W.1; telephone 935-3515

Childminders of Harley Street, 67 Marylebone High Street; telephone 935 9763/2049. This is the one we used successfully; about 75 cents per hour.

Babysitters Unlimited, 313 Brompton Road, S.W.3; telephone 730-7777/8, day and evening.

Universal Aunts Ltd., 36 Walpole Street, Kings Road, Chelsea, S.W. 3; telephone 730-9834

Nursery school and Homes for Part Time Care of Babies and Small Children

The House on the Hill, 33 Hooplane, Hampstead N.W. 11. Open 8:30 am–5:30 pm, closed mid-July through mid-August. Age: two–six years.

Walton Day Nursery, 239 Knightsbridge, London S.W. 7.

Pipers Hill, By Fleet, Surrey. Mrs. W. Dean, S.R.N. Age: Babies–12 years.

Norland Nursery Training College, Denford Park, Hungerford Berkshire. Age: two weeks–six years.

Children's London For information on activities for children in London telephone 246-8007

The British Museum Great **Russell** Street; telephone 01-636-1555. Nearest underground stations are Holborn (Kingsway) and Tottenham Court. Open weekdays 10 am–5 pm, Sunday 2:30–6 pm. Admission free.

Madame Tussaud's Wax Museum, Marylebone #1, on Road, near Baker Street underground station. Open daily 10 am–6:30 pm, in winter until 5:30 pm. Admission fee: Adults $1, children 48 cents.

The Tate Gallery, on Millbank. Take bus No. 88 from the Westminster underground stop. Houses modern art primarily. Open weekdays 10 am–6pm. Admission free.

Trafalgar Square Stop here to feed the pigeons before visiting the National Gallery.

Changing of the Guard, Buckingham Palace. N Daily at 11:30 am

Changing of the Horse Guards, Buckingham Palace. At 11 am Monday–Saturday; Sunday at 10 am.

Speakers Corner at Hyde Park, near Marble Arch. Go on a Sunday to hear a variety of speakers.

The Tower of London, on banks of Thames. Take underground train of Inner Circle or District lines to Tower Hill Station and then walk just a few steps. Open daily, May–September. (Never go on Sunday unless you want to fight the crowds) Closed Sunday, October–May. Admission fee: Adults 72 cents.

Play Outdoors at Hyde Park, Kensington Gardens, St. James Park and Green Park

Free shows for children that include magicians, clowns and puppet plays during the summer. Check the "Open Air Entertainment" pamphlet sold at newsstands.

Little Angel Marionette Theatre, 14 Dagmar Passage, Cross Street, N.I. Performances during school vacations and on Saturday mornings.

Pollock's Toy Museum and Toy Theatres, 44 Monmouth Street, Cambridge Circus, W. C. 2. Antique toys, dolls and games. Open weekdays 10 am–5 pm.

Nottingham Hill Adventure Playground, corner of Worington and Telford roads, Notting Hill Section. A creative playground built by children for children out of scraps of wood, spring and rope. Telephone 01-969-7919 for other playground locations.

Steam Age, 59 Cadogan Street, S.W. 3. Working models of early locomotives, aircraft and steamships.

The London Dolphinarium, 65 Oxford Street; telephone 437-9694. Open 10 am daily; 45- minute performances. Admission fee: Adults $1.25, children 62 cents.

Greyhound Races, White City Stadium; central tube line to White City. Held on Tuesday, Thursday and **Saturday.**

Greyhound Races, Wimbledon Stadium. On Monday, Wednesday and Friday at 7:45 pm. Call 946-561 for reservations.

Royal Windsor Safari Park, Royal Windsor, Berkshire; telephone Windsor 65083. Drive through lion, cheetah and baboon reserves; children's corner. Open 10 am daily.

Hampton Court Palace and Gardens, in Middlesex. Henry VIII lived here. Gardens include a hedge maze where children can wander. The State Apartments are open weekdays 9:30 am–6 pm, Sunday 11 am–6 pm.

At Greenwich see Cutty Sark (clipper ship), National Maritime Museum and old Royal Observatory. Boat service in the summer from Westminster and Charing Cross piers to the Tower and Greenwich downstream and to Battersea and Richmond upstream.

Windsor Castle and Great Park, Windsor, Berkshire. World's largest inhabited castle. Queen Mary's Dolls' House may be viewed when the court is not in residence. Open from 10 am–dusk.

Chessington Zoo, Chessington, Surrey. Take bus No. 65 (Monday–Friday) or bus No. 65A (daily) from Ealing, Richmond and Kingston. Or take Green Line Coach 714 (daily) from Luton, via Baker Street and Hammersmith to zoo entrance. Circus, aquarium, playground. Open 9:30 am–dusk.

Regent's Park Zoo is most easily reached by underground to Camden Tower, then bus No. 74 (daily) or No. 74B (Monday–Friday). In summer a waterbus runs along the Grand Union Canal to the zoo from Little Venice (Warwick crescent). Aquarium, animal rides. Open 9 am–dusk.

Whipsnade Zoo, near Dunstable, Bedfordshire. In winter, Green Line Coach No. 712, 713 or 714 to Luton, then district bus No. 43. In summer, Green Line Coach No. 726 direct from London every day, except Saturday. This line direct from London every day, except Saturday. This line uses the M. 1 motorway and stops at the zoo gates. Animals in natural habitat. Open 10 am–dusk.

Woburn Abbey Park Zoo, Woburn, Bedfordshire. Pets corner, deer, bison, boating, playground. Open daily 11 am–5 pm.

Shopping in London of Interest to Children

Foyle's, children's department, Charing Cross Road, W.C. 2. Famous London bookstore.

Times Book Shop, 42 Wigmore Street, W 1.

Paul and Marjorie Abbat, 94 Wimpole Street, W. 1. Toys

Hamley's, 200 Regent Street. Huge toy store.

General Shopping
Flea Market, Portobello Road. Open Saturday only.

London Silver Vaults, Chancery Lane.

Marks and Spencers, Oxford Street. A good department store with reasonable price children's apparel.

Special Events
St. Edmund's Fair, Abingdon, Berkshire. June.

Royal Cornwall Show. June

Horse and Pony shows: Royal International, Wembley, London, end of July; Windsor Berkshire, mid-May; Surrey, mid-June

Eating Out with Children
The Dell, Hyde Park. A circular, glass-walled building overlooking the Serpentine Lake. Self-service.

Old Kentucky Restaurants. Large restaurant chain offering a lollipop to each child who finishes his lunch.

Old Georgian Coffee House, Goodwins Court, W.C. 2. Salads and light meals.

Wimpy chain of short-order restaurants offering fries and hamburgers.

On the Road, forte Motorway Service Station Restaurants have special menus for children.

Good Restaurants for Adults
Golden Bamboo, 41 Wardour Street, just off Shaftesbury Avenue. For an inexpensive, delicious, authentic Chinese meal.

The Vega, Panton Street, off Leicester Square. Vegetarian restaurant.

Wheelers, Old Complou Street. Fish restaurant; good for lunch.

Indian restaurants, clustered on Rupert Street near the Eros statue and Piccadilly Circus.

Budget restaurants serving foreign cuisine can be fond on Charlotte Street.

LONDON TO DOVER

From London one can drive to Dover to cross to either Boulogne or Calais, France. There are many sights along the way.

Sidcup A small town in the midst of the *crays* (ancient and picturesque villages to which the River Cray gives its name). In the springtime, the hills of this rich fruit-growing area are covered with wildflowers and blossoms.

Wrotham A settlement of ancient Britons. The area is often called "the Garden of England" because of its natural beauty. A noteworthy feature is the 13th century church of Saint George.

Maidstone A small country town of Kent built on the site of an old Roman settlement. The archbishops have a palace here, and several of the adjacent buildings are unique for their external staircases.

Canterbury Capital of Ethelbert, King of Kent (560 A.D.). It was here that Saint Augustine founded a small church, which became Canterbury Cathedral, one of England's greatest architectural masterpieces.

Sittingbourne A brick-making center, formerly a stopping point for pilgrims traveling to Canterbury.

Rochester Charles Dickens immortalized Rochester in his "Pickwick Papers." Visit the ancient Norman cathedral here, built in the shape of a double cross.

Blackheath Common Once the haunt of highwaymen, this was the gathering place for many notorious rebels.

Camping in the County of Kent

Wrotham Thriftwood Camping Site, Stanstead Road. Take A20 Maidston-London road, right at Wrotham to Stanstead Road. Open all year; showers, laundry facilities, shopping, camping gas, swimming, fishing. Admission: Caravan 29 cents, tent 22 cents.

Ramsgate: Nether Court Farm Road. From Ramsgate turn off B2050 at St. Laurence church. Open April–September; showers, camping gas, fishing, canoeing, riding, tennis, water skiing. Admission: Caravan 86 cents.

France

On leaving London we were once again wayfarers and happy to be out of the city and on the open road to Dover. From there we took the much-acclaimed new mode of transportation across the English Channel, the Hovercraft. The cost was about $23. It was impressive to see this monstrous aquatic whale-like structure draw up out of the sea to its landing dock. We found taking some dry English wafers along helped with stomach queasiness, and luckily, we made it to France with no accidents.

We landed on a crisp, autumn morning in Boulogne, an uninteresting, industrial city. The grayness of the overcast atmosphere was a perfect introduction to France, for the one color, which most typifies the north of France is gray, lovely, rich French gray. Now the gray was accented everywhere with the colors and smells of autumn. The fields, which lined the country roads lay fallow for the winter. They were separated from the roads by long straight rows of trees forming tunnels. Now and then we would pass an old man in dark shirt, pants and black beret carrying *fagots* (small bundles of sticks, fuel for a fire), or riding his bike with a baguette tied to the back.

We headed for the village of Montreuil, hoping to arrive there to change English pounds into French francs before noon. This can be a problem in any country if you have forgotten to exchange your money at the border or, as in this case, at the departure and arrival point. Train stations, ports or airports all usually have exchange offices. In France we found the BNP (Banque National de Paris), with branches in almost every town, to be very dependable; our only problem was getting to one before noon when they usually close for two hours. We soon learned to make a quick currency check each morning in order to plan ahead.

Our first purchases in Montreuil were made at the local *boulangerie* (bakery). We bought two *baguettes* (long slender loaves of bread perfect for sandwiches and French style hot dogs) for about 30 cents. Our visit to an *alimentation* (general grocery store) added some rich, unsalted butter, a liter of wine and some cheese and fruit, which came to $1.80. For only $2.10 our first French picnic was complete. We were later to discover even more economical and more typical picnic combinations such as salads and pâté from the *charcuteries* (delicatessens) and small tarts from the pastry shops. This first picnic was the beginning of an epicurean adventure in this gourmet's paradise.

In his fascinating portrait of a people, *The French*, author Sanche de Gramont says, "Every French commune has a church, a café, and *monument aux morts.*" Montreuil was the perfect example: it typified all the other small towns we were to see in France with their rows and rows of gray stucco buildings, muted red-tile roofs, surrounding Romanesque or gothic churches and a central square with a cafe and a small monument to the dead of the First World War. It is in the cafes and at their sidewalk tables where so much of French life is led. Over a *Dubonnet* (French sweet red wine) one might discuss the latest move of Pompidou, the new cinema, the latest fashions in *Elle*, the best way to prepare *poulet Basquaise* (Basque-style chicken), or the bouquet of vintage '69. Spend some time in a tiny French café, and even if you have not brushed up on the language, just make keen observations and you will come closer to the French way of life. When ordering you might ask for a *Pssitt* (a popular soft drink) for the children and a glass of *vin ordinaire* (house wine) for yourself. If you are not a wine drinker, order a cup of *café* (coffee). You can sit as long as you wish with just one cup for it is considered impolite to hurry a customer and the waiter should not bother you.

When you wish your bill just get the attention of your *garçon* (waiter) and ask for your *billet* (check). Remember the total charge should include the tip if the ticket says *service compris* (service charge included). If it is not noted, make sure you are not being charged more than 15 percent for service.

Eating out—a rare occasion, but fun at an outdoor café in France. This was at a café on Boulevard St. Michele in Paris, often called "Boule Miche."

In **Montreuil** we found a free camping spot in a narrow parking area on a hill, just behind a large and rather foreboding-looking girls' school. It was a perfect place, a little out of the way and sheltered by some trees that lined a walking path. Luckily, we were not bothered all night and awoke the next morning to the aroma of fresh croissants from a nearby bakery.

We ate breakfast at a tiny café on the square; for $1.60 each. We each had a croissant, with hot chocolate for the kids and coffee for us, the typical French breakfast. Later we discovered we could buy twice as many croissants, with a few *brioches aux chocolates* (a delicious flaky pastry roll with a piece of chocolate in its center) thrown in, for the same amount at a *boulangerie* (bakery) and prepare our own hot chocolate. We soon became accustomed to this light and tasty breakfast along with a new regime, that of eating our largest meal midday with a light meal at night as the French do.

If your budget will allow, you might try stopping at a *routier* one day. These are small truck-stop-like bistros where a hearty, always tasty French meal is served for a low rate and with little fanfare. By ordering just one plate from each course for the kids and then asking for an extra plate to divide the quantity in two, we fed them amply at half the price. The meal for four came to about $5. A glance into another part of French culture, the life of the truck driver, heightened the enjoyment of the meal. It is primarily truck drivers and traveling businessmen who frequent these restaurants where conversations are jovial and the ambience unique.

From Montreuil we drove south to **Amiens** and stopped for a brief tour of the famous 13ᵗʰ century Gothic cathedral. The next stop was Senlis, just 50 kilometers outside Paris, a lovely old town where one can view an ancient Gallo-Roman wall and the early gothic cathedral with its famous 150-foot spire. This small town is worth a brief stop, though it does not hold much to interest children under the age of 13. Joan of Arc left her mark in Senlis, where in August 1429, she led the forces that defeated the English commanded by the Duke of Bedford.

Our arrival in Paris was poorly timed, as we were unable to avoid the inevitable turmoil caused by an existing *une grève* (metro strike), a not-too-infrequent occurrence in this city. The traffic was abominable, and the erratic French drivers increased our exasperation. While moving bumper to bumper down the **Champs Élysées** in the direction of the Bois de Boulogne where we hoped to camp, the lights of the Arc de Triomphe came on, a Parisian sight you should not miss at dusk. We finally arrived at the Bois de Boulogne, a beautiful old English-style park in the northwestern part of Paris on the Right Bank. The campground is a bit difficult to find, but if you can stop a friendly-looking passerby, pen and paper in hand if you do not speak French, and ask "*Où es le camping, s'il vous plait?*" you should get directions. Remember the campground borders the Seine, which will help you find its location.

We found the metro (subway) the best way to get around. It is easy to use and far less exhausting than trying to fight the traffic in the car. The most economical thing to do is purchase a *carnet* (booklet) of 10 tickets for $1.60. This saves about 40 cents, one ticket usually being 20 cents. Children, age three and under travel free. One important rule when riding the metro is to plan out your route in advance, knowing which connections to make. At least one change will probably be necessary to get to your destination. This might seem complicated at first, but large lighted wall maps next to the ticket booths in most metro stations will make it easier. By pressing a button opposite the name of the station at which you wish to stop, a row of lights will mark out your route, showing the times to take which connection. With this aid and a carefully planned route, there should be no problem of missed stops or wrong connections.

To familiarize yourself with Paris, one of the first things you should do is find a place with an overall view of the city. The **Eiffel Tower** is an obvious choice, but it is quite expensive and usually very crowded. Though the view is beautiful, one can get the same vista of Paris from other points less crowded and at no cost. One of the best views of Paris is the one from the roof garden of the **Samaritaine Department Store** on the Rue de Rivoli. Another choice might be the top of the **Arc de Triomphe** overlooking the *grands boulevards*, including the famous Champs Élysées and the whole area called Étoile. Another interesting panorama of the city may be seen from **Sacre Coeur**, which sits atop the tallest hill in Paris and is home to the quarter referred to as **Montmartre**.

The trip down the Seine on one of the many tour boats (*bateaux mouches*) is another good way to get to know the different districts (*quartiers*) of Paris. It also affords the opportunity to take some of the best pictures of the city and to get a good idea of the major sights to take in on foot later. The view of the **Notre Dame Cathedral** is particularly spectacular, with a wonderful glimpse of its flying buttresses at the rear of the nave. The tiny park behind the cathedral is a good place for a picnic.

One of the first places to stop after arriving in Paris, is the **American Center for Students and Artists.** Not only will it afford a chance to check out current activities, many of which are in English, such as plays, classes and concerts, but it's a great place to meet up with other traveling Americans. We stopped by on a gloomy day in January and to our delight were invited to join some African, French and American students in the lounge for coffee. We ended up spending the day there in front of the big fireplace in conversation with our new friends, while the girls met other children and we learned of an art class and dance lessons they could attend. Membership in the Center is encouraged, but no one seemed to mind our stopping by just to pick up information and to meet people. **Update: Sadly, this center no longer exists.**

Two additional sources of information on what's happening in Paris are the small magazines published weekly, *L'Officiel des Spectacles* for about 12 cents and *Une Semaine de Paris, Pariscope* for 20 cents. They are both in French but are fairly easy to follow; one can easily decipher movie schedules, for example.

The parks of Paris were especially enjoyable for our family. **Luxembourg Gardens** is beautiful in the autumn with the fall leaves forming a carpet of color along the pathways and the vendors selling roasted chestnuts at the entrance. Inside the park we discovered a children's play area with a 50-cent entrance fee, much to our surprise and disdain. (We found that France was the one country that seemed to provide little in the way of *free* recreation for its youth. Even Spain offered more, with at least one children's playground in every little village). However, the girls loved riding the carrousel and spending

Tiffany and Dawn playing by the big pond in the Luxembourg Gardens

the afternoon playing with the French children on the swings, slides and seesaws. We had a picnic with food purchased at a local "charcuterie." This delicatessen-type shop offers a wide assortment of gourmet appetizers, cheeses, salads and pâtés **at reasonable prices. In the Luxembourg area try the ones on the Rue St. Jacques just two blocks from the gardens.** Then pick up a loaf of *pain de compagne* (country bread) at the local *boulongerie* (bakery). Though a few centimes higher than the baguettes, we liked it better and found it went further.

One of the most entertaining days for the children in Paris was their visit to the **Children's Art Atelier** on the Rue de Vaugirard. **(See Appendix for art workshops for Children today.)** For 3 francs each, the girls spent two and a half hours in a delightful studio for children's art making. Operated by a young Parisian art student and her husband, its purpose is to let children use their imaginations in the creative exploration of several different mediums, including paint and clay. We had two blissful hours to explore our favorite museum, the **Jeu de Paume**, devoted to the French impressionists and far more enjoyable for us than the Louvre while the children were being creative. If you have time when visiting the Jeu de Paume you might walk over to the **Museum of the Orangerie** afterward (both the small museums are at the other end of the Tuileries from the Louvre and look out onto the Place de la Concorde). The Orangerie houses special exhibitions, and during your visit be sure not to miss the two large oval rooms on the ground floor where Claude Monet's paintings of mammoth size and liquid colors, "Les Nymphéas" ("Water Lilies"), are hung. Another of our favorite museums was the Musée Rodin, where the originals, of the famous sculptures "The Thinker" and "The Kiss," are located. **(Note: See Updates in the the Appendix for both the Jeu de Paume and the Orangerie).**

There are other activities the children will especially enjoy. At the **Jardin d'Acclimation** in the Bois de Boulogne where you will be camping, there is a marionette show every Thursday, Saturday and Sunday at three, four and five o'clock. There is an admission price to the park, but the marionette show is free. Though the script is in French, the children can follow the story easily from the actions of the puppets. Of all the museums in Paris we think the Palais de Chaillot offers the most for children. It houses the **Maritime Museum** (*Musée de la Marine*), The **Anthropology Museum** (*Musée de l'Homme*), the **Museum of French Monuments** (*Musée des Monuments Français*) and the **Aquarium of the Trocadéro Gardens,** the one the girls enjoyed most. All the museums are easy to find and can be browsed through in one afternoon, which seems to be about the limit for a child's attention span. **(See Updates under Paris in the Appendix)**

Although the famous farmer's market *Les Halles* no longer exists, there are still many tiny neighborhood markets throughout Paris. One to visit on a Wednesday or Saturday morning is in the Fauboug St. Antoine just off the Boulevard Diderot. Full of local color, it is a perfect place to do the daily shopping. One of our favorite things to buy was a large *citrouille* (pumpkin), which makes a delicious pumpkin soup when cut up with some potatoes and other vegetables. We all loved this very French dish and found it to be one of our most economical meals.

In the old section of *Les Halles* there is a delightful kitchenware shop called **Déhillerin** on Rue Coqilliére. If you are interested in French cookery, this is a perfect place to pick up some of the tools of the trade at reasonable prices. Although we do not encourage shopping on a $10-a-day budget in Europe, a few other specialty shops in the area offer interesting gift items. Avoid the department stores in Paris; they are no different from those in America.

Some of our most memorable days in Paris were spent strolling in the different quarters, sailing boats with the children in the small lake in the Luxembourg Gardens, window shopping on the famous street of Parisian haute couture, **Faubourg St. Honoré**, walking in the gardens of the Palais Royal and bartering and browsing at the famous Paris flea market, **Marché aux Puces**. Though the latter was a great experience, do not expect to walk away with Napoleon's sword for 20 cents. The vendors know the worth of the French "junk", but it's still fun to look. You may outlast the children in this endeavor. Be conscious of their tolerance level for browsing.

If doing art, like life-drawing, is your interest, be sure and visit the **École de la Grande Chaumière** on the Rue de la Grande Chaumiére off the Boulevard Montparnasse. It offers an afternoon life-drawing class at a reasonable cost of about $1.40. The models change positions frequently, and if you are there on the right day you might even get a critique by one of the art teachers. Do not be shy if you do not speak French; no one talks while drawing and the atmosphere is very relaxing. While this is not an activity for children, parents who are artists may enjoy taking a break from the kids for a drawing session while the other parent babysits.

While in Paris you will want to take some side trips to the suburbs to see **Versailles**, the great palace of Louis XIV, and the new children's park and zoo, **Thoiry**, at Vincennes. The best way to reach Versailles is by municipal bus No. 171. You can catch it at the Pont de Sèvres. It is a 15-minute ride to Versailles and by packing a lunch and going early you can leisurely spend the day seeing it all. The children will appreciate this, too. Be sure and not go on a Tuesday when many of the most interesting parts of the palace are closed.

We prepared many of our own meals in Paris but did want to try a few of the restaurants and cafes, although for the most part they are too expensive for a family of four on a serious $10-a-day budget. A good idea for an inexpensive snack is to stop at one of the many "*crêpes*" stands, which are as popular in France as hamburger stands in America. They feature delicious paper-thin *crêpes* (pancakes) with a variety of fillings, rolled up into a neat package easily eaten in the hand. There are *crêpes au sucre* (with sugar), *crêpes au rhum* (with rum), and *crêpes au confiture* (with jam) to name a few; they are all delicious and a perfect way to start a day in Paris.

For lunch one day, stop at a sidewalk café along the famous Boulevard St. Michel, or "*Boul Mich*" as the students call it. We tried the **Restaurant St. Michel** at 10 boulevard St. Michel choosing a table outdoors to be able to watch the passersby, one of the most interesting entertainments Paris offers. For about $5.50 we had three delicious *prix fixe* (fixed price) meals, one of which we split for the girls. Each meal included an hors d'oeuvre, an entrée or *plat garni,* a vegetable, cheese or dessert, plus a glass of wine. Look for the *pris fixe* menus in the bistros as they usually are the best buy for the least money.

In case you want to splurge on an evening out without the kids, we have included the names of babysitting organizations in Paris in "Summing Up." Our choice for a restaurant on the one special night out was **La Fagoterie** at 14 Rue Grégoire de Tours on the Left Bank. It is small and intimate, with a fire around which you can sit with a group, or if wishing to be more alone, you can choose a small table. Another excellent restaurant in the area is **La Grillerie** on the Rue St. Jacques, but prices are higher, and it was no more enjoyable for us than La Fagoterie.

BRITTANY AND THE MAGNIFICENT NORTHERN COASTLINE

In mid-October we left Paris via Route 12 for Brittany, camping that night in a campground about five kilometers outside of Le

Mele-Sarthe, the next day was overcast and gloomy so we made good time driving to reach our destination of Mont-Saint-Michel before too late in the day. On the way is a *"Parc aux Promenades Parmi des Animaux à Liberté"* (a park with trails where animals freely roam) with an entrance fee of $1. It is well marked by signs along the road.

We reached **Mont-Saint-Michel,** one of the 10 wonders of France, about four o'clock, just in time to arrive breathless at the top of the hundreds of steps to the abbey and begin the last tour of the day. The abbey is a fascinating ancient dwelling of monks who worshipped the memory of St. Michel. This is a must when visiting France but beware of the tourist-trap-type shops on the way up and down from the abbey. One can take the tour and enjoy the surrounding panorama in just an hour and then head for the beaches of the north coast, the home of the proud Breton who considers his land almost separate from the rest of France.

We left Mont-Saint-Michel and drove along N.176 to **Saint Malo,** via the tiny fishing village of **Cancale.** Saint Malo is famous for its ramparts and the part it has played in the history of the French navy and the overseas expansion of France. We spent the night at a campground nearby, **St Servan-sur-Mer** on the peninsula near N.137, and the next morning set off for Trégastel, stopping first at the **Le Cap Fréhel**, a gorse-and-heather-covered moor ending in a multicolored rugged wall of rocky cliffs pierced by caves from which one can see a magnificent view of the whole Breton coast. There, you can visit the memorable **Fort La Latte**, planted on a dramatic site amid these cliffs. If you have time visit the Île-de-**Bréhat**, a beautiful small island off the coast.

Trégastel is a beautiful village frequented by Parisians during their summer holidays. Many of the more affluent have magnificent old summer homes here which are boarded up in the winter. Autumn is the perfect time to visit this village as it was quiet and peaceful, the weather was sunny with crisp, cool evenings and the beach was ours alone to explore. We spent two nights here, with first one camped down by the beach and the second one at a nearby inn. The delightful inn, **Auberge de Vieux Églises,** is at **Bourg,** just three kilometers inland from Trégastel. For $10.40 we had a warm, clean provincial room and a delicious seven-course dinner including sea trout (*truite de mer*), a specialty of the region.

The area surrounding Trégastel is called the **Rose-Red Granit Coast** (*La Côte de Granit Rose*), because of the great masses of red rock, which divide the beaches and emerge unexpectedly from fields and gardens. The port of **Perros-Guirec** is the center of much sailing activity and if you are a sailing enthusiast you might visit the nautical club there to get information on the frequently held regattas. The setting is beautiful and the temperatures mild. The region is also full of lakes and rivers for fishing, *La Guer* and *La Rence*, to name only two. Between February and April, the salmon fishing is excellent.

Campgrounds are abundant on the northern coast, a few of which are listed in "Summing Up". Also, you may want to visit some of the many beautiful little islands in the area. Be sure and stop at the *Syndicat d'Initiative* of Perros-Guirec where they will supply you with brochures on what to do and see. Almost every town in France has a *Syndicat d'Initiative*, the French tourist information bureau. From Perros-Guirec, we left for **Quimper,** a small town noted for its pottery. Though it is fun to browse in the shops the prices are high and the streets are crowded; shop browsing is not a favorite activity for children anyway, and often becomes just a frustrating experience for adults when traveling on a tight budget. From Quimper we drove to **Concarneau,** a 14th century town enclosed by ramparts. Here we parked by the beach and prepared dinner. As we ate by candlelight (keeping a supply of candles not only saves on the use of battery-operated lights in the car, but lends more romance to meals), there was a beautiful sunset to enjoy at Concarneau. Later we camped at the municipal campground in **Conleau,** a suburb of Vannes off the road to Nantes and Poitiers. The price was $1.10, and the campground though adequate, was nothing special. We did find that the campgrounds in France were not kept up as well as those in Scandinavia and England.

LOIRE VALLEY: POITIERS

France is divided into departments, of which **La Vienne** located in the Loire Valley is one. **Poitiers** lies at its center and offers much to the visitor in terms of historical interest, natural beauty of its surrounding countryside, and a diversity of offerings in the small villages a short distance from it. It is undergoing great changes now as is every major town of France. On the outskirts are groups of modern, unattractive apartment buildings and shopping centers. The *super marché* (supermarket) has unfortunately hit France, but none of this negates the still present, historically significant buildings of the past, nor the richness of the natural environs.

Poitiers, Saint-Savin, Civray, Chauvigny and many other villages of La Vienne have astonishingly, in the midst of this modernization, managed to preserve and restore their many celebrated historical monuments. It was in this region that we truly became acquainted with French life and culture, for it was here that we had the opportunity to stay with French families due to my earlier connection when I worked in Poitiers for my first job out of college. The major sights are within a day's side trip from Poitiers and there is an excellent campground, **Le Porteau**, just three kilometers north of town on the Rue du Porteau where you can stay. Thus, Poitiers is a good home base for touring this area.

Poitiers, often under English domination during the 13th and 14th centuries, retains a certain English flavor in the twisting streets and the gray stone houses with their respectable and prosperous air. The town is most known for its ecclesiastical architecture. You should definitely visit the **Church of Notre-Dame-la-Grande** located at the Place Notre-Dame-la-Grande, and perhaps combine this with a walk around Centre-Ville (the center of the town). The church was constructed in a style representing the transition from Romanesque to Gothic architecture and the western façade, with its center steeple bordered by two beautiful bell towers, is famous for the richness of its sculptural ornamentation. In the vault of the apse there is a large

12th century fresco of the Virgin and Child. Behind the main altar is the revered statue of "Notre Dame des Clefs" (Our Lady of the Keys). If particularly interested in ecclesiastical architecture, you should also see the **Church of St. Hilaire le Grand,** the **Cathedral of Saint Pierre, the Church of St. Radegonde** and the **Baptistery of St. John.** Be sure and schedule these visits on different days as this becomes quite boring for the children. One day in the midst of this rather heavy sightseeing you might take a ride up to **Le Parc de Blossac** set in the center of town on a high promontory overlooking the River Clain. Here you can picnic, and the children can play.

An enjoyable side trip from Poitiers is to the little village of **Angles-sur-l'Anglin,** a picturesque *bourg* (defined as a market town) on the Anglin River dominated by the imposing ruins of the **Chateau des Eveques de Poitiers** standing atop a large rocky cliff. We picnicked by the mill down at the river and then walked around the town square. There is a particularly interesting wood craftsman's shop on the square. It features unique handmade articles, for all quite reasonable prices, and the woodcarver and his son work in the shop so that one can watch the articles being made.

Spend another day visiting the church and the chateau at the village of **Chauvigny,** just 30 kilometers outside of Poitiers on Route 151. You can take a picnic lunch, visit the interesting church and museum containing scenes showing the life of the early French peasant, and then go on towards **Chatellerault,** the home of the famous French philosopher, Descartes. Here visit the **Museum of Descartes,** if the kids have not lost their patience with all this sightseeing. On the way to Chatellerault stop to see **Chateau Touffou,** a very interesting example of the medieval Renaissance style, sitting on a high promontory overlooking the valley of the Clain. You can see another extraordinary Renaissance-style chateau on your return to Poitiers from Chatellerault along Route 10, **Chateau Dissay,** situated between the River Clain and the vast Moulieve forest. The charming village of Dissay, clustered around its chateau and church offers the tourist riverside beaches and a campsite to stay the night before heading back to Poitiers.

The town of **Cognac,** where the famous brandy is made, is a two-hour drive from Poitiers. By the time we got to Cognac and toured the interesting medieval chateau with its vast vaulted cellars where the Otard firm matures their brandies, we could appreciate the tasting room where a small snifter of Cognac was served. As the Cognac trickled down our throats and warmed our spirits, our patience with the children increased considerably. On hectic days you might try this mellowing influence. The tour was well worth the visit as we learned about this interesting and ancient art of distilling the wine of Charente to reach the colorless, heavily perfumed, acid-tasting alcoholic beverage called Cognac.

You may also want to take in a "degustation" (wine tasting) at one of the many wine festivals in the region if there at the right time. While visiting friends in the country outside of Poitiers, a neighbor came by to invite us all to be the first to taste this year's sweet, fruity one and the acrid brandy as a topper. We also suggest that you read about the French wines before this experience. The Frenchman is very proud of his wine and for him the tasting and appreciation is as much an art as the growing of the grape and the distillation.

One of the most curious sights in the region around Poitiers is the **Marais Poitevin** or marshes of Poitou. Between Niort and the sea, and covering an area about 30 by 40 kilometers, the old Gulf of Poitou has been won back by the sea. The result is a farmland of half water and half land where all the work is done on the water, including transporting animals and the harvest. A fleet of flat-bottomed barges (*plattes*) propelled by men and women with paddles are the only means of transport. It's a picturesque sight to see them laden with hay, silently gliding over the marshy water as they slip in and out of the small isles. Regular boat trips are organized from the little villages of Coulon, Damvix, La Garete and La Grève-sur-le-Mignon. Reservations can be made for the Coulon tour at the *Syndicat d'Initiative* of Niort. There are two good itineraries listed in

"Summing Up." We felt that the two-hour trip was best for the kids, for that was just the right amount of time to hold their interest.

From the Marais you can head toward the sea and the port of **La Rochelle.** Originally known as Rupella (Little Rock), La Rochelle came into being as a village around the ninth century when people from the neighboring swamps moved to this one small area of dry land and built their huts. Today it is a bustling seaport full of all the color imparted by marine life: French sailors in their jaunty hats, crêpe stands, fish sellers in the street, marvelous seafood restaurants, colorful sail boats tied up at the harbor and fleets of fishing boats. Besides these admirable features, it is the takeoff point for a small island off the coast of France called **Île-de-Ré.** Camping is readily available on the island. St.-Martin-de-Ré is a large, well-equipped campground, open from June through September, or during the winter months you can always pull up to a parking spot at one of the many beautiful beaches. One of our favorite beaches was *Trousse-Chemise* (which means "Lift Skirts") where the girls had fun playing in the surf and collecting some rare and beautiful shells. This was October and still quite warm. Some French friends solicited our help in finding mussels (*moules*), left on the rocks during low tide, and taught us how to prepare *moules à la marinière*, a delicious dish in which *moules* are steamed in a sauce of white wine and garlic. Along with *moules-à-la poêle*, these are two of our favorite dishes. We later used this knowledge in preparing mussels in Spain, a delicious, economical meal. It's fun and simple to prepare *moules* on a campstove.

If you are in this region during the summer, we can also recommend the beaches at *Les Sables d'Olonne*, a well-frequented seaside resort and an important fishing port along the Vendean coast about 59 kilometers north of La Rochelle, and another beach, Royon to the south of La Rochelle. Situated on the mouth of the Gironde, Royon had been for generations a quiet holiday place. Then came the war. This coastal town was occupied by the Germans, partly evacuated, surrounded with blockhouses and pillboxes, and eventually destroyed by American bombs. After the war Royon was rebuilt by the Allies. Today it is the most modern sea resort in western France. A roofed promenade along the sea, a ferry with regular departures, a park and a city garden with miniature golf bring many tourists. During the summer months you will see bright-colored tents lined up, side by side, on the beaches all along the coast. This is the way the French preserve their privacy, a very important factor in French life, even on the beach. These small tents can usually be rented at most beach towns at fairly reasonable daily rates.

LIMOGES

From Poitiers one can drive a short distance south along N-147 to Limoges. This city is famous as a center of goldsmiths and for the minting of coins in medieval times, an industry founded by St. Eligus, the patron saint of goldsmiths and a craftsman of the court. The manufacture of the famous Limoges enamels reached its zenith in the 16th century and then completely disappeared by the end of the 18th century, but the prosperity of the town was maintained by the manufacture of porcelain following the discovery of china clay at St. Yrieix in 1755. The enamel industry was revived in 1875, and today porcelain factories and enamel workshops may be visited free of charge. For information go to the *Syndicat de la Porcelaine*, 7 Rue de General Cerez.

We found the tour of the porcelain factory most interesting and not too lengthy for the kids. They were delighted when a kind worker handed them each a miniature porcelain piece (*bibelot*) for their dolls. We later purchased a miniature tea set for them, which became a favorite distraction during the trip. This may not hold true for little boys. There is also a showroom where one can purchase china at very reasonable prices. For instance, in the Havilland factory we were able to purchase a small luncheon set of six plates, six cups, and two saucers for $5. These were seconds but flawless in our eyes and though short four saucers, we were told they could be ordered later.

LE LOT

From Limoges we headed for the department of **Le Lot** in the region of Quercy. It is not only an area of rich history with its prehistoric caves and medieval villages, but also one with a great variety of terrain, magnificent and rural at the same time. There is so much for one to see in Le Lot that it is difficult to say what the best itinerary is. One needs at least four or five days to do justice to this beautiful region, but if you are traveling with young children about two days is enough before their interest begins to wane; unfortunately, there is little here for children to do.

Our first stop in Le Lot was **Rocamadour,** a remarkable and beautiful village built in superimposed tiers on a vertical, rocky cliff. The ancient streets with medieval gates and the many charming squares make Rocamadour a real attraction. While there, climb the interminable flights of stone steps leading up one part of the cliff where three sanctuaries, one after the other are located. They contain precious relics, including a miraculous bell and the antique Black Virgin.

From Rocamadour take the narrow road going east to **Saint-Céré,** a tiny medieval village. Here is located **La Grotte de Presque,** famous subterranean caves open to the public for viewing every day from the 25th of March to the 10th of October.

One of the most memorable villages in Le Lot is **Saint-Cirq-Lapopie,** in a picturesque corner of Quercy. Built on the face of a cliff 250 feet above the River Lot, the medieval town is reached via Route N. 653 from Cahors through the valley of Le Lot to Route N. 662, then to D. 40. It is a steep ascent up the cliff on which Saint-Cirq rests. From this perch you can view the face of the cliff where the town's ancient half-timbered buildings stand. We later wandered through the cobblestone streets admiring the buildings, many dating back to the 11th and 12 centuries. Visit the 15th century church here, after which you may want to picnic on the hill where it stands.

We left Le Lot reluctantly as we had made arrangements to visit friends in the Pyrénées for a few days before going on to Spain. We

114

were thankful to have friends to visit from time to time to break the monotony of being in such confined quarters. It is a good idea to plan on staying in a small inn or hotel once every two weeks or so. Listed in "Summing Up" are a few reasonable ones in the region of Le Lot, the Loire Valley area and around the Pyrenees. If you plan this into your budget ahead of time, you will be able to make up for the extra expense on other camping days. For example, we found our daily costs to be very low while in Le Lot, as most of the sightseeing was free, our meals were prepared in the car and our only major expense was gas, which runs about 90 cents per gallon in France.

We further combated the feeling of being cramped by a change in our sleeping arrangements. Expecting both girls to sleep in a hammock over the front seats was a bit too much to ask. They were crowded and consequently could not sleep well. While in Poitiers we had gone to a ***bricolage*** (a sort of do-it-yourself store) and bought enough plywood to build a small box, which fit down between the two front seats. Its purpose was twofold: to serve as storage for all our maps and books, and with the two front seats on either side, it made a nice bed for the smaller of the two girls. It was made more comfortable by adding a small piece of foam rubber to the top. This arrangement worked perfectly and is one you may consider if you need that extra sleeping room for a small child. We were lucky to be able to borrow tools from a French friend while in Poitiers. You may have to make this box before you leave the states.

We had also added other accouterments to our camper to make her more like home. At a small carpet store in London we were able to buy a remnant of indoor-outdoor carpeting for about $2 to lay on the floor in the back. This made a nice cushion for our feet on some of the icy cold mornings. With the addition of paintings by the girls bedecking the walls and a clothesline strung across the back, our camper had taken on quite a homey air.

PYRENEES

A reprieve from our crowded conditions was provided by our friends' home in the small city of Oloron-Saint-Marie in the Pyrénées. We spent just two days with them at this visit but returned later for the Christmas holidays.

The town of Oloron-Saint-Marie has much to offer the traveler. Situated at the junction of two rivers, the Gave d'Aspe and the Gave d'Ossau, Oloron is composed of narrow winding cobblestone streets, medieval buildings, and views of the surrounding mountains. There are many buildings of historical interest among which the highlight is the 12th century cathedral, one of the most beautiful and ancient in southwestern France. It merits a prolonged visit. Before entering be sure to look closely at the much-celebrated portal with its relief of salmon fishermen.

A pretty place to stop for a tea break on one of your afternoon explorations is the little "salon de thé" on the Rue Barthou, **Climatisé,** specializing in pastries typical of the region; a balcony overlooks the Gave d'Ossau. There is also a wonderful small park, **Park Pommé**, where the kids enjoyed playing on the swings and slides and performing impromptu theater in the old-fashioned bandstand. Municipal camping is available in Oloron; locations and hotel accommodations, too, are listed in **"Summing Up"**.

The highlight of the mountainous area surrounding Oloron is the availability of ski facilities near the villages. Our favorite place was **La Gourette,** a beautiful little town in the heart of the Pyrénées standing at the foot of Le Col d'Aubisque. Situated in the region of a famous hot springs and health spa, **Les Eaux Bonnes**, it lies just 50 kilometers from Pau and between Larun and Le Col d'Aubisque. With an altitude of 4000 feet, La Gourette offers its visitors magnificent views of the surrounding valleys. In the winter it is a ski center; in the summer, a mountain-climbing region with guides available to lead the hiker through the many mountain trails. It is also a good takeoff point for excursions into the surrounding areas of Vallée d'Ossau, Vallée d'Aspe, la Bigorre and the Basque country. At Les Résidences du Valentin in La Gourette, one can rent rooms for four at $56 a week, a bit high for a $10-a-day budget, but an alternative to the camp mobile, if necessary. There are also good camping facilities at both Les Eaux Bonnes and La Gourette. The campground at La Gourette is open all year, and even in December we saw many French families in small caravans camping there in order to make their ski holidays more economical.

One day our friend volunteered to babysit for the girls so we could have a day of skiing. First, we went to the sporting goods store, Sport-Loisir, on Rue Barthou in Oloron, and rented skis, boots and poles for a reasonable rate of $5.60 a day for the two of us. We drove through beautiful countryside arriving at La Gourette and Le Col d'Aubisque in just about an hour. The chair-lift tickets were $2 each for half a day. There is also a funicular for non-skiers going up to some of the high points, providing spectacular views. The one-way charge on the funicular is $1; a round trip is $1.60; special price for children under 3 provided that the child is held on the lap of an adult. The skiing is excellent with a wide choice of slopes offered: a beginner's slope, another for moderately good skiers and finally one for the real pros. Incidentally, a parka is not only practical if you go skiing in Europe, but makes a good coat for in the car, warm and less cumbersome while sitting than a full-length coat.

The region around Oloron is designated as a national park for the preservation of wildlife. Comprised of a great variety of flora and fauna, the park covers an area of 125,000 acres and contains many different types of terrain, lakes, waterfalls and animal reserves that one can freely explore with the aid of park rangers who provide helpful information. In "Summing Up" we have listed some of our favorite scenic spots for picnicking while taking one-day side trips from Oloron.

You may also want to visit **Pau**, one of the largest cities in the area, ancient capital of the kingdom of Béarn. Pau has much to offer the tourist with the **Chateau de Henri IV** and the **House and**

Museum of Bernadotte, former King of Sweden and Norway, the highlights. The favorite place for the children, however, was the **Parc de Beaumont**. Here they could feed the swans in the central pond and use up their surplus energy by playing hide-and-seek in amongst the trees.

From Pau we drove to **Bayonne**, a large and rather uninteresting city, and then to the small and charming town of **Saint-Jean-de-Luz** where one begins to notice his/her proximity to Spain. The white-washed buildings with tile roofs resemble those across the border, and the people seem more Spanish than French. In Saint-Jean-de-Luz we camped along the beach on a small boardwalk. There is also a year-round campground, **Chibaou-Berria**, just three kilometers northeast of the town on Route N.10. Bungalow rental is also available here.

Chibaou-Berria, three kilometers northeast on N-10. Open all year; showers, shopping, camping gas, bungalows for rent, swimming. Admission: Adults, caravan and tent each 50 cents, car 20 cents.

Erromardi, two kilometers on D-10. Open Easter September 30; showers, shopping, camping gas. Admission: Adults 46 cents, car 50 cents, caravan and tent each 44 cents.

Luz Europe, four and a half kilometers northeast of St. Jean-de-Luz. Open all year; shopping, restrooms, bungalows for rent.

FRENCH FOOD SPECIALTIES

HORS D'OEUVRE

Salade de tomates, sliced tomatoes in oil and vinegar dressing.
Artichauts vinaigrette, artichokes with oil and vinegar dressing.
Salade de chou rouge, red cabbage salad.
Tranche de melon, a slice of melon
Filet de hareng, filleted herring
Escargot a la Borguignonne, snails with herbed, garlic butter.

118

PLATS GARNIS (MAIN DISH OR ENTRÉE)

Moules á la marinière, mussels steamed in white wine.
Sauté d'agneau, sautéed lamb aux fines herbs.
Canard a l'orange, duck in orange sauce.
Poulet rôti, roast chicken.
Coquilles Saint-Jacques, scallops, mushrooms in white wine sauce.
Gigot rôti, roast leg of lamb.
Foie de veau a la Lyonnaise, calves' liver with onion.
Ris de veau, sweetbreads.
Côtes de veau, veal cutlets.
Côtes d'agmeau, lamb chops.

LEGUMES (VEGETABLES)

Pommes frites, French fries
Haricots verts, string beans.
Haricots, dried white beans
Petits pois, peas
Épinard, spinach
Asperges, asparagus.
Chou, cabbage.

POTAGE (SOUP)

Potage Saint-Germain, puréed fresh pea soup.
*Consomm*é, A clear soup
Bisque, at thick soup usually made from shellfish.

ENTREMÉTS (DESSERTS)

Pâtisserie, pastry.
Babas au rhum, a small cake soaked in rum.
Tarte aux fruits, fruit tart.
Macédoine de fruits, fruit salad with kirsch.
Marrons glacés, glazed Chestnuts.
La glace, ice cream.

SUMMING UP FRANCE

For France we have listed campgrounds by region with some of the major points of interest. Information such as baby-sitting, post offices, shopping facilities, things to see and launderettes will be given only for the major towns and cities we visited. Admission fees are in dollars computed at the exchange rate of 5 francs to $1.

NORMANDY

Boulogne Camping

Le Moulin Wibert, 500 meters north of N. 40. Open all year; showers, shopping, camping gas, swimming. Admission: Adults 33 cents, caravan and tent each 15 cents.

Amiens, an important industrial town on the Somme River between Lille and Rouen. Of most interest are the famous 13th century Cathedral of Notre Dame and the Picardy Museum of prehistoric collections and paintings.

Rouen, the ancient capital of Normandy, is closely associated with the history of Joan of Arc. In the 14th century abbey Church of Saint Ouen she was sentenced to death in 1431. The Cathedral of Notre Dame there has a 525-foot spire that dominates the town. Other points of interest are the 14th century Church of St. Maclou and Grosse Horloge, a Renaissance building with a unique 14th century clock.

Camping

Bonsecours, three kilometers southeast of Rouen. Open all year; showers, swimming in a river. Admission: Adults 36 cents, tent and caravan each 15 cents.

PARIS

Paris is divided into several *arrondissements* or neighborhoods, each with a number. In giving addresses, the number is included where possible, for easy map reference. We also recommend you pick up a metro map at the first metro station you enter.

Camping

Bois de Boulogne, park with campground five kilometers west of the Place de L'Étoile (the Arc de Triomphe). Open all year; showers, laundry facilities, shopping, limited children's play area, post office, restaurant, camping gas. Family of four and caravan $1.05, 20 cents for showers.

Tourist Information

American Express, Rue Scribe across from Place de l'Opéra (metro stop Opéra).

American Center for Students and Artists, 261 Boulevard Raspail, Paris 14. Membership ($2 for non-Parisian residents) enables one to use the center's facilities including library, pool, art studios, music practice rooms, restaurant, lounge, garden and gymnasium as well as the center as a mailing address. The center sponsors dances, plays films, lectures, art exhibits and classes in art, dance and swimming. It also furnishes information about inexpensive travel and vacation possibilities in Europe and sponsors transatlantic charter flights for low-cost return transportation to the United States.

Note: This center is no longer in existence.

Babysitting (Garde d'Enfants)

Association des Étudiants en Médecine, 8 Rue Danté; telephone Odéon 25-44. Office open from 10 am–7 pm. Fee is $1 an hour plus transportation. Minimum of three hours.

Comité Parisien des Oeuvres des Étudiants, 39 Avenue de l'Observatoire; telephone Dan 07-49, extensión (poste) 330. Open weekdays 9:30 am–1 pm and 2–5:45 pm. Care provided for evening only at $1.10 per hour and $1.20 after midnight plus transportation. Minimum of three hours.

H.E.C.J.F., 108 boulevard Malesherbes. During the week call 924-57-23 until 6 pm; after 6, and on Saturday and Sunday call 833-34-59. Fee is $1 per hour, $1.20 per hour after midnight.

Institut Catholique, 21 Rue d'Assas. Office opens from 10 am–noon and from 2:30–5:30 pm. Fee is $1 per hour, after midnight $1.20, plus transportation. Minimum of three hours.

Institute d'Études Politiques, 24 Rue St. Guillaume; telephone 22-35-59, poste 706. Open between 3 and 6 pm. Fee: $1 per hour plus transportation. Minimum three hours.

Note: If you do not speak French, the best way to get a babysitter is to ask one of the multilingual student attendants at the campground office to assist you by telephoning the agencies and trying to find an English-speaking sitter. The attendants can then tell you how to reach the babysitter's residence in order to pick him or her up. Check their credentials and references. We did not use these babysitting services as we were fortunate to get some breaks from the children via our friends. We know not everyone is as lucky as we are to have friends in European countries, one of the benefits I, to this day, appreciate from my early career days working in France.

Launderettes

Economy Laverie Pressing, 34 Rue Delambre, Montparnasse, near the Gare Montparnasse (take the metro to Vavin, Montparnasse-Bienvenue or Edgar Quintet). Open 8 am–midnight, seven days a week; 60 cents for five kilos of laundry, 20 cents for drying. Inexpensive dry cleaning available also.

Selsa Service, 216 Rue St. Jacques (Latin Quarter area on Left Bank of Seine), on stretch of Rue St. Jacques beyond Rue Soufflot (uphill). Cost is 60 cents for a five-kilo load, 40 cents for drying.

Of the numerous neighborhood launderettes, our favorite was the small one on the Place de Chérioux just off Rue de Vaugirard. Take the metro to Vaugirard stop. The cost is $1.10 for each load.

A picnic at the laundromat while waiting
for our clean clothes to dry

Hotel Suggestions

Eden Hotel, on Rue Blomet right off the corner of Place de Chérioux (metro stop Vaugirard). Walk up Rue de Vaugirard to Place de
Chérioux, turn right then left on Rue Blomet. Rooms for about $3
to 4.50 a night; clean, not fancy

Restaurants

We have listed only a couple that we tried and found fairly reasonable
(or with so much atmosphere they shouldn't be missed).

Restaurant St. Michel, 10 Boulevard Saint-Michel, Paris 6. This tiny
restaurant with outdoor tables right on the boulevard makes people
watching good entertainment while eating. It offers a *prix fixe* meal at
about $1.15 that includes a drink, hors d'oeuvre (note: this does not
mean a small snack that can be anything from a platter of tomatoes to
a piece of fish fillet or an artichoke), *plat garni* (entrée) and a choice of
legume (vegetable), *fromage* (cheese) or dessert. We highly recommend
you accustom yourselves to the French custom of a piece of cheese and
some fruit at the end of a meal. It is not only good for the waistline

but tasty as well, with the variety of cheeses offered far broader in scope than in America. You may want to stop for a pastry in one of the many patisseries along the streets for your mid-afternoon snack.

La Fagoterie, 14 Rue Grégoire de Tours, Paris 6. Though not a particularly economic choice we found the atmosphere of this restaurant unbeatable. A great place for fondue bourguignon on that one evening out in Paris.

La Grillerie, Rue St. Jacques, Paris n5, near the Petit Pont. Also, good atmosphere; prices a bit high, but food is delicious.

Chez les Fondus, 19 rue des Trois Frères (up the street from Au Coin Fleuri), in Montmartre. For $3 you will be served a cocktail, fondue bourguignon, cheese and fruit, with service included.

The Balkans Restaurant, Rue de La Huchette, Paris 5, just off Place St Michel. Good food, reasonably priced.

Also try one of the North African restaurants on Rue de la Huchette and be sure to order couscous, a dish of steamed grain served with a variety of vegetables and meats (go lightly on the red sauce unless you prefer very spicy and hot). There are several inexpensive restaurants on Rue St. André-des-Arts just opposite Place St. Michel. For an inexpensive lunch go to the department store, *Au Printemps*, at 64 Boulevard Haussmann, near the American Express office. Go two blocks from American Express down the Rue Auber to the store. Enter at the building marked *"nouveaux magasins"* and ascend to the sixth floor to the large rooftop dining room offering a *prix fixe* lunch for about $2. This includes salad or melon, entrée, dessert, wine and service charge. Closed Sunday and Monday.

Shopping in Paris

Most stores in Paris, including the supermarkets, are open from about 9:30 am until noon and then close until 2 pm for the midday meal. Plan your schedule accordingly.

Shopping for Food

We found that the best way to buy food was to follow the natives and buy most of our fruit and produce at the neighborhood open markets (*marches*), which one finds everywhere in Paris. These markets are usually open every day except Monday. One of the best known is that on the street, *La Rue Mouffetard*, known as *Marché de la Mouffe*; another that we frequented was the one in Faubourg St. Antoine, open on Wednesday and Saturday. Take the metro to the Reuilly Diderot stop, follow Boulevard Diderot to Rue de Reuilly where you will turn left and walk until you find the open stalls. We bought our bread at the *boulangerie*, our meat at the *boucherie* and our cold cuts at the *charcuterie*. The most fun was the *pâtisserie* where we drooled over the many delicious-looking pastries. For wine, canned goods, juice and some dairy products you can go to an *alimentation* or épicerie. Supermarkets (*super marchés*) are occasionally found in small residential neighborhoods, but more often you will have to go to the big department stores such as Galerie Lafayette or Au Printemps to find a supermarket.

Shopping for Clothes

Au Printemps, 64 Boulevard Haussmann.

Galerie Lafayette, Near Place de l'Opéra.

Prisunic, a giant store, like a US five-and-ten-cent (or five-and-dime) store, on right-hand side of the Champs Élysées as you walk toward Arc de Triomphe (corner of the Rue de la Boétie).

Sumaritaine Department Store, on Rue de Rivoli.

Unishop Shopping, 61 Rue de la Verrérie, Paris 4. An odd-lot clearance shop featuring fine quality women's fashions at reasonable prices.

Specialty Shopping

There are some delightful small shops and galleries where one can buy old books, prints of famous paintings and contemporary as well as ancient art objects along the Boulevard du Montparnasse and in the small side streets off the main boulevard, particularly Rue de la Grande Chaumiére.

Le Griot, 167 Boulevard du Montparnasse, Paris 6. A fascinating shop of African hand-crafted objects.

Galerie des Peintres Graveurs, 159 Boulevard du Montparnasse. For graphic arts, prints and paintings.

For Prints. Most of the art museums have small shops where one can purchase prints of good quality for considerably less than one would pay in the United States. Another source is the **Laboratoire de Calcographie du Louvre,** located on the third floor of the stairway on the riverside entrance to the Louvre, just a few yards from the main selling room. Here prints are made from old engraving plates, selling at from 70 cents to $2. We found they made great gifts, lightweight and easy to carry in between clothing in our suitcases, or to send in a mailing tube that most shops will provide.

For cookware, *Déhillerin,* 13 Rue Coquilliére.

For Wine and Spirits, *La Maison de Vrai Rhum*, Rue de Renard off the Place de l'Hotel de Ville. They sell 500 different kinds of spirits. Run by the friendly Ginot family who founded the shop in the 19th century.

For Perfume (*Parfumeries*) and High Fashion (Haute Couture) the area of Rue du Faubourg St. Honoré is renowned for its elegant shops featuring fashions of many "grands couturiers": *Balenciaga* **and** *Givenchy*, Avenue George V; *St Laurent, Lanvin-Castillo* and *Jacques Esterel*, rue du Faubourg St. Honoré; *Maggy Rouff, Ungaro and Balmain,* Avenue Montaugire.

126

The Paris Flea Market (*Marché aux Puces*) is at the Porte de Clignancourt (metro stop Porte de Clignancourt). It is open on Saturday, Sunday and Monday. We found prices high, but it's an experience you shouldn't miss.

Sightseeing in Paris

Note: Virtually all museums and monuments of Paris (including the Louvre and the Palace of Versailles with the exception of the gardens) are closed on Tuesdays. This would be a good day to take a side trip to the beautiful town of **Chartres** or to just stroll in the **Luxembourg Gardens** and along the quays of the Seine and let the children play.

Bateaux Mouches: A boat tour is a good way to see the main areas along the Seine as well as to familiarize yourself with the layout of Paris. Tour boats leave every half hour between 10 am and noon and 2 and 7 pm from the dock on the Right Bank next to the Pont de L'Alma (**metro stop:** *Alma-Marceau),* directly across from the Eiffel Tower. For our family of four, it cost 2.60francs ($1 for each adult and 30 cents for the children). The tour lasted one and a half hours. There is also a longer tour, which costs more and lasts two and a half hours (a bit too long for children).

Notre Dame Cathedral (see note added to this edition at the end of this section about France) Open every day except Tuesday from 10 am–4 pm (until 5 pm in the summer). A 40-cent ticket must be purchased to go up in the tower. This is a long walk for the kids, however, and we might suggest you forgo this or take turns so that one adult can stay down below with the kids. After you visit, picnic in the little park on the **L'Île de la Cité** just behind Notre Dame. You can spend the two-hour lunch break enjoying the local scenery or walking along the quays in front of the cathedral and browse in the book stalls (*les boquinists*) filled with art prints and old and new books.

Rodin Museum Take the **metro to Invalides or Varenne** and proceed to 77 Rue de Varenne. Here you will enter a garden and museum filled with sculptures of Rodin. The museum is open every day except Tuesday and 10 am–12:15 pm and 2–5 pm for a rather high admission fee of 60 cents each. If you schedule your visit for a Sunday, you can get in for 20 cents.

Luxembourg Gardens: Metro stop is Odéon or St Sulpice. A great place for the kids with a lake where they can sail boats, take pony rides and play in the playgrounds. For the playground, be prepared to pay a small admission fee of 30 cents each. Admission into the park is free.

Children's Art Atelier Take the metro to rue Vaugirard and walk one and a half blocks to the Art Atelier, on your left just before you arrive at Rue de l'Abbé Groult. Go down the short alley to a central courtyard where signs will direct you the rest of the way. For $3 each the children can spend two and a half hours in a delightful and creative studio playing with clay, paint and other craft materials.

Boulevard Montparnasse While the kids are at their art class take the metro from Vaugirard to metro stop Montparnasse-Bienvenue and explore this fascinating boulevard of galleries and small shops. The side streets are just as interesting, especially the **Rue de la Grande Chaumiére** where you can browse in small bookstores or art supply shops. You may also want to take a class at the **École de la Grande Chaumiére where** an afternoon life drawing class is offered for only $1.40.

The Jeu de Paume Take the metro (stop Place de la Concorde) to the Garden of the Tuileries to visit this exquisite little museum devoted to impressionist paintings. We found it more enjoyable than the Louvre, which was exhausting with children. The Jeu de Paume is open every day except Tuesday from 9:45 am–5:15 pm. Tickets are on sale until 4:40 pm and admission is 60 cents, 30 cents on Sunday (free to those with a student identification card on Sunday and on Thursday afternoons).

The Place de la Concorde and the Arc de Triomphe Upon leaving the Jeu de Paume enjoy a walk through the huge and beautiful sculpture and fountain bedecked square, the Place de la Concorde, to the grand boulevard of the *Champs Élysées* toward the Arc de Triomphe. Stop at a local sidewalk café and watch for the lights to come on: it is beautiful and free! You may want to take in an early cinema in one of the big theaters on the boulevard before heading back to camp that night.

The Palais de Chaillot Located at **metro stop Trocadéro**, this complex of museums is open from10 am–5pm (in summer until 6 pm) every day except Tuesday. The museum admissions range from 40 to 60 cents (some offer half-price tickets on Sunday). There is a maritime museum, an anthropology museum and an aquarium, with a park and cafes facing the Eiffel Tower.

The Museum of Modern Art, Located at 13 Avenue du President Wilson (**metro stop Iena**). This museum is open every day except Tuesday from 10 am–5 pm for an admission charge of 60 cents (half price and sometimes free on Sundays).

City of Paris offering changing exhibits of contemporary Parisian artists and open every day except Tuesday from 10 am–noon and 2–5 pm with an admission of 60 cents. In the same building is a **Museum of Costumes** with fashion exhibits from the 18th century up to the present. Admission is 40 cents, free on Sunday, with the same hours as at the Museum of Modern Art of the City of Paris.

A Walk and a Picnic Suggestion
A fine way to break up the normal round of sightseeing is with a walk through the oldest quarter of the Left Bank to work up a good appetite for a picnic. Start at the *Rue de la Huchette* just off the Place St. Michel. During the day shops here sell pastries and

Arab specialties. This would be a good place to stop and pick up your picnic dessert. Be sure and take a basket or canvas bag along. This street is the heart of the St. Severin quarter, which has taken over from *St.-Germaindes-Prés* and Montparnasse as the center for non-tourist Paris nightlife. After 9 pm the cabarets and discotheques open their doors and the young Parisians pack such places as *Le Chat qui Peche* and *Storyville*. At the end of *Rue de la Huchette* cross *Place St.-Michel* in front of the fountain and follow Rue St. André-des-Arts straight ahead to get a marvelous view of one of the oldest church towers of Paris, **St. Germain-des-Prés**, above the rooftops. Continue to *Rue de l'Éperon*, the first street to the left; enter it, then turn right at *Rue du Jardinet*. Don't be fooled when it appears to be a dead end. Through the gates are the three court-yards of Cour de Rohan, a charming sight that even Parisians often miss. At the end of these cobblestone courts another gate leads into a covered arcade where the critic Sainte-Beuve once lived. Turn left into the arcade, then right as soon as possible. You are now on *Rue de l'Ancienne Comédie* where Molière and the original *Comédie Française* had their first theater in a handball court. Turn right and follow the street the distance of a long block to the place where five streets form a star. On the right you will pass the **Procope**, the oldest café in Paris where Voltaire and Ben Franklin were frequent visitors. This intersection, *Carrefour de Buci*, has been a key point in several revolutions and was the scene of the massacre of the priests during the revolution of 1789.

Buci Market begins here and continues to the right on Rue de Buci. This is one of several street markets in the city where goods are exhibited in open stalls as they were in medieval times. At a number of "charcuteries" you can buy salads, pies, roast chickens and pâtés. (We particularly like *"pâté de la compagne."*)

You can supplement your main dish with a loaf of bread and a bottle of wine. Return to Carrefour de Buci and take Rue Dauphine to Pont Neuf, about two long blocks in distance. **Pont Neuf** is the oldest bridge in Paris and the first built without houses on it. The round bays along the side were used at one time by traveling gypsies, entertainers and jugglers. Behind the equestrian statue of Henry IV are stairs leading down to the garden of **Vert-Galant**, a good spot for a picnic. From the tip of the island you see the Louvre to the right, and to the left, the **Monnaie** (the mint) and the institute where the French Academy meets. There are usually fishermen under the willows and, to the left, the barges and boats of the fire stations.

Zoos in and around Paris

Zoo de Paris, metro stop Porte-Dorée. Open daily from 9 am–6pm. Until 6:30 pm on Sunday. Entrance: Adults 60 cents, children up to 7 years, 30 cents.

Chateau de Thoiry, Thoiry (Yvelines). Forty kilometers from Paris (autoroute de l'ouest, route de Dreux), from Porte Mailot. Open Monday through Saturday, 11:30 am–5:30 pm. Animals in a natural setting.

Marionnettes *Jardin d'Acclimatation*, Bois de Boulogne, Paris 16. Shows on Thursday, Saturday, Sunday and vacation days at 3, 4 and 5 pm. Free admission. Entrance to the garden is 25 cents for adults and 13 cents for children.

Circus *"Cirque d'Hiver,"* 110 Rue Amelot (metro stop Filles-du-Calvaire or Oberkamp). Seats cost from \$1.30–\$5; performances on Thursday 4:30 pm, Saturday at 9 pm, Sunday at 2 and 5 pm.

NOTE: On April 15, 2019 just before 18:20 hours, a structural fire broke out in the roof space of the Notre-Dame de Paris. By the time the fire was extinguished the cathedral's spire had collapsed, most of the roof had been destroyed, and its upper walls were severely damaged. When we visited in 2022, we appreciated all the restoration work that was going on to restore Notre Dame, and the well-done billboards along a walkway next to the Cathedral that described the reparations project.

SIDE TRIPS FROM PARIS

Palace of Versailles: You can either go by train from the Saint-Lazare station or by bus No. 171 that you catch at the Pont de Sèvres exit (take the **metro to Pont de Sèvres**). The 60-cent bus ride takes 15 minutes. The advantage of the bus over the train is that it runs more frequently, and it also will let you off right at the front gates. You can bring a picnic lunch and eat it in one of the many splendid gardens.

Chartres this makes a marvelous one-day trip from Paris if you leave early enough. We suggest you take the car as you may decide to stay a little longer. The town is picturesque and the cathedral magnificent. Take autoroute N. 10 from Paris to Chartres. You could combine the Versailles and Chartres trips, seeing Versailles and then proceeding along the same autoroute to Chartres, spending the night at a campground in Chartres before seeing sights there and going south or back to Paris.

Camping

Vieux Moulin, on N-817, Avenue des Déportés. Open April 1–November 1. Admission: Adults 25 cents, car 11 cents, caravan and tent, no charge.

BRITTANY

From Paris take Route N. 12 towards Dreux. This road will take you all the way to Mont-Saint-Michel. The following are campgrounds and special sights to see on the way.

Le Mêle-Sarthe Small village between Mortagne and Aleçon; watch for campground signs. Very nice grassy area, clean restrooms and showers. We paid about 80 cents for our family and the camper.

Mayenne Raymond Fauque, 454 Rue de St. Leonard on N. 12. Open May–October; showers, shopping, bar, pool, camping gas. Admission: Adults 30 cents, car caravan and tent each 15 cents.

Du Mont-Saint-Michel, two kilometers south at crossroads between N. 776 and d. 275. Open Easter–September; grassy parking area, showers shopping. Be sure and walk to the top to visit the famous Abbey of Saint Michel. Tours run every hour until 4 pm. Admission is 50 cents for adults, children free.

Col-De-Bretagne Ferme-Camping le Vieux-Chêne, five kilometers east on N. 176. Open April–October 30; showers, shopping, chalet for rent, swimming in lake or sea.

Dinard, Le Port Blanc, Rue du Sergent-Boulanger, one kilometer west on N. 786. Open Easter–September 30; showers, shopping, camping gas, swimming in the sea. Admission: Adults 35 cents, car, caravan and tent each 18 cents. The villages of *Cancal* and *Dinan* should both be visited. They are picturesque and typically Breton in character. Watch for the women wearing the Breton cap or *coiffe* made of starched white lace.

St. Malo At St. Servan-sur-Mer, Cité d'Aleth, on the peninsula near N.137. Open all year; shopping, restrooms, camping gas, swimming. Admission: Car 18 cents, adults, caravan and tent each 36 cents. See the ramparts, which date back to medieval times, and the tower *Tour-Quic-en Groigne.* Visit the office of the Syndicat d'Initiative for schedule of boats leaving for Le *Cap Fréhel.* If you drive inland along N. 166 to Dinan and then take D. 221 to Les Iffs you will come to a village well known for its beautiful stained glass; also see the *Montmuran* Castle, a kilometer from the village in lovely woods overlooking a deep gorge.

Plérin Villes-Fontaines, three and a half kilometers northeast on Route des Rosaires. Open all year; showers, shopping, camping gas, swimming in the sea. Admission: Adults 47 cents, car 14 cents, caravan and tent each 13 cents.

Trégastel Camping Caravaning Le Golven, reached via N. 786, near the sailing school (Ecole de Voiles). A very agreeable site with play area, 100-meter beach, a small store, sailing school and riding school. *Camping de Roch Uzon*, on N. 786. This is an agreeable site with fishing, sailing school, beach.

Camping Ajonc d'Or Convenant Bihan, on the Route de Tourony Beach. Laundry room, recreation room with ping pong, volleyball green, swings and play area for children, fishing, beach, walking paths. You might al want to consider one of the following inns:

Auberge de Vieux Églises, at Bourg, two miles inland from Trégastel. Very reasonable prices clean and cozy rooms, delicious food served in a pleasant dining room.

Hotel "Le Caboteur," in the center of town; telephone 35-28-33. Open only in the summer.

Perros-Guirec Ploumanac'h Le Ranolien, reached via route N. 786; watch for signs and small driveway. Beach, fishing, sailing. La Claire-Fontaine, by N. 786. Play area for children, shopping, beach, fishing and sailing.

Plougastel-Daoulas Le Clé des Champs, one and a half kilometers southwest of Plougastel-Daoulas. Open all year; showers, shopping, camping gas. Admission: Adults 30 cents; car, caravan and tent each 15 cents.

Du Moulin Sylvain, about three kilometers southeast of Concarneau. Open all year; showers, shopping, camping gas, beach. Admission: Adults 60 cents, car 20 cents, caravan and tent each 40 cents.

Camping des Menhirs, near Carnac, St. Michel, 56340, one kilometer on N.781. Open all year; shopping camping gas, beach. Admission: Adults 30 cents caravan and tent each 15 cents.

Les Ombrages, two and a half kilometers north D.119, road to Auray, taking turning to left. Open Easter–September; showers, shopping. Carnac is at the center of a huge megalith-strewn area that runs 5 miles coastwise across fields and moorland as far as and even beyond *Locmariaquer*. Note: this is a Breton name and the region is very interesting to explore.

St. Nazaire At St. Marc: L'Eve, seven and a half kilometers west of St. Nazaire. Open May 15–September 15; showers, shopping, camping gas, swimming. Admission: Adults 40 cents, car, caravan and tent each 20 cents.

Angers: *Parc de la Haye*, four and a half kilometers northwest on D. 122. Open all year; showers, swimming in a lake. Admission: adults 27 cents, car, caravan and tent each 18 cents.

THE LOIRE VALLEY

Camping

About 22 kilometers from Tours at Amboise, *Île d'Or*, north on N. 52. Open Easter–September 30. Admission: Adults and car each 34 cents, no charge for tent and caravan.

Mont-Louis-Sur-Loire, one and a half kilometers west on N. 751, halfway between Tours and Amboise. Open all year.

Sightseeing

Poitiers: A university town and center of the Chateau Region, this is a lovely city to stroll in; be sure and stop at the Hotel de Ville on the Place Jean Jaures, building typical of most French city halls.

CHATEAUX OF THE LOIRE

Start in Tours. The best thing to do while in Tours is to pick up a Michelin guide to the castles in the region and work out an itinerary. We present some suggestions here.

Follow Route N. 76 from Tours 24 kilometers to the **Chateau Chenonceaux**, one of the most beautiful in the Loire Valley. Visiting hours are 10 am–noon and 2–7 pm, March 16–September 15; 9 am–noon and 2–6 pm, September 16–October 31; 2–4 pm, November 1–January 31; and 2—5 pm, February 1–March 15. Entrance 50 cents. Sound and light show in the summer.

Next take Route D. 31 to *Amboise*. The chateau is magnificent, the town interesting. Visiting hours for the chateau are 9 am–noon and 2–7 pm, until dusk in the winter. Entrance: 40 cents. Don't miss *Clos-Luce*, Leonardo de Vinci's studio. Follow the Rue Victor-Hugo. Visiting hours are 9 am–noon and 2–7 pm. Entrance: 30 cents. Plan on camping at Amboise as you will probably be tired after these visits and kids under age 12 may be bored to tears. (**Note:** Leonardo da Vinci was commissioned by Francois I to move to the Chateau Clos Luce in 1516, where he spent the rest of his life. DaVinci is buried here).

From Amboise, continue on Route N. 751 to *Chateau de Chaumont.* Visiting hours are 9-11-45 am. And from 2–6:30 pm, April 1–September 30; 9–11:45 am and 2–5 pm in October; 9–11:45 am 2–4 pm., November –March 31. Entrance: 20 cents, 10 cents on Sunday and holidays.

From Chateau de Chaumont continue on Route N. 751 to *Blois*. Visiting hours are 9 am–noon and 2–6 pm, in the summer and 9 am–noon and 1:30–dusk in the winter. Entrance 40 cents. There are Sound and Light shows in the summer; entrance 50 cents. These are definitely worth seeing.

By this time, you may be "chateau'd out", but if not, others you may want to see are: *Azay-le-Rideau*, at the convergence of Route N. 751 and D. 17; *Chinon*, southeast of Azay le-Rideau on N. 751; *Richelieu*, south of Chinon on Route N. 749.

POITIERS

Camping

Le Porteau, three kilometers north of town on the Rue du Porteau. Open all year: showers, shopping, camping gas. Admission: Adults 45 cents, car 23 cents, caravan and tent each 30 cents.

Tourist Information, Syndicat d'Initiative, Place du Maréchal-Leclerc; telephone 41-21-24. Branch office, Place de la Gare (train station); telephone 41-34-50.

Post Office, Rue Arthur-Ranc.

Restaurants

Auberge de la Belle Aurore, at St. Benoit, route de Ligugé, about five kilometers outside of Poitiers on the River Clain.

La Petite Marmite, Chez Jacqueline, 16 Rue du Mouton, near the Porte de Paris. A small student restaurant with family-style dining at one long table.

Places of Interest:

St. Johns Baptistry, in the middle of Rue Jean Jares where it meets a tiny street called Rue Roche d'Argent.

Notre-Dame-la-Grande, one of the oldest Romansque churches in Europe on the Place de Notre-Dame-la-Grande.

Le Parc de Blossac. This park provides one of the most beautiful walks to be found in a provincial town. Enclosed within the ancient ramparts, the park overhangs the Clain Valley some 150 feet below.

THE COUNRYSIDE AROUND POITIERS

Les Grottes de la Norée, amidst lovely scenery in the Loire Valley, four kilometers southwest of Poitiers at *Grottes de La Norée*. These grottoes were formed by an ancient underground water course and consist of caves and stalactites in a fairyland-like setting. They can be visited all year round.

Dissay lies halfway between Poitiers and Chatellerault on the main road N. 10, but it is advisable to take the local road (*route departmentale* N. 4) that follows the right bank of the Clain. Visit the chateau at Dissay.

Angles-sur-l'Anglin, a picturesque village reached by taking route N. 151 to St. Savin where you turn onto D-11 to Angles.

Chauvigny, 23 kilometers outside Poitiers on N. 151.

Marais Poitevin Take route N-11 to Niort. Pick up reservations for a boat tour through the marshes at the Syndicat d'Initiative, 43 Rue Chabuady. Two itineraries: (1) By boat take the triangle cruise-Coulon, La Garette, La Soiterio, Coulon. About 2 hours. (2) For the whole day, from Coulon to La Garette, follow the "Rigole de La Garette" by Irleau to Arcais or Damvix where one can have lunch, returning up the Sèvres, being pulled by towline.

Cognac, reached by taking Route N. 10 south to Ruffec, southwest on N. 736 to Jarnac and west on N. 141 to Cognac. Visit the Otard distillery there.

Camping

Aussac, on Route 10 outside of Angoulème. Open all year; extensive facilities, small play area.

LA ROCHELLE

Camping

Lagord, Les Trois Lys, northwest of La Rochelle on D. 104. Open all year; showers, camping gas, bungalows for rent, swimming in a pool or sea. Admission: Adults 34 cents, car, caravan, and tent each 18 cents.

Tourist Information *Syndicat d'Initiative*, Place de Verdun.

Sightseeing

This is one of the most interesting towns in France with a history that has been full, heroic and tormented. It is famous for its three towers of *St. Nicolas, La Chaine* and *Tour de La Lanterne* and the ramparts, which fortified the city. *Charruyer Park* lies along one side of the town and forms a pleasant link between the old town, the beach and the modern sector. Watch for a *"criée aux poissons"* (public auction of fish) when the fishing boats return to harbor.

Island of Île-de-Ré: Take a ferry from the pier at La Rochelle ($4.80 round trip) to this beautiful little island, a good place for a few days rest from sightseeing, where the children can run on the beaches, make sand castles, visit lighthouses, and the family can rent bikes and bicycle around the island and its many picturesque villages. Again, we were very lucky to have French friends with whom we could stay. The children loved this place. One can now take a bridge to the island.

Restaurants in La Rochelle

There are numerous restaurants in La Rochelle. One of the most famous is *Andrés* on the quays, specializing in, you guessed, seafood.

LIMOGES

Camping

At *Bonnac-la-Côté Chateau*, 10 kilometers from Limoges, north on Route N.20, *Chateau Leychoisier*, Open April–September 15; showers, shopping, bungalows for rent, swimming in a lake. There is a park, lake and waterfall here and it is not far from **Chalus Tower** where Richard the Lionhearted was killed. There is also a playground here and small swimming pool for children.

Tourist Information: *Syndicat de la Porcelain*, 7 Rue de Général Cerez.

Sightseeing

The most interesting thing to visit in Limoges is the porcelain factories. Even the children will enjoy this as they will receive a little piece of china at the end of the tour (referred to as a *bibelot*)

THE REGION OF LE LOT

Go south from Limoges on N.20 to Brive and from Brive to Souillac. From Souillac go south still on N.20 to Payrac where you should turn east on N.683 to Roc-Amadour, Take N, 681 to N.677 and continue southwest to N.20, south to Cahors, which is a good central home base for further exploration into this beautiful region. You can pick up further information and suggested itineraries at the Syndicat d'Initiative in Cahors.

Camping

Brive: Ferm des Isles, Open all year; small shop, restrooms.

Souillac: Les Ondines, one kilometer southeast on road to Sarlat, take a left turn. Open June 15 to September 15; showers, shopping, bar, swimming.

Cahors: Municipal Campground, in city center; watch for campground signs

Figeac: Les Carmes, N.140 Avenue de Paris. Open a year; showers, shopping, camping gas, swimming. Admission: Adults 36 cents, car, caravan and tent each 18 cents.

Roc-Amadour: Be sure and see the Abbaye on top of the cliff, the small chapel of the Black Virgin and the Hotel de Ville down in the town.

Saint-Céré: Visit *La Grotte de Presque*, 11 Rue de la République, on route N. 673, five kilometers outside of town. Open to the public every day from March 25–October 10, 8:30–12 and from 2 to 7. Tour of the grottoes lasts a half hour.

Saint-Cirq-Lapopie: One of the most beautiful and picturesque villages in all of France; an ancient town of artists and poets. This town cannot help but evoke the romance of medieval times. Its tiny winding cobblestone streets invite exploring, and the architecture of its old buildings with their strange sculptural decorations fascinate the viewer. We loved this village and could have spent weeks there if time had permitted.

Toulouse: Camping at **Municipal Campground,** Chemin du Pont de Rupé, six kilometers north of town by route N.20. Open all year.

THE PYRÉNÉES

PAU

We did not find any good camping spots in Pau. However, this is a good place to stop and pick up information on the region of *La Béarn*. Information is available at the Syndicat d'Initiative in town.

Sightseeing: Le Parc Beaumont, Le Chateau d'Henri IV, House and Museum of Bernadette.

OLORON-SAINT-MARIE

Col de la Marie Blanque, reached by taking Route N. 618 as far as Escot where you will turn and follow the road straight. There are beautiful grassy areas here along the way where you can picnic and explore

Aydis this is a very old village near Oloron in the valley of Aspe. Take N618 south to intersection near Bedous. Turn left toward Laruns and you can't miss Ayduis. It is a lovely place to walk and enjoy the view of the mountains.

141

Col d'Aubisque You will find a good restaurant here, Les Crètes blanches, with a prix fixe menu for about $2.

St.-Jean-de-Luz This charming Basque village is a worthwhile stop on your way to the Spanish border.

Spain

To understand Spain, one must know something of her rich history and topography. Located at one end of the European continent, the Iberian Peninsula, and separated from Africa by only a brief sea voyage, Spain has been constantly open to invasion by other cultures that have left their indelible mark. From a thousand years before Christ through the eighth century, the Iberian Peninsula aroused the ambitions of a series of invaders who brought it into contact with the great civilizations of the world, Romans, Visigoths and Moors who remained in Spain for long periods and produced lasting racial mixtures and cultural infusions.

Spain is also characterized by a geographic diversity, which has created many almost separate cultures within a culture, such as the contrasts between the Catalonian and the Castilian. The distinctive feature of the Spanish topography is the great central plateau with an area of 120,000 square miles and an average altitude above sea level of more than 2000 feet. It slopes gently toward the Atlantic, the valleys of the Ebro, and the mountain ranges that border its coastline of huge, sweeping beaches.

On arrival in any Spanish city you should first find the tourist office and pick up a list of the government-operated inns called *paradors* and *albergues*. The Ministry of Tourist Information operates this unique network of hotels throughout the Spanish countryside, offering the tourist excellent accommodations at very modest rates. These hotels or inns are often in old restored castles, palaces and convents,

143

located in regions of historical and natural significance. You may even want to write to the Spanish National Tourist Office (see "Summing Up" for address) before your departure for Europe and request the list. It may be helpful in planning your itinerary for the country.

When touring Spain, you should also be aware of the Spanish custom of closing down all the shops and many of the museums during the hours of siesta, from 1:30 to 3:30 pm in most cities. At first this practice may be a bit frustrating, especially to North Americans who have never learned the value of spending a few hours each day in repose or reflection. We came to appreciate the value of this custom though, and began looking forward to our daily siesta, whether it be a nap along the road or a quiet time with the children during a break from our busy sightseeing schedule.

SAN SEBASTIAN

San Sebastian is one of the most elegant and cosmopolitan cities of northern Spain. Situated between the mounts Igueldo, Urgall and Ulia, its palms sway in the breezes that blow off the Cantabrian Mountains running parallel to the northern coast. Best known as a resort and vacation spot for wealthy Europeans, San Sebastian is a striking contrast to the small medieval villages we were to see in the next few days. For a marvelous view drive to the top of Igueldo and look out over the magnificent **La Concha Beach** with its exceptionally clean, fine golden sands. Atop Igueldo is a large amusement park, a good spot for the children.

The old sector of San Sebastian, with its narrow streets and little shops, makes for interesting browsing. Even the children enjoyed time spent here, for there are a number of toy stores. The area is also noted for having the best places to eat in the city. Anxious to try some Spanish cuisine, we stopped for lunch at the first restaurant we passed going into the old sector. Its exterior showed the name to be simply **Restaurante**. The interior was clean and inviting with tile floors, heavy wooden furnishing and friendly waitresses to serve you.

For about $2.75 our lunch was a delicious platter of paella, enough for us all, with big chunks of chicken, clams, shrimp and mussels adorning the saffron-flavored rice, a small glass of wine and milk for the children. We rejoiced that in Spain one almost always finds an inexpensive restaurant. Being on a budget was not at all difficult here. In fact, on $10 a day in Spain one can live almost luxuriously, eat well and still have money left over. It was here that we were to make up for some of our more expensive days in Scandinavia.

This became particularly evident when we went grocery shopping in the big *Mercado*, a large exposition building across the street from the main post office. The children were enthralled with the huge colorful stands of fresh vegetables and fruit, big trays full of whole fresh fish, and geese, chickens and rabbits hanging from their feet.

Burgos is famous as both the birthplace of El Cid and the home of one of Spain's finest Gothic cathedrals. Also, of interest is an archaeological museum, but the city was less attractive and lacked the charm we were to later see in Segovia.

Driving along N.1 toward Madrid, it is easy to miss the turnoff to Segovia, N.110, a narrow, deserted road weaving its way across flat plains and through the center of the small villages of *Sequera, Casla, Pradena, Arcones, Matamala and Matabuena*. Here an interesting symbol decorates the buildings: an ox with four arrows pointing up and passing through the center, the ancient symbol of rural Spain. In one of these villages a young boy was selling kitchenware on the street. Brightly painted, crude pottery was spread out on heavy blankets and women were gathered around inspecting his wares and dickering over prices. We spoke briefly to a friendly man on a donkey who responded warmly to the children. These brief encounters with the Spanish people of the villages made us love Spain.

SEGOVIA

Upon entering Segovia, the first sight is the huge **Roman Aqueduct**, a sign of Spain's earliest invaders and one of the best-preserved Roman relics in existence today. It is still working with the help of a modern siphon system, carrying water brought from the hills 15 kilometers away. We proceeded to the huge open square to look in the small shops. It was easy to see that this was a tourist town, for everywhere there were vendors and stores offering curios. Browsing can be fun here but wait to buy later in the less auspicious villages where prices are lower and the quality of merchandise more authentic.

We hiked up a steep hillside along cobblestone streets to the Alcázar, standing some 262 feet above the point where two rivers, the Eresma and the Clamores, meet and surround the city. This royal palace, once the home of King Ferdinand and Queen Isabella, is well worth visiting for a striking example of the Moorish influence in architecture and surface decoration, especially in the heavily gilded motifs of the ceilings. Be sure and look up in all the rooms. The girls seemed more interested in this building than in others we had visited, perhaps because of its colorful and almost fantasy like interior decoration. The tiny park at the entrance of the Alcázar is a pleasant spot for a picnic lunch.

MADRID

The road from Segovia to Madrid winds through the pine covered Guadarrama Mountains. At Camping Madrid, we had to watch carefully for signs as it is a bit difficult to find being off a long narrow dirt road. There was a grassy parking area, modern restrooms, showers that were not working and a small store at our disposal.

Our first day in Madrid we drove into the Plaza de Castilla, parked the car and hopped onto a bus going down the Avenida Generalísimo toward the center of town. Our destination was the main post office on the Plaza de Colon. We found that having friends and relatives send letters to the main post offices in each major city care of *poste restante* (general delivery) was an efficient way of receiving our mail. The American Express offices, although having client's mail service, are usually bulging with tourists and one must wait in long lines.

146

We also suggest you economize by limiting the amount of mail you send. You can buy a tablet of aerogrammes, which saves considerably on postage.

From the post office we walked over to the large, beautiful **Retiro Park,** just behind and a block east of the Prado Museum. It is the Luxembourg Gardens of Madrid. The children's play area is complete with swings, slides and teeter-totters. On the other side of the park, we found the zoo, a big disappointment to us. It was poorly cared for, and the animals did not appear to be very healthy. The time would have been better spent letting the children play.

One of our best experiences in Madrid was a Sunday at the **Rastro,** the flea market on the **Plaza de Cascorro.** The entire square and the long street extending out from it is blocked off each Sunday, and stalls are set up selling everything from antiques to birds, a colorful display of fascinating articles. Never hesitate to bargain over a price, for that's the fun of the Rastro. Two hours later we walked away carrying a huge old copper pot on a copper chain, purchased for only $10, and the girls each had a little Flamenco doll as a souvenir of Spain.

Nightlife in Madrid was limited to the campground as we usually found ourselves exhausted at the end of a big day in the city and enjoyed the evening back at the camp getting to know our neighbors and learning of their adventures. Our fellow campers were like walking information bureaus and we relied a great deal on their recommendations.

The prize of Madrid for us, if not for the children, was the **El Prado,** one of the greatest museums of art we were to visit in Europe. Since the entrance fee was not prohibitive, we decided to see it in three installments so as not to tire the children. Bringing a small box of crayons and paper along for them saved the day; they sat on the benches in the big gallery rooms drawing while we looked at the paintings. The museum opens each day at 10 o'clock and is one the few places you won't have to hurry through before the closing at noontime, for it stays open all day until six, except on Sundays when it closes at two. Saturday afternoon's admission is free. We scheduled one of our three visits for then, being budget conscious, but later wished we hadn't because it was so crowded.

Looking back at my journal we find less was written about our stay in Madrid than any other city in Spain, perhaps because its cosmopolitan polish hid the essential Spanish qualities we found in the villages. Also, as in most cities, it was tiring and frustrating: the traffic was extreme, the prices high and the streets crowded. The children, too, became more irritable in the cities. This colored our experiences. By the fifth day we were anxious to leave for Toledo and points south, but before departing we took a side trip highly recommend to **El Escorial**, 50 kilometers northwest of Madrid.

El Escorial is many things: a palace from which kings ruled Spain, a mausoleum holding the sarcophagi of royalty, a monastery and an enormous church. We highly recommend you read the pages from Michener's *Iberia* that so aptly describe this strange and awesome building, and help you understand why it reflects so well the Spanish character. Plan on a whole day for your visit, as the main building and nearby structures are quite extensive.

We left for Toledo early the next day. The weather was becoming quite cold forcing us to eat our meals inside, and we were beginning to experience the first inconveniences of not having a pop-top. Preparing meals was quite a chore in such crowded conditions.

TOLEDO AND CUENCA

We passed through the Toledo Gate in Madrid and headed for Toledo, once the Moorish capital of Spain; on the way is the unspoiled medieval village of **Illecas** where the **Hospital and Sanctuary of Our Lady of Caridad** is located. Admission is only 7 cents and the visit is well worth the time in seeing the paintings of El Greco as well as other art treasures shown by the gracious nuns in these quiet and simple surroundings. Leaving there continue on the route to Toledo, about 70 kilometers from Madrid.

Toledo spans an enormous crag that hangs out over the River Tagus, and its ancient walls seem anchored in a natural moat. The silhouette of the city stands out in sharp relief against a background formed by the crest of the encircling hills and more distant mountain ranges. It is the one city in Spain that seems to capsulize the entire history of the country. Everywhere are vestiges of all the civilizations, which occupied the Iberian Peninsula.

Today, Toledo is the center of damascene work, a method of decorating swords, ashtrays, jewelry and other articles with fine gold thread hammered into the background in intricate designs. We stopped on the outskirts of the town to visit the **Fábrica Garrida**, just opposite the bullring, where much of the damascene work is done. A most interesting free tour is offered visitors

Our campground was **Camping El Greco**, easily found by turning right at the Puerta de Biscagra, the main gate into Toledo, following Paseo de Recaredo, Paseo de La Ronda Nueva and crossing the bridge of San Marin. A right turn here brings you to Camping El Greco; a left turn will bring you to one of the national *paradors,* Nacional Conde de Orgaz, named after the subject of El Greco's masterpiece that hangs in Toledo. A bus going into the center of town stops at the entrance of the campground. This is a good mode of transportation in Toledo as parking is difficult to find on the narrow streets and very expensive, with someone always greeting you, hand outstretched. Also, the streets are very narrow, making it difficult to drive through them.

The church of San Juan de los Reyes was our first stop in Toledo. It was originally built in the 15th century by Queen Isabella and King Ferdinand, who favored Toledo as an intended burial place. Though they were later to change their minds, the church is worthy of two such prestigious tenants. It has recently been restored and offers a wealthy assortment of Gothic decoration. The upper cloisters have beautifully sculptured fruits and flowers entwining the columns and an ornate ceiling in the characteristic *Mudéjar* style showing the influence of the Arabs in the Christian world.

149

From there walk up the street and push open an old wooden door that leads into the sunlit gardens of the **Church of Santa Maria la Blanca,** a Jewish synagogue taken over by the Christians in the 15th century. Its gardens, now a bit shabby, are none-the-less lovely with their rows of citrus trees. The interior of the synagogue is the real highlight, though, with its graceful horseshoe arches and fascinating ornamentation in the *Almohade* style. Though converted to a Christian church, the synagogue retains much of its original quality. Wandering between the columns, we became keenly aware of a ghostly silence and of the cold dampness, which penetrates the walls, now crumbling in some places from the moisture.

We found the Spanish cathedrals quite different in character from those in England and France. They were often filled with artificial flowers, many candles and much flamboyant ornamentation. Built in 1226, the **Cathedral of the Primate of Spain** at Toledo is perhaps the most unusual and genuinely Spanish of the churches built in Spain during the Gothic period. For us the sacristy, a veritable museum containing paintings by El Greco, Van Dyck, Tristán, Goya and others, was the most interesting part.

Another interesting church is Santo Tomé, a modest 14th century chapel now very famous as the home of the masterpiece of El Greco, "The Burial of the Count of Orgaz." Later you will want to see more of his work at the El Greco Museum, not far from San Tomé on the Calle de los Alamillos. Nearby is the House of El Greco.

We also recommend a visit to the Alcázar. Dominating the skyline of Toledo, it is most famous for the role it played in the Spanish Civil War during a 70-day siege in 1936. Today, the government has turned the Alcázar into a Museum of the Army honoring the memory of those who lost their lives in the siege. The building was interesting for us but not for the children who preferred playing in the gardens and on the steps outside. Again, we would suggest you take turns visiting this monument and leave one parent outside with the kids. Be sure to take in the impressive view from the fortress walls of the Tagus and the surrounding region of Toledo known as La Mancha.

One of our best discoveries in Toledo was a little marzipan shop, the factory of Rodrigo Martinez at Calle de Santo Tomé, 5. In Spain this confection is called *mazápan*, and tradition has it that the Moors were the first to introduce this candy, now an institution of Toledo. The children were not only delighted with the sugary almond taste of the candy, but also with its many charming shapes and colors. We could not resist buying one of the marzipan eels with scales of sugar, eyes of candy and a filling of crystallized cherries and other goodies. For the children it was like a real serpent coiled up in its brightly decorated, round box, ready to be a traditional Christmas surprise for some Spanish child.

Another purchase we made was almond soup paste, also a Christmas tradition in Spain. You can make the soup in your camper by taking 200 grams of the paste and adding one liter of cold milk to it. Beat it together with a bit of cinnamon and serve warm at Christmas, cold the rest of the year.

For lunch one day try the small "hostería" on the Calle de Santo Tomé, about a block up and across the street from the marzipan store. Our meal there included a rich fish soup, chicken, potatoes, wine and dessert. We found one portion split in two was plenty for the girls, bringing the total cost of the meal to $4.30. Also be sure to stop at the stand selling "churros," hot fritters served laden with sugar, a popular delicacy in Spain.

CUENCA

One of the most picturesque villages in Spain is Cuenca, about 200 kilometers east of Toledo, via Aranjuez and Taracón. It has only recently been discovered by tourists and is not yet spoiled.

The main thing to do in this town is to explore on foot its many little alleyways. Be prepared for some climbing, as much of the most interesting part, the old sector, is built on high cliffs overhanging deep gorges. You can pick up a map at the tourist bureau in town at 28 Calderón de la Barca and go directly to the Museum of Spanish

Abstract Art on the Calle los Canonigos. The most striking feature of the museum is its mélange of the old and new. Outside it is another of the ancient cliff houses. Inside it's a world of tomorrow with paintings by Spain's young artists who, if they do not outshine Velásquez and Goya, will certainly equal them in talent. We talked with one of the young artists working there in the studios built by one of Spain's contemporary artists, Fernando Zobel. He explained the difficulty of surviving as an artist in a country so steeped in tradition that to compete with the great masters is practically impossible. The new artists are more known in New York, Paris and London than in their own country. We were also struck by the beauty of the interior of the museum that, though exquisite itself, did not compete with the paintings or sculptures, but enhanced them.

(**Note:** while there we purchased a small abstract print by Fernando Zobel, which we display in our home today. It brings back good memories for us.)

From Cuenca drive to Ciudad Encantada, meaning enchanted city, about 40 kilometers northeast of Cuenca in a mountainous and rather deserted area. Here nature has fashioned sculptures of rock in curious designs. Three huge rock formations called "*Los Barcos*" stand out above the others like huge battleships pulled into a harbor. Cuenca and her environs still remain one of the highlights of our Spanish travels. We recommend a visit, even if it means a side trip of 200 kilometers.

ALICANTE AND COSTA BLANCA

We headed south from Cuenca via a small road to Motilla de Palancar, then to Albacete and Murcia. The scenery through Don Quixote's La Mancha is vast and barren, and we were happy to finally arrive at the coast with its large mountain ranges breaking the monotony of the flat stretches of land. One shock was the equally large apartment buildings that line the coast. They are monstrosities to behold and quite alien to the small Spanish villages we had enjoyed

152

so much. Built either by Europeans who spend their holidays in Spain, or more recently by the Spanish government to encourage tourism, they reminded us of something one might see in Southern California or Miami Beach. Feeling a bit disenchanted, and anxious to find some beautiful, secluded beach with a Spanish fishing village nearby, we drove right through Murcia to Alicante, hoping to find a campground for the night.

Finding a campground in this part of Spain is no problem, for there are signs all along the main route advertising camping. The one we chose was La Bahia, just outside Alicante on the road to Valencia. Though there was no play area for the children, the beach was seconds down a path, and we had great fun tossing the Frisbee on the sand, running and playing. It felt good to toss aside our heavy clothes and go without coats for the first time since arriving in Madrid three weeks earlier. Through early December, the weather was moderate, and we enjoyed the soft ocean breezes.

The ride along the coast from Alicante to Valencia is beautiful, marred only by the presence of so many ugly, high-rise apartment buildings. We were heading for the little town of Calpe, with a quick side trip to Elche between Alicante and Murcia. Elche is famous both for the age-old Mystery Play performed there each year from August 13th to the 15th, and its groves of date palms. It is the area that supplies most of Spain with its palm fronds for the Palm Sunday processions. After stopping there to picnic we continued on our way to Calpe.

Late that day, upon rounding a bend a short distance outside the small village of Altea where the high-rises finally seemed to be thinning out, we came upon a cluster of charming whitewashed houses scattered down a sharp hillside that seemed to slip into blue waters of the Mediterranean. Slowing a bit to see the sign, it read La Galera. We stopped to inquire if any of the small cottages were for rent and learned this small neighborhood of houses is primarily owned by German families for use as summer homes. Within a half hour we had rented a charming little two-bedroom cottage with kitchen, fireplace and a veranda shaded by deep-purple bougainvillea for just $2.50 a day. Our *casita* had a beautiful view of the Mediterranean, and just 1000 yards away was a small private beach. There was even a small bathroom with a hot shower.

We did our shopping in Altea, just a few kilometers south of La Galera. The marketing street is about two blocks west of the main street and full of much activity, people hurrying here and there buying their fresh produce at one market, their staples at another. We even found a wonderful little market that obviously catered to the many Europeans who had homes in the area. It carried such delicacies as candied fruit, fresh coconut, tiny French pastries, and, amazingly, peanut butter.

Calpe is about 15 kilometers beyond La Galera on the road to Valencia. It is a picturesque little town, much like the Spanish fishing village we had hoped to find. Its highlight is the *Peñon Ifach*, a huge piece of granite that explodes out of the sea at the Calpe Peninsula. We drove to its base and began climbing to the top. Near the peak we came to what we thought was a big cave, but upon exploring it, we found it was a tunnel to the other side of the rock. The view was magnificent looking over the Mediterranean and the little harbor of Calpe. Later we climbed down the rock and headed for the small beach where fishermen were mending nets and the sun was warm and soothing, an ideal place for a picnic. Before leaving town, we stopped at the wharf. The fishing boats had just come in after a bountiful day and the fishermen were displaying their catch. We bought some *mejillones* (mussels), to take home and prepare.

Another interesting side trip in this area is a drive up into the mountains to the little town of Polop near Callosa. The road passes through verdant orange and lemon groves in rugged, mountainous terrain that farmers have formed into terraces edged with rock walls to support their citrus trees. Here and there donkeys walk slowly alongside the road; their backs piled high with orange crates. We stopped at one of the farms and asked if we might buy some oranges. The farmer graciously picked some of the best and filled our red bag with what must have been about three kilos of oranges for just 15 cents.

The main attraction of Polop is El Sotano Medieval, the caves under a 15th century house. Today this medieval house is a fantastic museum of antiques with room after room of copper pots, cooking utensils, Valencia pottery and ancient Spanish furniture. There's also a shop selling modern, hand-crafted Spanish art objects and the studio of the renowned sculptor, Ribera Girona. The town surrounding El Sotano is picturesque with steep, winding streets, fountains and old buildings.

Another village in the same vicinity is Guadalest, just 15 kilometers from Callosa by way of a winding road. Guadalest sits high on a peak, its Moorish tower rising above the valley of orange groves. As we parked the car, a Spaniard walked up to us leading his donkey and asked if the children would like a ride. For just 45 cents he took us on a walking tour of Guadalest while the girls rode on Andes, the donkey. Up a steep hillside are some castle ruins. We paid a small admission fee to enter, deciding later it really wasn't worth it. The magnificent view could be enjoyed from outside.

Dawn and Tiffany riding on a donkey in the village of Guadalest, Spain

VALENCIA

Seeing the rice paddies along the road leading into Valencia reminded us that it is famous for its *paella* and, hungry upon our arrival, we decided to try some to compare with that we had thought was so good in San Sebastian. There proved to be no comparison. We stopped at a small restaurant called Casa Cesáreo on Guillen de Castro, 15. It was charming, with a beautiful dining room upstairs

155

complete with fireplace and old Spanish, hand-painted tiles lining the walls. For about $3.75, our meal included wine, bread, the most delicious paella one could imagine piled high with steaming fresh shrimp, mussels, clams and chicken and a dessert of fresh sherbet.

A highly recommended visit is to the Museo Cerámica on the Plaza del Marqués de Dos Aguas. It is a combination of *rococo* and *churrigueresque* architecture on the exterior and houses a most heterogeneous collection of oddities on the inside, including a collection of beautiful coaches and 18th century costumes. Moorish rooms are full of remnants of the Arab rule of Spain. There are rooms of pottery and an amusing Gallery of Humorists with caricatures of famous personages from Einstein to Truman. Its great variety kept the kids content for two hours, a particular highlight for them being the room full of elegant coaches. From there stroll down the street adjacent to the museum, a rich quarter of the city where aristocratic-looking, heavy wooden doors open onto private courtyards.

Leaving Valencia, we headed for Castellón, stopping at a nearby beach for a picnic and to gather seashells. That evening we found a beautiful little camping spot just off the road outside of Cambrils in a tiny grove of trees next to a railroad track (fortunately, the trains did not seem to be running very frequently).

The next day, about 25 kilometers south we followed a tiny road that turned off the main highway and led us to the small village of Sitges, a resort town of some fame, but rather quiet and untouched in the wintertime. We found a perfect picnic spot by the sea on a bluff where there was a children's park.

BARCELONA

Coming into Barcelona we watched for good campgrounds. There were many along the road just outside town, but desiring to be closer to the central section, we went on into the city. We fund the local tourist office at Avenida de José Antonio, 658, and picked up information on what to see and do in this cosmopolitan city, center of the Catalan culture. The temperatures here in the winter are mild with overcast mornings, occasional light showers and usually sunny afternoons. Barcelona is considerably easier to get around than many of the other big European cities. We decided to camp for the night in the big Montjuich Park on Montjuich Mountain. The park is full of beautiful sculptured gardens, an archaeological museum, an ethnological museum, a museum of Catalan art and a stadium, swimming pool and modern fun fair. We found a good parking spot near the Japanese gardens, which was quiet and secluded.

First on the list of sights to see was the ***Pueblo Español***, or Spanish Village, at the base of Montjuich Mountain. Erected in 1929 at the time of the International Exhibition in Barcelona, the Pueblo Español, remains one of the highlights of the city. Its purpose is to reproduce in a comprehensive manner the most characteristic aspects of Spanish architecture, and the buildings are grouped according to the old geographical divisions of the Iberian Peninsula. Also interesting are the many workshops of traditional crafts. The children loved watching the glassblowers at work, and all of us enjoyed the print shop where works of the great masters are reproduced, and the studio of the woodcraftsmen. A highlight of the Spanish Village for children is the Museum of Catalan Crafts with a room filled with ancient handcrafted toys. We were the only ones in the small museum and could browse at our leisure, pleased we were touring when it is possible to avoid the summer crowds.

Across town from the Pueblo Español is the ***Parque Güell***, where sculptures of the great 19th century Spanish artist-architect Gaudí adorn the park. Parque **Güell** is a child's fairyland in stone. There are caves, where one can rest and towers that lean at a dazzling angle, flights of stairs lined with rocks of all hues and strange anthropomorphic sculpture, a joy to behold despite their dilapidated state. There is also a children's play area in the center of the park. To see more of Gaudí's sculptures, visit the Gaudí House Museum on the Carretera del Carmelo.

Another of Gaudí's creations you will want to see is El Templo de la Sagradea Familia. This fantastic cathedral, which seems in appearance to be a bizarre mixture of art nouveau and baroque decoration, is still in progress after nearly 90 years of construction.

If you're in Spain in December, we'd recommend a visit to Barcelona during the holiday time. One of the special features of our visit was the Christmas Creche Market in front of the Sagrada Familia. An annual event, this special market has tiny stalls decorated in fresh pine boughs where miniature manger scenes with holy figures made in every medium from ceramic to wood are being sold. Another festive area is near the central city park, Parque Ciudadela. Calle de la Princesa was invitingly lit with Christmas lights and was the site of much activity. We window shopped along this street, finally arriving at a huge square, the Plaza San Jaime, in the middle of the Gothic Quarter, to behold a huge 70-foot Christmas tree aglow with strings of lights. The kids were dazzled. Further along we arrived at Las Ramblas, one of the most famous thoroughfares in Europe. Every kind of trade and business is to be found on Las Ramblas, which is in a continuous state of bustle and full of color. One can walk along the central island of the street and buy anything from birds to flowers. We even stopped at one stall selling pet monkeys, which delighted the girls. On the way back to our car by way of Calle de la Princesa, we stopped to buy some candied nuts in a sweet shop, looked into the windows of an interesting wholesale spice shop, drooled outside the windows of the pastry shops and again marveled at the beauty of the giant Christmas tree.

One of the most highly recommended visits while in Barcelona is to the Picasso Museum located in an old converted palace at 15 Calle de Moncada, off the Calle de la Princesa. Near the Gothic Quarter, the museum stands on a street reminiscent of the Middle Ages. The entire collection is fascinating, though one section particularly remains in my memory. It is the part of the museum devoted to drawings and paintings by Picasso in his youth, with his great talent already apparent. Unfortunately, we did not both tour the museum, fearing the children would become bored. This was later regretted, for the children would probably have enjoyed some of the famous and colorful paintings. They were able, though, to take in the Barcelona Zoo, agreeing it was one of the best sights they had seen.

The **Mercado San Jose on Las Ramblas**, with its hundreds of colorful stalls, was one of the most interesting marketplaces we visited in all of Spain. One of our real finds in the market was the delicatessen where we bought big containers of pickled cauliflower, carrots, onions and fresh tuna and made a delicious lunch salad for less than a dollar. With a big loaf of freshly baked bread, some cheese and fruit, a gourmet meal was prepared.

A day in Barcelona can be spent at the flea market, Los Encantes, at the Plaza Glorias. The best way to get there is to park your car at the Plaza de España and take the metro out to the Plaza Glorias. Here you cross a large pedestrian bridge and end up right in the center of the flea market. We bought a trunk and after lugging it all the way to the metro station learned we could not take it aboard so ended up taking a taxi, a ride that fortunately cost us very little. We would suggest, therefore, that if you plan to buy anything of great size you bring your car to the Plaza Glorias. That trunk was later to come in handy.

From Barcelona the ride along the Costa Brava was beautiful. We decided to take one more quick side trip before heading for the border to see Cadaqués, the village where the great surrealist artist, Salvador Dali, makes his home. Lying at the extreme northeast corner of Spain, about 88 kilometers from Barcelona, this beautiful white-washed pueblo is reached by traveling through the mountains and then descending a steep and windy road to the Mediterranean. One sees in the distance the gleaming white buildings with tile roofs grouped around a small cove of crystal blue water. Dali's house is located in the small cove of Port Lligat, about two kilometers from Cadaqués. A white mosque-like house with two huge cement eggs on its roof, it stands alone looking out at the Mediterranean.

We went back to town to do some shopping before beginning our drive back to France. On the main square, we stopped in a little wine shop to buy some Spanish wine for our friends in Oloron. The owner of the store was very warm and friendly. We soon learned that he had once worked for Dali and we enjoyed listening to some of the tales he had to tell about their adventures. Reluctantly we said good-bye to our new friend and his beautiful country that had come to mean so much to us.

SUMMING UP SPAIN

We found camping sites to be quite numerous along the coast but much less so inland. Except in the mountain areas, camping outside officially authorized sites is permitted provided there are no more than three tents or caravans and 10 campers at one place and that they do not remain for more than three days. If you camp outside official sites you should have an International Camping Carnet or a National Tourist Camping Permit obtainable from the Spanish Forestry Service. For sites along the coast, it is recommended that you book in advance if going between late spring and mid-October, as they tend to become crowded at the height of the season. Charges per person usually range from about 20 to 40 cents for adults with similar prices for caravans. There is a reduced price for children under 10 years of age.

Spain also has a highly developed network of government operated inns and hotels. These are known as *paradors* (national tourist inns), *albergues de carretera* (highway inns), *refugios* (mountain lodges) and *hosterías* (typical restaurants). They are often in restored castles or other buildings of artistic or historic value that have been adapted to the requirements of a first-class hotel. In most cases the prices are very reasonable. We have listed these where possible as they offer a good alternative to camping for the budget traveler.

As noted in the text, the climate of Spain is as varied as its scenery, and so it is important when planning your itinerary for this country to know which regions have the most agreeable temperatures during each season. For example, in the winter, Alicante, Murcia, Almería, Málaga, all on the southern coastline, have exceptional climate with temperatures from 55 to 60 degrees even in January and February. Spring is loveliest in the eastern regions and the Balearic Islands. This is the season to visit the cities of Andalusia. Fall is classically gentle and mild in Madrid and surrounding regions and in Barcelona. In general, this is an excellent season to see the whole Iberian Peninsula. The Canary Islands have a spring like climate all year round.

Prices are listed in dollars computed at the exchange rate of 68 pesetas to $1. *They represent quotes as of December 1971.*

SAN SEBASTIAN

Camping

Igueldo, five kilometers west of Monte Igueldo; telephone 23-03-6. Showers, shopping, camping gas, swimming. Admission: Adults, car, tent and caravan each 34 cents.

Rosaleda, telephone 55-362. Open April1-October 30; showers, shopping, camping gas, bungalows for rent, swimming. Admission: Adults, car, tent and caravan each 29 cents.

Parador

Parador Nacional El Emperador, Fuenterrabía, Guipúzcoa, three kilometers from Irun, 21 from San Sebastian. Picturesque surroundings pool and gardens. Rooms with showers and two double beds, minimum $7, maximum $8.90.

Tourist Information Office Andia, 13; telephone 41-17-74. Across the street from the small park along the waterfront.

Post Office Urdaneta.

Sightseeing

San Sebastian is the capital of the Basque province of Gulpuzcoa. The region known as the Basque Coast offers attractive scenery and interesting villages and towns, noteworthy among which are **Oñate and Loyola**. The sites in and around San Sebastian are many and varied.

La Conca Beach, with excellent swimming in the spring and summer; in the autumn it is a beautiful place for a stroll. There is a small park in center of town; a perfect place for the kids to play.

Mt. Igueldo Amusement Park, offering a magnificent view of the city. You may want to stop and take a few rides with the kids at the amusement park.

The Old City: The best thing to do in this sector of town, to your right as you leave the tourist office, is to explore. There are some good and inexpensive restaurants here as well as interesting shops and old buildings. Art Gallery, in the Escuela de Artes Oficios contains an extensive collection of Goya and El Greco.

San Telmo Museum contains murals by José M. Sert, noted Catalan artist.

SIDE TRIPS FROM SAN SEBASTIAN

Pasajes de San Juan, a charming fishing village about 11 kilometers from San Sebastian. Drive or take the bus from Calle Aldamar in San Sebastian (leaves every 15 minutes) to **Pasajes de San Pedro**, from where you can walk to the village of San Juan.

Loyola Lying about 60 kilometers southwest of San Sebastian, Loyola is where St. Ignatius, the founder of the famed religious order of the Jesuits, was born. The Santa Casa (Saint's house) may be visited free from 10 am-12:30 pm and from 4-7 pm.

Guernica After leaving Loyola continue northwest toward Bibao and on the way stop at this Basque stronghold and subject of a famous Picasso painting, *Guernica*.

Bibao this is the other great city of the Basque Coast. Bilbao holds major bullfights during the spring and summer. Check with tourist information to find out the date of the "Semana Grande," week of celebration.

Parador Nacional El Emperatriz, Lequeitio, Viscaya, 54 kilometres from Bilbao. Picturesque surroundings. Rooms with showers and two double beds, minimum $7, maximum $8.90.

PAMPLONA

The ride through the mountains from San Sebastian to Pamplona is beautiful. Everywhere there are rugged crags and small water-falls. This city, about 80 kilometers from San Sebastian, is most famous for the annual Bull Run in July. Ernest Hemingway's book, *The Sun Also Rises*, has inspired many to participate in this event. Though this is the main attraction of Pamplona, those with less courage (and more smarts; not a good activity with kids) can enjoy a stroll around the town. Be sure and take a look at the Cathedral of Pamplona, a Gothic church, begun near the end of the 14th century.

Camping San Juan. Open June-September

Parador Nacional Santo Domingo de La Calzada.
149 kilometers (two and a half hours) from Pamplona, 67 kilometers from Burgos. Room with shower and two double beds, minimum $7, maximum $8.90.

BURGOS

Camping
Fuentes Blancas, four kilometers east on Rio Arlanzon. Open March 1-November 1; shopping restrooms, camping gas, swimming.

Costajan, Aranda de Duero, north on N. 1 at kilometer 162.3. Open April-September; showers, shopping restrooms, camping gas, swimming pool. Admission: Adults, car, tent and caravan each 29 cents.

Albergue Nacional de Carretera in Aranda de Duero, 79 kilometers south of Burgos. Room with shower and two double beds, minimum $3.15, maximum $4. Good dining.

Tourist Information Office Paseo del Espolón, 1; telephone 20 1846.

Sightseeing
Situated on a high northern plain of Old Castile, Burgos is a historical town with a wealth of medieval architecture. It is famous as the birthplace of El Cid, Spain's national hero who defeated the Arabs in the 11th century. The Cathedral is a Gothic structure founded in 1221. The interior contains some superb chapels and cloisters, the most famous of which is the Chapel of Condestable. Behind the main altar, is found a fine example of what is called the Isavelline-Gothic style of architecture.

Royal Monastery of Las Huelgas. A monastery that was once a summer retreat for Castilan royalty and nuns of royal blood. Its interior is interesting and worth the visit. The monastery is reached by going out the Valladolid road for more than a mile (the turnoff is clearly marked). The convent is open from 11 am-2pm and from 4-4 pm, charging an admission of 14 cents. If a guide shows you around, which is optional, you are obliged to tip.

SEGOVIA

Camping
Piscina Florida, two kilometers southeast on N. 601. Open April-October; showers, shopping, café, bar, camping gas, swimming pool. Admission: Adults 31 cents, car, caravan and tent each 29 cents.

Alberque Nacional de Carretera in Villacastin, 33 kilometers southwest of Segovia, Rooms with showers and two double beds, minimum $7, maximum $8.90.

Tourist Information Office Plaza del General Franco, 8; telephone 1602; Plaza de Facundo, 1; telephone 1792.

Post Office San Facundo, 2.

The Aqueduct dates from Roman times. Its 118 arches span a total distance of 728 meters and rise to a maximum height of 96 feet.

The Alcázar, a fantastic 12th century castle visible from below at the confluence of the Clamores and the Eresma rivers. To reach the top of the hill where it sits, we suggest you park in the central Plaza de Pranco, then take the narrow street opposite the cathedral and walk up to the Alcázar. It is a pleasant walk and will give you an opportunity to become more familiar with your surroundings. The castle is open to visitors from 10:30 am-7:30 pm (until 6 pm in the winter) and the price of admission is 21 cents. There is a nice little park for a picnic just outside *"La Dama de las Catedrales."* This is the affectionate name given to the magnificent Gothic cathedral located on the Plaza de Franco. Visiting hours in the summer are from 9 am-7 pm. And in winter from 9 am-1 pm and 3-6 pm. Admission is 14 cents, admitting you to cloisters, chapel room and museum.

SIDE TRIPS FROM SEGOVIA

Since you will be close to the famous Guadarrama mountain range you will be within easy access to one of the most beautiful ski areas of Spain in winter and a maze of lovely mountain pathways in summer.

Puerto de Navacerrada Situated 60 kilometers from Madrid and just 28 kilometers from Segovia, this is one of the most popular ski areas in Spain. It is usually open from September to March. The following inns and shelters are suggested for lodgings.

Alberque del Club Alpino Español at the 60-kilometer mark from Madrid. The albergue, standing at 5,907 feet, has central heating, running water, a canteen and service year-round.

Another, *Albergue del Club Alpino Guadarrama* at a height of 6,039 feet, accommodates 90 guests (12 with complete bathrooms, 22 with showers, and the rest with running hot and cold water). Restaurant and snack bar, personal lockers, special rooms for juvenile and children's section of mountaineering and skiing.

Refugio de Grupo Castellano de Montaña Cumbres Shelter at 6,155 ft. has running water, a canteen and electricity. Accommodates 39 guests.

Albergue Coppel Situated at the pass of Puerto de los Cotos or Puerto del Paular at a height of 6,171 feet, an hour and a half from Puerto de Navacerrada and 68 kilometers from Madrid. Accommodates 35 guests. Running water and canteen. Service all year round. Owned by the Club Alpino Español; write the manager, Don Lucio Bartolome.

A TOUR OF THE CASTLES IN THE PROVINCE OF SEGOVIA

Leave Segovia on the road leading to the little town of *Santa Maria la Real de Nieva* (where there is an interesting Gothic church with a pretty cloister). Soon you come to Coca, whose castle is one of the finest and best preserved in Spain. (Note the Moorish influences in the architecture). Some 35 kilometers northeast of Coca you come to *Cuellar*, a walled township commanded by the Moorish-style towers of its parish churches. In the upper part of the town stands the castle, built in the mid-15th century by Don Beltran de la Cueva, Duke of Albuquerque. From there follow the road east to Fuentiduena, about 30 kilometers away, where you will see the remains of two Romanesque churches and a mighty castle. Thirty-two kilometers further on you will come to one of the most important towns of the province, *Sepulveda*, the scene of many battles. From the natural lookout point you will behold a breathtaking view, and the narrow treacherous streets of the town afford countless vistas over the gorges of the Duraton and the Castilla. The churches are of the Romanesque style. Leaving Sepulveda on the Pedraza road, you will pass Castilnovo Castle, on your left. Now privately owned, it was once a fief of the Counts of Castile who enlarged an earlier fortress that was probably of Arab origin. The castle stands in the center of a large park. Pedraza, believed to be the birthplace of the Roman Emperor Trajan, is one of the most colorful places in the area. Its walls are intact, and it is commanded by a stout, severe-looking castle standing on an enormous crag. Not far south of Pedraza lies Turegano, an old Episcopal town. The local castle was built in the late 15th century around the Romanesque church of San Miguel. A district road leads back to Segovia.

MADRID

Camping

Cerro del Aire, Cerro del Aguila, seven kilometers on road to Burgos; telephone; 202 28 35. Open all year; showers shopping camping gas, bungalows for rent, swimming pool. Admission: Car 22 cents, adults caravan and tent each 29 cents.

Madrid Camping, seven kilometers on the Madrid-Burgos road. Open all year. Watch carefully for the camping signs; this is a tricky one to find, so tricky we cannot even describe it other than to say that when you end up on a very bumpy dirt road, you are almost there—don't give up. It has showers, shopping, camping gas, swimming pool. Admission: Adults 34 cents, car, caravan and tent each 29 cents.

Osuna, Canillejas Madrid 17, at kilometer 15.5 on Carretera Ajalvir-Vicalvaro; telephone 205 05 10. Open all year; showers, shopping, bungalows for rent, swimming pool. Admission: Adults, car caravan and tent each 34 cents.

Tourist Information:
American Express Office, Plaza de las Cortes; telephone 222 11 80. American Visitors Bureau, Avenida Jose Antonio, 68; telephone 247 03 33. The Post office is on Plaza de Colon.

Shopping
The Mercado de la Cebado. This very colorful spot specializing in fresh fish, rabbits and poultry, is not only the best place to get a good buy on meat and fish but is also one of the most enjoyable sightseeing adventures. The walk there leads through the oldest and least "touristy" quarter of this city, via the ancient street of Cava Baja at the end of which is the market. Calle de Fernando VI is another interesting shopping street. Take Avenida Generalísimo to the Plaza de Colon, turn right on Calle de Genova, go as far as the Plaza de Santa Barbara and turn left, then left again onto the Calle de Fernando VI (the third small street from the Alonso Martinez circle where you turned).

El Cortes Ingles, just off the Plaza de Castilla, is a huge department store in the basement of which is a fabulous supermarket with everything one could imagine. Be careful though; we found prices a bit high. The most important thing to remember is to eat like the natives—large amounts of fish, rice, fresh fruit. You can get some good packaged items here but be discriminating as they are expensive.

Sears Roebuck is located on the main boulevard running parallel to Generalísimo, one block to the east in the direction of the center of town. We found the prices high there too and preferred to shop in the small markets on the residential streets.

Camping gas can be found at the Plaza de Olavide off Calle de Genoa via the streets Marato and Feliciano.

Flea Market, *The Rastro*, Madrid's flea market, is held on Sunday on several hilly streets just south of the Plaza de Cascorro. This can be a real experience even if you don't buy anything. Most stall keepers start shutting down about 2 pm in the afternoon.

City Transportation: The best way to get around Madrid is to leave your camper at the Plaza Castilla (there is a convenient parking-lot area just to the right as you enter the Plaza) and from here proceed down the Avenida Generalísimo to the city center by bus. The buses run frequently and are very reasonable (kids go half fare). For intra-city traveling, the best means of transportation is the subway or "metropolitan system," where the three major lines all converge and cross at Puerta del Sol. The charge is only 3 cents to any point in town, a round trip on weekends is 4 cents, and you can transfer from one line to another by looking for the red signs reading *correspondencias*. It operates much like the Paris metro, once you know your destination, just make the appropriate transfers to get to that point.

Retiro Park, Located behind the Prado with the entrance on Calle de Alfonso XII. This big central park has a large children's play area—a good place to let the kids exercise and for picnics between sightseeing excursions. There is a zoo at one end that we do not highly recommend, but a possibility if the kids have their hearts set on going to a zoo. The zoo is open daily from 10 am-1:30 pm and 4-8:30 pm, 7 cents admission.

El Prado Museum, a great art museum full of masterpieces by El Greco, Goya, Velásquez, Titian, Rubens, Ribera and many others. Open 10 am-6pm daily. Admission is 29 cents every day but Saturday afternoon when it's free. Closed Sunday afternoon after 2.

Plaza Mayor, a large formal 17th century square, center of Madrid life. The surrounding neighborhood with its shops, markets and restaurants is an interesting place to explore.

Bullfights at the Plaza de Toros are presented every Sunday and on holidays from Easter until the end of October, beginning late in the afternoon, often as late as 6. Tickets can be purchased ahead of time at the midtown ticket center at 9 Calle de la Victoria (just off the Puerta del Sol walk one short block up the Carrera de San Jerónimo, and then turn right on Victoria), open on Saturday 10am-1 pm and 5-9 pm, and on Sunday, 10 am-5 pm. Tickets for normal fights (those not featuring a celebrated matador) start as low as 60 cents for the worst seat (*sol*, in the sun) and go as high as $6.65 for the best seats (*sombra*, in the shade). We do not suggest this as a good activity for children. If one of you has your heart set on seeing a bullfight, one of you can go to the Plaza de Toros and the other can take the kids to the park.

Flipper Dolphin Show: An aquatic show at the Plaza de Castilla.

Ice Skating: Take bus No. 24P and ask the driver to tell you where to get off for the *patinadero* (skating rink).

Evening Entertainment: Teatro de la Zarzuela, at Jovellanos 4. The music hall usually offers variety acts at its matinee and evening performances. Check with tourist information for specifics.

SIDE TRIPS AROUND MADRID

El Escorial Located 50 kilometers northeast of Madrid on the slopes of the Guadarrama Mountains, the highlight is the **Royal Monastery of San Lorenzo de Escorial**, considered the eighth wonder of the world. Visiting hours are 10 am-1 pm and 3-6 pm, until 7 pm in the summer. For 71 cents you will receive a ticket that will include admission to the palace, the mausoleum, the charter halls, the royal library, the Prince's Cottage and the Upper Cottage.

El Pardo Located about 14 kilometers north of Madrid, this is the seat of government of modern Spain. Though you cannot enter the main palace you can visit the Casita del Principe (Princes Cottage), a small hunting-lodge-type palace that was built during the reign of Charles III in the 18th Century. Open 10 am-1 pm and 4-6 pm, with an admission of 21 cents. The surrounding town and countryside offer much of interest.

AVILA

An ancient walled city, 115 kilometers west of Madrid, this fascinating town is completely encircled by a well-preserved 11th century wall. We suggest you make this a two-day stop, staying overnight along the road or at the parador before continuing on.

Parador Nacional Raimundo de Borgona in Avila. Double rooms with shower, minimum $7, maximum $8.90.

Convent of St Teresa St. Teresa is said to have been born in Avila and this 17th century baroque church and convent was built on the site of her birth. The convent is open from 9 am-1:15 pm, in winter until 8 pm. There is no admission charge.

The Cathedral A most unusual cathedral built into the walls of Avila, both Romanesque and Gothic in design and decoration, it has a fascinating interior of red and white stone. The cathedral is open 10 am-2 pm and 2-8 pm in the summer, until 6 pm in winter.

If you're not tired of churches by this time and the kids are holding up, too, you can also visit the **Basilica of St. Vincent**, outside the city walls, open from 11 am-1 pm and 3-8 pm. On Sunday it's closed until 12:30 pm. Also, The Church and Monastery of St. Thomas. Open from 9 am-1 pm and from 4-8 pm, St. Thomas may be visited free of charge unless you wish to visit the cloister, admission 7 cents.

TOLEDO

Camping

El Greco, two kilometers southwest of Toledo on C 401; telephone 22 00 90. Open all year; restrooms, laundry area, some shade, small store, river. We paid about $1 a day here while visiting Toledo, 63 kilometers from Madrid open N.401, the Madrid-Toledo road. Open May 1–September 15; showers, shopping, bungalows for rent, pool. Admission: Adults and car each 31 cents, caravan 37 cents, tent 29 cents.

Parador Nacional Conde de Orgaz: telephone 221850, 221854 and 221858. Located in a beautiful setting just outside Toledo with a spectacular view, said to be the very spot that El Greco selected for his "View of Toledo." Rooms here range from $6 to $17.40. You may not wish to splurge on lodging but rather save it for a special Castilian meal at the Parador's fine restaurant. A fixed-price meal, including Spanish hors d'oeuvre, followed by fish, meat and dessert cost about $2.70.

Tourist Information Puerta de Bisagre : telephone 220843. The office is to your right just before you enter the main "Puerta" from Madrid.

Post Office Plata, 1; telephone 213611

Launderette Pasqual, in the new sector of Toledo to the left of Avenida de la Reconquista. Take first street after "Ruinas del Templo Romano" to your left and ask the first person you see, "*¿Donde está Pasqual lavadero?*" Follow their gestures if you cannot understand what they say. About $2.50 for two small washer loads.

Fábrica Garrida, a damascene factory just outside the entrance to Toledo and across the street from the bullring. A most interesting free tour of the factory is offered to visitors from 10 am-6 pm daily. Here you can see workers producing beautiful damascene jewelry, ashtrays, swords and other items, for which Toledo is famous. You'll also have an opportunity to buy a souvenir in the small shop. We suggest not only the damascene ware, but also the fantastic wood-carvings of Jésus Ballesteros. Be sure and ask to see his work bench. He is a charming man besides being a gifted craftsman and enjoys practicing his English with visitors.

Plaza de Zocodover: The main square and meeting place of Toledo. Try the Bar Español; you will begin to feel like a Toledan.

The Church of San Juan de los Reyes At the end of Calle de los Reyes, this Gothic monastery was founded by Ferdinand and Isabella in 1474. Note its cloisters with their Mudéjar style. Open in the summer 10 am-2 pm and 3-7 pm, until 6 pm in the winter. Admission is 14 cents, no charge for children.

Synagogue de Santa Maria la Blanca Just a few doors up from the Church of San Juan de los Reyes, open from 10 am-1 pm and 3-7 pm, until 6 in the winter. Admission is 7 cents, no charge for children.

Museum of El Greco and House of El Greco: Open 10am-2 pm and 3:30 to 7 pm, until 6 pm in the winter. Admission is 21 cents, no charge for children.

The Church of Santo Tomé: The main reason to visit this church is to see El Greco's masterpiece "The Burial of the Count Orgaz." The church is open 10 am-1:30 pm and 3-7 pm, until 6 pm in the winter. Buy a ticket (only 7 cents, no charge for children) in the souvenir shop across the street.

The Alcázar: Visiting hours are 9:15 am-7:34 pm in the summer, until 6 pm in the winter. This will be boring for the children, so we suggest you alternate your visits here. Admission charge is 14 cents.

Shopping in Toledo

Avoid the little tourist shops around all the places of interest as prices are high and merchandise poor.

Food Shopping: there is a supermarket in the new sector of town. Take Avenida de la Reconquista, turn right at the third street, park and walkup some steps to cross Calle Talavera where you will find the market. We also enjoyed shopping at the fruit and vegetable stalls and the fish stalls along the Calle de Santo Tomé. Be sure and get your shopping done before one o'clock as most shops close then until three.

Camping Gas: Ferreteria Marcial is a good place to buy camping gas, right on Zocodover Plaza, across from the Bar Español.

The Marzipan Factory of Rodrigo Martinez: Located at Calle de Santo Tomé 5, this was one of our favorite shops in Toledo especially when it came to bringing satisfaction to our sweet tooth.

Restaurants

Hostería, one block up from the marzipan shop on the opposite side of the street. We had a delicious *prix fixe* lunch for just $1.45.

Placido For a little bit more of a splurge, go to Calle de Santo Tomé 6. This one-time Franciscan convent has lots of atmosphere and offers a good prix fixe meal for $1.85.

Be sure and stop at one of the *churros* stalls along the street that sell these delicious fritters coated with sugar.

CUENCA

Camping

La Moraleja 18 kilometers from the Cuenaca-Tragacete road. Venta de Contreras, Puerto de Contreras (Minglanilla).

Tourist Information Office 18 Calderón de la Baria.

Shopping for Food: A large *Mercado* (market) can be found across from the main post office at Parque de San Julian 18. There is a butcher shop off the Plaza Mayor, a few blocks from the Museum of Spanish Abstract Art.

Sightseeing

The most worthwhile sight in this fantastically picturesque village is the village itself, with its cliff houses called *casas colgades*. The highlight of the town is the Museum of Spanish Abstract Art on Calle los Canonigos. Be sure and see it. We found the kids enjoyed this unusual museum.

Ciudad Encantada is a good side trip from Cuenca. Here you'll see some fascinating rock formations.

INLAND ROUTE TO ALICANTE

From Cuenca, we took the inland route through the small towns of Matella del Palancar, Alvacete, Almansa and Villena to Alicante and Costa del Sol. There were virtually no campgrounds in the region, but we did find that there were many ideal pull-off points where we could create our own secluded campsite with no problems. Of course, we didn't have running water, but by refilling our water tank before we left Cuenca, we found this to be no great disadvantage. In Alvacete, there is the **Albergue Nacional de Carretera**, 188 kilometers from Valencia. Double rooms with baths start at $5.90. The alternative route would be from Cuenca to Valencia and then along the coast where there are many campgrounds.

ALICANTE

Camping

La Bahia, Albufereta, reached by taking N. 332 Valencia-Alicante road, turn left at kilometer 96.4, right at kilometer 15, then left southwest of Playa de San Juan; telephone 23 25 42. Open all year; shopping, restrooms, laundry area, beach. Admission: Adults 29 cents, children 22 cents, caravan 29 cents.

Lucenturm Internacional, Albufereta, three kilometers northeast of Alicante on N.332; telephone 23 11 97. Shopping, restroom, camping gas, bungalows for rent, beach. Admission: Adults, car, caravan and tent each 22 cents.

We did not find Alicante a particularly attractive nor interesting city for the sightseeing visitor; it served merely as a good stopping point for a night's rest and a run on the beach before going on to the small coastal villages, which have far greater appeal than the cities. We would recommend that, if your itinerary permits, you explore more of the region west of Alicante, such as Málaga, Algeciras and inland, Granada and the small town of Ronda. Following are campsites between Alicante and Calpe.

BENIDORM

Although this is a noted European resort town, it completely turned us off! However, you might wish to camp here for a night.

Camping

Benidorm Camping, 400 meters off N. 332 at kilometer 117. Open April-September; showers, shopping, restrooms, camping gas, bungalows for rent. Admission: Adults, car, caravan and tent each 37 cents.

La Cala, 200 meters west in direction of Villjoyosa on N. 332 at kilometer 117. Open all year; shopping, restrooms, camping gas, bungalows for rent, swimming. Admission: Adults, car, caravan and tent each 37 cents.

ALTEA

We found this to be a rather interesting little village and were lucky to find a cottage to rent for a week just outside of Altea at La Galera, on the right side of the main road.

Camping

Miami, 100 meters left of N. 332 to Alicante toward the sea, between kilometer 129 and 130. Open March 15-November 15; shopping, restrooms, camping gas, bungalows for rent, swimming.

Santa Clara, beyond Altea between kilometer 129 and 130 on a hill west of the road; telephone 196. Open June 1-October 1; showers, shopping, restrooms, beach. Admission: Adults, car, caravan and tent each 29 cents.

*House Rental
Write to: Manuel Alvarez Santana, Admistrador de Fincas Coligido, Altea (Alicante) Spain. Refer to La Galera and mention your interest in renting a small house there, specifying the length of time you plan to stay.*

CALPE

A small and delightful fishing village just north of Altea and La Galera. We did much of our shopping here in the local markets and down at the harbor where the fishing boats would come in each evening, set up their stalls and sell the fish. From Calpe there are several very interesting side trips.

Camping
Ifach, from Moraira between kilometer 9 and 10, 300 meters from Ifach rocks; telephone 199. Open April-October; shopping, restrooms.

Peñon Ifach A huge rock that rises out of the sea at the end of the Calpe Peninsula, this is an excellent place to take a hike if you think your kids are up to it. The view from the top is magnificent. It does involve a lot of hard climbing and would not be safe for children young children under 10 years old.

Calpe Park is a small children's park in the center of town.

Calpe Beach is a nice place for a picnic and swimming.

Polop Take the small road between Calpe and Altea to Callosa; watch for signs. Polop is a short distance from Callosa. The road runs through the beautiful citrus orchards of Spain. At Polop be sure and see **El Sotano Medieval** on the main street to your right as you drive into town. There will be a sign directing you to it. It is a fascinating medieval house, now the studio of sculptor Ribera Girona, and a combination museum and antique shop.

Guadalest is an ancient Moorish village reached by road from Callosa and situated in a most picturesque fashion atop a mountain, overlooking a valley of citrus groves and rugged, rocky terrain. Well worth a visit. Let the kids ride on a donkey here for just 45 cents.

DENIA

Another interesting little town along the coast. We found some great shops here with reasonably priced baskets, straw and raffia rugs and wicker furniture.

Camping

La Brisas, reached by turning off N. 332 in Vergel, going east in the direction of Denia; after going north for about four kilometers turn left at the beach. Open April-October; shopping restrooms, camping gas, beach.

Les Basetes, 100 meters toward sea, off road from Vergel and Las Marinas to Denia. Open April-September; two kilometers from shopping facilities, restrooms, camping gas, beach. Admission: Adults, car, caravan and tent each 22 cents.

Olé, just beyond Denia at Oliva. Open May-September; shopping facilities, bungalows for rent.

Parador Nacional Costa Blanca at Javea, 87 kilometers north of Alicante. Picturesque surroundings. Prices start at $5.90 for a double room with bath.

VALENCIA

Camping

El Saler, at kilometer 7 on the outskirts, south of Valencia; telephone 21 33 03. Open all year.

Alternative to Camping: Parador Nacional "Luis Vives" at Saler (Valencia), 10 kilometers south of Valencia, 95 from Javea. Picturesque surroundings. Double rooms with bath start at $5.90.

Tourist Information office: Officina de Turismo, Plaza Alfonso El Magnanimo; American Express, 1 Jerusalem, in the Viajes Taber office.

Post Office Central Office, Plaza del Caudillo, 24. Open daily 9 am-2 pm and 3-10 pm, Sunday 10 am-noon.

Shopping:

There is a supermarket in the huge department store of El Cortes Ingles, just up the street from the Officina de Turismo.

Open Market, Calle de Julio Antonio, near American Express office.

The City Market Across the street from La Jonja at the Plaza del Mercado is a Gothic building housing the *mercado*. Walking through the markets of Spain was one of our greatest pleasures. This one is particularly spectacular with more than 1200 stalls. The market is open every day.

Restaurant Suggestion: *Casa Cesáreo*, 15 Guillen de Castro. This restaurant not only serves the best paella we've ever tasted, but also has atmosphere and low prices. Try the 'menu del dia" for just $1.45, or order paella from the á la carte menu for about $4 for two adults and two children. This will include bread and wine.

Museo Cerámica, Plaza del Marqués de Dos Aguas. A fascinating structure of rococó and Churrigueresque architecture. The kids enjoyed this museum as much as we did. Highlights were the coach and

179

costume room, the Gallery of Humorists and the Moorish rooms. Visiting hours are 11 am-2 pm and 5-9 pm, until 8 pm in winter. Price of admission is 14 cents.

CAMBRILS

Cambrils is a small town, south of Barcelona. A nice stopping point along the way.

Camping: Cambrils Puerto, 800 meters from N. 340 at kilometer 262. Open all year; showers, shopping, restrooms, camping gas, beach. Admission: Adults, car, caravan and tent each 37 cents.

SITGES

A picturesque town 40 kilometers south of Barcelona on the Costa Dorada; in summer, a popular resort town for young Europeans. There is a small children's play area down by the water that makes a perfect picnic spot.

Camping

Los Almendros Europe, from Barcelona, at kilometer 26.1 before level-crossing, turn right and continue for 200 meters telephone 294 11 01. Open May-October; shopping, restrooms, camping gas, beach. Sitges, at kilometer 38 on Barcelona-Santa Cruz de Calafell road; telephone 294 10 80. Open all year; shopping beach.

BARCELONA

Camping

Barcino, from Plaza Gloria via Avenida del Generalísimo Franco through town to junction with N. 11; telephone 249 30 47. Open all year; shopping, restrooms, restaurant, camping gas, swimming pool.

Though there are many other campgrounds on the outskirts of Barcelona we decided to find our own spots within the city limits; this made for quicker and easier access to the places of interest. The authorities didn't seem to bother us as long as we remained quiet and fairly inconspicuous.

Tourist Information Office, Avenida de José Antonio, 658; American Express, Viajes Taber Office, Caspe 21; telephone 232 59 00.

The Institute of North American Studies, Via Augusta, 123; telephone 227 31 45. We found this to be a good place to pick up information and to meet English-speaking Spaniards.

Post Office Plaza Antonio López.

Babysitting

Though we did not have the occasion to use a babysitter in Barcelona and were unable to find any official agency, we suggest you call the Institute of North American Studies listed above, as they may be able to suggest student babysitters or where to find an agency. Another suggestion is to call the American School of Barcelona, Plaza Eusebio, **Güell**, 8; telephone 203 79 01 or 13.

Shopping

Open Market, *Mercado San José*, off Las Ramblas.

Flea Market **Los Encantes**, Plaza Glorieas. Take the metro from Plaza Cataluña **to Plaza Glorias.**

Bookstore: *Librarea Francesa*, on the corner of Generalísimo and Calle de Muntaner, three blocks from Plaza Grazia and the metro stop Diagonal. Children's books in English are available here.

Camping Gas: Available at the 19 Pinto Fortuny, two blocks from Plaza Cataluña **from the Mercado San José off Las Ramblas.**

Launderettes

There is a *lavanderia* one block from the Sagrada Familia on Calle de Mallorca, the corner of Napoles. There is another one on the right side of Calle de Luis, going toward Calle de General Sanjurjo.

Sightseeing

Montjuich Park At the south end of town, this park is a great place from which to view the city. There are fountains, romantic pathways, gardens, outdoor restaurants, an amusement park and museums. The most exciting way to go is via funicular from the **Calle del Marqués del Duero.** On weekend nights, usually Saturday, there is an illuminated fountain display near **Plaza de España**, lasting from about 9:30-11 pm. In the summertime a play is staged on Thursday nights.

Pueblo Español (The Spanish Village): This was the best part of our visit to Barcelona. Built in 1929, the Spanish Village reproduces in a comprehensive manner the characteristic aspects of Spanish architecture. One also has the opportunity to see some of the ancient crafts still being performed today such as glassblowing, printmaking, woodcarving, engraving and textile design. Visit the small Catalan Museum with displays of Ancient, handmade toys. The Village is open all day, every day and charges 22 cents admission for adults, children free.

Parque Güell: this delightful park displaying the whimsical sculpture and architecture of Gaudí is at the slope of Mount Tibidabo, overlooking the city from the north. Entrance into the park is free and there are numerous play and picnic areas. This makes a good spot to take a break from the general sightseeing. After seeing the park, you can continue up the mountain to the top of **Tibidabo** for a panoramic view of Barcelona.

El Templo de La Sagrada Familia: A brief stop here will suffice but make a point to go by this bizarre Gaudí masterpiece still in the stages of construction almost 90 years. It is at Calle Mallorca, Provenza y Marina-Cerdena. For 22 cents you can go inside the grounds and an elevator will take you up to the top of one of the towers for another 8 cents.

The Picasso Museum: Located in an old converted palace at 15 Calle de Moncada off Calle de la Princesa, the museum is open daily 10 am-2 pm and 5-8 pm, charging 22 cents admission.

A Walk Through the Gothic Quarter: The old aristocratic quarter of Barcelona lies east of Las Ramblas and is reached via the Calle del Carmen. Highlights of the quarter are the cathedral at the Plaza de la Catedral, and the 18th century Bishops Palace at 5 Calle del Obispo Irurita. Both are worth a visit. If you visit the cathedral on a Sunday at noon, you may be lucky to see a *sardana*, a Catalan folk dance performed in front of the church.

Parque de la Ciudadela (Central Park) The kids will enjoy this well-designed zoo that has just recently been renovated, making it one of the most up-to-date zoos in Europe. It is open every day from 9 am to dusk with an admission of 22 cents. For a small additional fee, you can tour the zoo in small open-sided buses that traverse it at all points. Also, in the park are museums of zoology, geology, and modern art, open every day 10 am-2 pm with an admission for each of 22 cents.

SIDE TRIPS FROM BARCELONA

Monserrat: The monastery of Monserrat is one of the most important religious pilgrimage sights in Spain. Situated near a spectacular work of nature, a cluster of finger-like protrusions in granite, it is well worth a visit. While there you can take the funicular for 37 cents to the peak, San Jerónimo, the tallest spot on the mountain. To get to Monserrat follow the general road leading to Lerida and Madrid as far at the crossing with the road to Monistrol (43 kilometers from

Barcelona). From Monistrol to the monastery (18 kilometers) the road goes straight up in continuous curves. Be sure and leave early, allowing a full day for this excursion.

Cadaqués This picturesque fishing village of whitewashed, tile-roofed buildings overlooking a lovely bay of the Mediterranean is situated about 150 kilometers north of Barcelona as you head toward the Spanish French frontier. You will turn off the main road at Figueras going east toward the ocean and follow this through the mountains to Cadaqués. Being quite secluded, one can understand why the surrealist artist, Salvador Dali, has chosen it for his home. To see his home go to the nearby cove, Port Lligat.

Camping Close to town, watch for camping signs; telephone 25 81 26. Open June 1-September 30; showers, shopping, restaurant, camping gas, bungalows for rent, beach. Admission: adults, car tent and caravan each 29 cents.

From Cadaqués the ride along the Costa Brava to the French border is magnificent.

SPANISH FOOD SPECIALTIES

In Spain, the choice of foods is unlimited, as the cost is considerably less than many other countries of Europe. Each region has its specialties that one can sample at the local hostería, restaurant or at a snack counter in the big department stores in major cities. Regional specialties that we encountered are listed below.

The Basque Country
Marmitako, a savory stew.
Bacaldo al pil pil, a savory dried cod dish.
Merluza a la vasca, whiting prepared in a Basque style.
Chacoli, wine or cider.

184

Segovia

Cochinillo asado, roast sucking pig, a famous dish in Segovia

Madrid

Pechuga, breaded breast of chicken dish.

Valencia

Paella, a wonderful combination dish of shellfish (mussels, shrimp and clams) with rice and chicken.

French Riviera and Northern Italy

The first stop in our drive toward the French Riviera was at the famous walled city of **Carcassonne**. This medieval city, located on the Aude River in southern France about 92 kilometers southeast of Toulouse, was founded by the Romans in the first century B.C Surrounded with double walls and guarded by 54 towers, the restored city stands virtually complete. The ramparts, towers, basilica and castle are illuminated every night from Easter to October. Since we were too late for that we decided to try and make it to Montpellier by nightfall.

We arrived in Montpellier in the late afternoon and stopped at the pretty central park to get some exercise. In spite of the fact that there were several campgrounds in the area, we again chose our own sheltered spot off the road that follows the coast to Nice. From Montpellier the road continues through **Vallauris**, a beautiful coastal town near Cannes, not as touristy and ostentatious as some of the other Mediterranean resort areas. It was once the home of Picasso. Watch for the ceramic factories there, as many do not realize that Picasso also developed his own unique designs in this media. Be sure and visit the interesting *Madoura* factory, which produces his designs.

We arrived in the large cosmopolitan city of **Nice** with its palm-lined boulevards and broad beaches about a half-hour later. Being warned of the exorbitant prices in restaurants, we decided to try the *pâtisserie* next to the train station for a *pan bagnet*, the famous *Niçoise* sandwich. Much to our disappointment and attesting to their popularity, the sandwiches were all gone upon our arrival. We continued the search, luckily finding a small Tunisian bistro on the Rue Pertinax that had them. If we ordered our sandwich and ate it in the restaurant at one of the small tables, it was more costly than if we bought it to go. Being budget conscious, we ordered two of the large *pan bagnets* filled with olive oil, tuna, hot sauce, capers and olives. Not being able to resist the temptation, we also ordered some of the tiny sweet Tunisian pastries, and took our lunch out to the camper. By splitting the sandwiches in two there was plenty for all of us.

Our first sightseeing on the French Riviera took us to some of the surrounding areas of Nice to see the **Henry Clews Museum** at the village of **La Napoule** just eight kilometers beyond Cannes, and the beautiful mountain village of Saint-Paul-de-Vence. We found the place most interesting and enjoyed seeing the bizarre sculptures of a former American sculptor in the villa, which was once his home. From there it was a short drive to Saint-Paul, an ancient and picturesque village of artists, writers and painters nestled in the hills behind Nice. Before reaching Saint-Paul, there is a sign pointing the way to the **Maeght Foundation,** a modern art museum formed from the cooperative efforts of several well-known contemporary artists and housed in a most unique architectural creation. The various paintings and sculptures donated to the Foundation, a gift of Aimé and Marguerite Maeght, permit a constant renewal of exhibitions, offering an ever-changing view of contemporary art. Within this fascinating structure one sees a blending of monumental works: Calder's mobiles, Miro's paintings, Giacometti's sculptures, mosaics by Chagall, Tal-Coat and Braque. Miro sculptures are found in the gardens, and there is a chapel exhibiting beautiful stained-glass windows executed by Braque and Ubac. The offerings of the Foundation are many, among which one of the most famous is the annual summer festival, *Nights of the Maeght Foundation,* devoted to music, theater and contemporary ballet. The Foundation also houses an extensive bookstore, a theater of contemporary films and a modern snack bar. Plan on spending at least two hours to get the full benefit of all there is to see, and afterward take a walk in the beautiful gardens surrounding the museum.

We approached the village of **Saint-Paul-de-Vence** near dusk, a beautiful time to see this charming walled town nestled in the hills above Nice. As we wandered down the extremely narrow cobblestone streets, we felt as if we were in some sort of fairyland. The shops are elegant and the windows full of beautiful objects to tempt the eye (just look as prices are high). The old houses dating back to the 16th and 17th centuries displayed beautiful, well-preserved façades. Our hour walk through the village was a highlight of the day and built up a good appetite for our dinner that evening in Nice. We chose the **Restaurant L'Escargot** on Rue Pertinax, serving Vietnamese cuisine. For $5 we had a delicious Vietnamese meal of chicken, rice, vegetables, salad, wine and tea.

After dinner we drove to the Italian border, arriving about 10 o'clock, stopped to buy the Italian gas coupons available for tourists, some auto insurance and to check on road conditions north of the Alps. Because of the late hour we pulled into one of the rest-stop areas along the autoroute and spent the night there. We were surprised at the maze of wide, smooth highways there were in this part of Italy and at the fast-moving traffic that traversed them even at this hour of night. One unfortunate factor of this convenience for the motorist is having to pay for it. To drive on just a short span of the freeway from the border to the outskirts of Genoa, we paid about $1.20. We would suggest that if traveling in the daytime and time is no problem, you take alternative roads; they are easier on the budget.

GENOA

We arrived in the largest seaport of Italy, Genoa, early the next morning after a rather fitful sleep along the noisy freeway. This chief commercial center is laid out like a huge amphitheater along the seashore. The most picturesque part of the city is near the harbor where white palaces and villas rise in terraces up steep hills of luxuriant gardens. The center of the city is crowded and fast moving. We stopped there briefly and then drove on to Milan.

As we headed north the weather became cooler and we were thankful that our small German gas heater was still serving us well. If we kept it on in the car from the time that we stopped each evening to prepare our dinner to the time we went to bed, the car stayed quite warm all night. The only problems were the cold mornings and the ice that formed on the windows. We hated to get up and even began sleeping in old blue jeans and sweatshirts to help break the shock. This worked well as we could always change after breakfast when the car had warmed up from the heater. The girls slept in pajama blankets, what we called "bunny suits," an indispensable item we were happy to have stuffed into their suitcases in spite of the bulk.

MILAN

Milan is the capital of the region of Lombardy and the second largest city in Italy. The best place to start from when visiting this Italian metropolis is the central square of the **Piazza del Duomo,** where most of its principal streets meet. Not only is Milan known for the most famous opera house in the world, **La Scala,** but also for the **Church of Santa Maria Delle Grazie** where the original of Leonardo DaVinci's "Last Supper" can be viewed.

On an important day, our young daughter's fourth birthday we also visited the Milan zoo, but found it rather shabby (it reminded us of the zoo in Madrid), although we did especially enjoy watching the polar bears. While observing the polar bears' antics, my talking French to the children attracted a passerby who greeted us with a friendly *"bonjour."* He explained that though he was from Milan, he had just returned from working in Belgium and overheard the "French family," which we quickly explained we were not. We told him we were celebrating our daughter's fourth birthday. With delight, he insisted we go back to his house where he and his wife would have a birthday party for her. He went on to say he had been married several years and had "no *bambini*" and was so happy to have children in his home. We returned to his apartment where his charming wife proceeded to order a birthday cake and friends arrived with balloons and *gelato* (Italian ice cream). We had a wonderful time and, most importantly, our young daughter was embraced by these warm and friendly Italians. His wife asked us if we had any laundry and when we said we did she insisted we give it to her to wash. The next morning, we found a basket of folded, clean laundry waiting by our camper door (we had parked in the street by their apartment). After thanking them we left with a very warm feeling towards the Italians. What hospitality!

We had a particularly delicious meal in Milan at a reasonable price by stopping at one of the many *salumerias* (delicatessens) to buy some lasagna, salad and antipasto. Shortly after we began our journey north towards Switzerland and the beautiful region of the *Tecino*.

Lying between the Alps and the northern part of the plains of Lombardy from northwest Piedmont to the Veneto and the western Trentino, this area offers a number of picturesque lakes, remains of the glaciers of the Quaternary period. We soon came to Lake Como, one of the deepest and most beautiful of the lakes. We stopped at one of the cafes on the edge of the lake for hot chocolate, and then crossed the border to Switzerland.

SUMMING UP THE
FRENCH RIVIERA AND NORTHERN ITALY

THE FRENCH RIVIERA

Note: Because campgrounds are abundant along the entire Riviera, we will list only the ones at the major spots where we stopped.

CARCASSONNE

On your way to the Riviera be sure and stop at this famous walled city. There is camping at *A. Domec*, Avenue Savrail.

MONTPELLIER

Camping

Lattes: Le Salamandre, autoroute Montpellier-Carnon, five kilometers southeast on D. 189. Open all year; showers, shopping, bungalows, caravans and tents for rent. Admission: Adults 36 cents, car 18 cents.

Sites

Aigues-Montes: Excursions may be made from Montpellier 40 kilometers to the west to this fortified medieval seaport left landlocked by the receding Mediterranean.

Grotto of the Demoiselles, about 27 kilometers north, near Ganges, one of the most beautiful grottoes of France. You can also take the Route N.113 north to the town of **Avignon.**

NICE

Camping

There are several campgrounds in and around Nice. The one we found that was open in the winter was at *Cros-de-Cagnes*, *Le Concordia*, 800 meters north on N. 7. Admission: Adults 32 cents, car 18 cents, caravan and tent each 28 cents.

Sightseeing

Stroll along the *grande promenade* down by the beach. Take a side trip to the beautiful little village of *St.-Paul-de-Vence* and visit the *Maeght Foundation* arts center. This arts center is open daily (including Sunday and holidays) October–April, 10 am–12:30 pm and

2:30–6 pm; May–September, 10 am–noon and 3–7 pm. Admission is $2 for adults and 60 cents for children, with a reduction available if you are the holder of an International Student Identification Card. Parking is available at the entrance. Take a side trip to *Vallauris*, former home of Picasso and famous for its pottery.

We were very disappointed in the French Riviera other than for these three sights. It was touristy, commercial, high priced and lacked the charm of many other regions in France.

NORTHERN ITALY

Unfortunately, we left this country for the end of our itinerary; the weather was cold and wet, our funds were running low and it was expedient that we get to Germany as quickly as possible to ship our VW camp mobile back to the US. Because of this, we toured only the northwestern section of the country. We would recommend though, that if you are traveling in the spring, this is a wonderful time to see all of Italy and then take in some of Greece, easily accessible from the southern Italian port of Brindisi. Included here is some camping information for the northwestern section of Italy. Prices are quoted in dollars at the exchange rate of 585 lira to $1.

Much like Spain, Italy has concentrated many of its camping facilities along coastal regions—the Adriatic Riviera from Grado to Pescara, the Gargano Promontory and the Tyrrhenian Riviera (the flat coastal area of Campania). There are also many campgrounds on the banks of the pre-Alpine regions. In the higher areas of the Alps there are some 600 Alpine refuge huts sited at points where they are most useful to those on excursions and climbs. Most of the huts are managed by the Club Alpino Italiano (C.A.I.), whose headquarters is in Milan at Via Ugo Foscola 3. Arrangements may be made either by mail or in person when you are in Milan. In other areas the sites are few and far between; however, we found that camping was allowed almost anywhere as long as permission was obtained from the landowner. Many times, we would just pull off the side of the road and were never bothered.

It is advisable to make reservations at some of the more popular camping regions during the tourist season. Local information bureaus, referred to as *Ente Provinciale per il Turismo*, are to be found in most towns and will provide details of campsites in their area. Fees for one night are generally from 40 cents to 65 cents per person, from 17 cents to 40 cents for a caravan, 25 cents to 50 cents for a car, and free to 40 cents for a tent. For a complete up-to-date list of Italian camping facilities, write to The Italian Camping Federation, Via Mameli 2, Florence.

IMPERIA

A provincial capital just beyond the Franco-Italian border and situated in a major olive-oil production center of Italy.

Camping

De Wijnstok, Via Poggi 4, two kilometers southwest of Porto Maurizio telephone 01 83-78 9 86. Showers, shopping, restaurant, camping gas, bungalows for rent. Admission: Adults 51 cents, car, caravan and tent each 43 cents.

SAVONA

Charly, Vado Ligure between AGIP and BP filling station inland from Via Aurelia telephone 85 1 21. Open May 1–September 30 showers, restrooms, camping gas. Admission: Adults, car and caravan each 34 cents, no charge for tent.

GENOA

Italy's chief seaport and leading commercial center, a large bustling city, the most attractive area being near the harbor where white palaces and villas in luxuriant gardens rise in terraces up steep hills. Other than that we found very little of interest to keep us there.

From Genoa going southeast along the coast you encounter the Italian Riviera, one of the loveliest areas of Italy. Dense vegetation (palms, pine, citrus, cypress and eucalyptus) covers much of this region and winding roads offer fresh vistas of the Mediterranean at every turn. The Roman road known as the Via Aurelia or N. 1 is the main drive along the shores. Some of the highlights you see along the way are Rapallo, Camogli, Nervi, Portofino and Santa Margherita. Between Pt. Mesco and La Spezia you will want to visit *"Cinq Terre,"* the Five Lands of the Italian Riviera, a fascinating group of tiny Italian fishing villages, accessible only by train. See the tourist information office in Genoa for more details on this interesting side trip. The American Express office in Genoa is the Societa Internazionale Turismo on Via San Vincenzo 22-r telephone 581-368.

Note: Many years later we hiked in the Cinque Terre. We stayed in Comogli, which we found to be a wonderful place to stay with easy access by a small cog railway to the Cinque Terre. Comogli had good restaurants and accommodations.

MILAN

Camping
Chiesa Rossa, Via Chiesa Rossa 168, four kilometers south of Porta Ticinese. Open May 1–October 31; within three kilometers of shopping restaurants, bungalows for rent. Admission: Adults and caravan each 43 cents, car and tent each 34 cents.

Tourist Information Tourist Information Office at Piazza del Duomo, near the corner of Via Mazzini.

Italian Touring Club, Corso Italia 10.

Shopping
PAM supermarket chain located throughout the city.

Sightseeing

The Cathedral, a magnificent Gothic structure crowned by 135 pinnacles of which the central one, on which rests a gilded stature of the Madonna, reaches 108.5 meters (355.7 feet).

"The Last Supper" the famous fresco by Leonardo da Vinci, in the former convent adjoining the **Church of Santa Maria delle Grazie.**

The Scala Opera House

The Public Gardens, Zoo and Planetarium, located between the Via Senato and the Corse Venezia

LAKE COMO

Camping

*Rivabell*a, four kilometers south of Lecco; telephone 31 205. Open May 1–September 30, showers, shopping, camping gas, swimming. Admission: Adults, car, caravan and tent each 43 cents.

Alto Lario, north of Poncia. Open April 15–September 30; shopping, restaurant, bungalows for rent, swimming.

Vigna del Lago, telephone 81-4-48. Showers, swimming. Admission: Adults 34 cents, car 26 cents, no charge of tent and caravan.

Del Sole, one and a half kilometers southwest; telephone (0344) 58. Open March 1–October 30; showers, shopping restaurant, camping gas, bungalows for rent, swimming. Admission: Adults 34 cents, car 26 cents, caravan 9 cents, tent no charge.

LAKE MAGGIORE

Camping

Lido, Via Piave 28; on Road 33 west side of Lake Maggiore; telephone 27 75. Open April 15–September 30; showers, shopping restaurant, bungalows for rent, swimming. Admission: Adults 43 cents, car, caravan and tent each 26 cents.

Tranquilla, on road 33 west side of Lake Maggiore, four kilometers from Stresa; telephone 21 58. Open all year showers, shopping, restaurant, camping gas, swimming (lake and pool). Admission: Adults 34 cents, car, caravan and tent each 18 cents.

GOOD SKIING AREAS IN ITALY

The **Dolomites,** South Tyrol (northeast of Milan).

Gardena, famous for its woodcarvers and one of the top-ranking regions for skiing in Europe.

ITALIAN FOOD SPECIALTIES

A typical Italian dinner, such as you might find in a *trattoria* or other inexpensive dining place, consists of minestrone or a clear soup with vermicelli and a pasta made of many varieties of macaroni with a tomato or meat sauce. The *entrée* is generally a meat dish (veal is an Italian favorite) with vegetables, followed by salad, cheese and fruit. Ice cream (*gelato*) in Italy is excellent.

There are many excellent varieties of Italian cheese; in the marketplace they will usually let you sample a small piece before deciding. The coastal towns of Italy are famous for *zuppa di pesce,* a fish soup. *Capretto* (kid) and *abacchio* (lamb) are especially favored for spring holidays. The food of the south is highly seasoned and heavy on the olive oil. In Northern Italy, most of the cooking is done with butter and the seasoning is subtle. For light snacks look for a snack bar or *spuntino*, or a *tavola calda*, a combination delicatessen and cafeteria.

The view of Zermatt from our chalet window

Switzerland

The snow-capped mountains in the distance heightened our excitement as we arrived in Switzerland. Our plans were indefinite, but we did hope to be able to see the Matterhorn and some of the other high Alpine peaks. We headed for Lugano and the region known as the **Tessin** (or Canton of Ticino), the southernmost canton of Switzerland. Italian Switzerland, as it is called, is most known for its beautiful countryside, lakes, forests, small villages, varied dialects and ancient architecture. We were in search of such villages as Indemini, Giornico, Marcote and others we had read about but couldn't find on a map. Lugano, Locarno and Ascona are all three favorite holiday centers of this region, but it is in the more isolated lake and valley villages that one can get a true picture of the unaffected Swiss Italian way of life. Unfortunately, time prevented us from visiting some of the smaller towns, so we are including some suggested itineraries from the tourist bureau in "Summing Up."

LUGANO AND LOCARNO

As we pulled into Lugano, we were struck with the beauty of this large but unspoiled city on the shores of the huge Lake Lugano. The old town, with its arcaded shopping streets is thoroughly Italian in character, with the hotels and villas on the shore and hills beyond giving it an international flavor. A fine promenade runs along the lakefront and provides panoramic views of the Alps on the other side. Strolling around town we looked in the windows of the elegant shops, stopped to have tea in a pastry shop, and walked in the beautiful park at the edge of the lake. Of course, the kids enjoyed this the most as there was a grand play area there, and in spite of the wetness of the ground, they had a great time sliding down the big slide into the snow.

Also, while in Lugano be sure and catch the magnificent view from the **Monte Bre** and the **Monte San Salvatore,** both ascended by funicular. Another interesting side excursion is to the curious old village of **Grandia** reached via lake steamer from Lugano.

From Lugano we went to Locarno, the first leg of our trek to Zermatt. Splendidly situated on a small bay on the north shore of Lake Maggiore, Locarno is famous for its International Film Festival held each September. We strolled along some of its streets under the arcades of the piazza, and then decided we had better quickly find a place to park for the night. We found a big empty parking lot in the center of town, which had public restrooms. The place was deserted, and our only worry was getting caught in the snow during the night as it was beginning to come down quite heavily. Most of the campgrounds in the area, listed in "Summing Up," were open only from April to September but we were determined to defy common practice and prove that camping is possible in Switzerland even in the winter. Well, we did, and, though we would recommend other times as better, we were pleased to have seen this majestic land in all her white winter splendor.

The following morning after some hot cereal and coffee (which we had to make from fresh snow as the water in our tank had frozen), we set off for the Simplon Pass.

From Locarno we followed the route to Golino, Intragna, Corcapolo and finally across the Italian border again through Re to Masera, Domodossola, Varzo, Bertonia, Iselle and across the Swiss border to Gondo, then on to Simplon and the Simplon Pass.

Of all these small villages, Re stands out most vividly, for it is there that we witnessed a most moving scene. We were stopped along the road for lunch when the bells of the large village church began to resound throughout the streets. Slowly the doors of the shops were closed, and a long procession of townspeople dressed in black and led by a priest and cart bearing a wooden casket filled the street. The scene was full of rich contrasts: the dark clothing of the procession against the white winter surroundings, the soft snow against the granite and slate roofs of the buildings, and the gleaming sunlight reflecting off the domes of the church against the darkness of the somber event.

This was one of our most memorable experiences in Italy, the Village of Re on a cold winter day

ZERMATT

We finally arrived at Randa, a small village where one must park to catch the train for Zermatt, the village near the base of the Matterhorn. No automobiles can go into Zermatt and, consequently, the town is serene and quiet. Boarding the train at Randa, 20 minutes later we descended at the station in Zermatt to behold horse-drawn sleighs laden with furry sheepskins waiting for visitors. Everywhere was the sound of sleigh bells, and the scene of people carrying skis over their shoulders or swinging ice skates in their hands. After asking the price of a horse-drawn sleigh, we decided to walk. You can enjoy their charm almost as much as a spectator.

Our first problem was finding an affordable room for the night. From the crowded conditions at the little train station we were beginning to fear that none would be available. With fingers crossed, we walked up the main street in search of the **Echo Chalet** some mountain-climbing friends had told us about. It is reasonable, but the rooms were all full. While crossing a bridge, we were approached by a woman who smiled at the girls and seemed to want to talk. When we told her that we were looking for a place to stay she invited us to her place, the **Sudlenz Chalet.** When we saw our lovely accommodations, including two huge bedrooms with down comforters on the beds and a view of the Matterhorn, a bathroom with shower and tub, and a big, fully equipped kitchen, we were a bit afraid to inquire about the price. Much to our surprise and delight she told us it would only cost us $7 for the first night and $4.70 thereafter. She also offered to lend us a sled for the children's use during our stay.

That night we splurged and went out to a small restaurant, **The Kanne.** On the main street midway up from the train station, it has a big white milk pitcher (the meaning of the word *kanne*) outside. We had been anxious to try the typically Swiss dish, *raclette* (potatoes in a fondue-like cheese sauce). It was delicious, but a bit expensive for the small portions we received. We would suggest trying this dish in a less touristy place than Zermatt, which is definitely overpriced in most aspects due to its popularity.

The next day after some time spent walking and sledding, we set out on an afternoon hike up to the village of **Zmutt** that stands at the base of the Matterhorn. Although the scenery along the way was magnificent, the hike proved a bit long and cold for the children. If you decide to make this hike, we suggest you start earlier in the day so breaks can be taken along the way and you return before dusk when the air turns cold. We had quite a scare when our youngest daughter started to turn blue; we piled her onto the sled with a blanket around her and Gary started back down the hill at record speed while her sister and I quickly followed them on foot. We were glad to find a chalet with a fireplace halfway down and quickly got some hot chocolate into both girls, deciding not to make the journey to Zmutt after all. It was too late in the day and too cold.

Gary, Dawn and Tiffany. Happy we made it down the mountain safely after a close call on the trail to Zmutt

After leaving Zermatt we set off for the small town of Oberwald where we hoped to drive through the pass. We later spent a very cold night there parked at the train station, as we discovered a bit too late that the pass was closed, and it would be necessary to take a car train through the mountain. Though we learned we would have to backtrack to Goppenstein, we were too exhausted to go on that night. In the morning we awoke to find our water frozen and a sheet of ice on all our windows. Once we defrosted the windows, we traveled back down the road we had come on from Randa, all the way back to Visp, then Turtig and finally turned right towards Steg, then on to **Goppenstein**. The beautiful scenery helped ease the pain of having to backtrack. We suggest that when traveling in Switzerland during the winter, you check the tourist information offices before leaving to discover which passes are open and which are not.

The train ride from Goppenstein was quite an experience. We rode sitting backwards through the longest and darkest tunnel we had ever been in. The 15-minute ride took us through a huge mountain to the village of **Kandersteg** from where we would continue our journey back on the road to Bern. In Bern we were to visit a delightful Swiss family we had met at the LA airport just before our departure for Europe several months earlier.

BERN

One of the highlights of our days in Bern was the tour with our Swiss friends through the old part of the city down arcaded walkways. We saw the famous **Bears of Bern** in their moat, which is said to have protected the old city from invasion years ago (the bears do tricks for the public who can reward them with small fig bars purchased at a nearby stand) and the statue and fountain of **Kindlifresserbrunnen,** the ogre said to eat children. At two o'clock we pulled up to a corner where we could watch the actions of the famous **Glockenspiel** or clock tower. As the hour strikes, a cock flops his wings, two bears go around, a wooden figure turns over his hourglass and a jester rings his bells three times. Then a sculptured man at the top knocks the big bell that resounds throughout the town the number of the hour.

On another of our daily excursions we went to **Guggershorn Mountain** at **Guggersberg**, a famous hiking spot about 30 kilometers south of Bern. After an exhilarating hike to the top we climbed about 60 steps to a high platform affording us panoramic views of the whole region, including the Ural Mountains and the Alps. Our friends watched the girls while we climbed, but Gary, who suffers from a fear of heights did not enjoy this as much as I did. The views were magnificent.

204

Another side trip we enjoyed was to the little village of **Aarber,** also about 30 kilometers from Bern. One day we walked a few short blocks from our friends' home to see the **Bern Natural History Museum,** one of the best in Europe with excellent exhibits of a wide variety of animals. It was a cold, brisk day and our walk home built up a good appetite for the delicious meal ahead. Our friend, Trudi, had made *roasti*, a popular Swiss dish with whipped potatoes fried in butter. Some of the other typically Swiss foods we had while there were black *brod* (farmer's bread), *vervicelli* made with chestnut paste and topped with whipped cream, delicious little pastries, and cheese fondue.

Dawn having fun climbing in the tree tower at the Bern park

On our last day we walked in the woods behind our friends' home to a delightful children's play area created by a woodcarver. Whimsical figures that children could climb on and explore were hewn from tree logs. The kids especially liked the tree tower where they could climb and hide from one another. (See "Summing Up" for directions on how to find this park.)

ZURICH AND ST. GALLEN

With much sadness we said good-bye to our Swiss friends, left Bern and headed for Zurich. We stopped there for the afternoon and enjoyed browsing in the beautiful shops along the **Bahnhofstrasse,** the famous shopping street of the largest industrial city in Switzerland. Our time for sightseeing was limited but we have listed some of the highlights of Zurich's many sights in "Summing Up." We would

205

also suggest that if it fits into your schedule you take an excursion from there to St. Gallen, the Swiss cotton center, to see some of the finest embroideries and laces in all of Europe.

While in St. Gallen be sure and see the magnificent baroque cathedral built on the site of the hermitage of the seventh century Irish monk, Gallus. It contains one of Switzerland's great cultural treasures, the gorgeous rococo Abby Library with its 2000 priceless manuscripts and 1700 *incunabula*.* The rural regions surrounding St. Gallen are most interesting and can easily be reached by rail or road. Appenzell is a small village where one can observe the still unspoiled life of the Swiss peasant and the kids would enjoy seeing the famous Pestalozzi Children's Village, established for orphans from almost a dozen nations, at nearby Trogen.

From St. Gallen we followed the main autoroute into Bregenze, Austria, then back across the border into Germany and to Lindau.

*Plural form of *incunabulum*, meaning early printed books, especially those before 1501.

SUMMING UP SWITZERLAND

Of the many camping sites throughout Switzerland, 90 are run by the national motoring organization, the Touring Club Suisse, which maintains offices in most towns and cities. There are sites along the main routes and in areas of interest to the tourist—along Lake Constance (Bodensee), Lake Neuchâtel (**the largest lake wholly within the country**), **and the beautiful lakes Lucerne,** Lugano and Thun. Camping outside authorized sites is permitted, except in the Swiss National Park (canton of Grisons) or where there are nature reserves. Fees range from 22 cents to 66 cents per person per night; a parking fee for caravans is free to 44 cents and a caravan tax is payable. At some sites there are additional local taxes. The height of the tourist season extends from April or May to September or October. A few sites are open all year, particularly those in winter resort areas.

Though the spring is a beautiful time to see the country when the hills and mountains are ablaze with wildflowers and the temperatures are warmer, we did see a certain advantage in seeing Switzerland in the winter. The winter sports of tobogganing, sledding, skiing and ice skating are a very big part of life in Switzerland; we did not meet one family, for instance, who was not avid in at least one of these activities if not all. If you like to ski, the winter is the time for you to see Switzerland. The choice of ski areas is fantastic and not all of them are expensive. (Note: prices are quoted in dollars at an exchange rate of 4.40 francs to $1).

BRIG

Camping
Geshina, one kilometer south of town center; telephone (028) 3 26 98. Open April 15–October 15; showers, shopping, camping gas, swimming pool. Admission: Adults 63 cents, car 23 cents, caravan and tent no charge.

ZERMATT

Camping is possible from June to October if you have a tent and equipment easy enough to carry on the train. We would suggest, however, that you stay in one of the many beautiful Swiss chalets for the most pleasant visit. We have recommended two below, which are both quite reasonable.

Chalet Sudlenz
Write for reservations if you plan on being there during ski season, Chalet Sudlenz, c/o Frau Peter Perren, Zermatt, Switzerland. Rooms with fully equipped bath and kitchen facilities available for $7 a night.

Echo Chalet
Write to Echo Chalet, c/o Josef Lauber, Zermatt, Switzerland. Rooms with baths and kitchens available.

Restaurant Suggestion

The Kanne (across the street from the post office).

Zermatt is the winter-sports center of Switzerland. We recommend a hike to Zmutt at the base of the Matterhorn, but start out early and wear very warm clothing (down jackets, for example)

BERN

This city, situated on the banks of the River Aar, has been the capital of the Swiss Confederation since 1848. Founded during the Middle Ages, Bern presents a medieval façade to its modern and up-to-date shopping, education and tourist facilities. Especially interesting is the old part of town which we have outlined below.

Camping

Eicholz, right near the large park south of the city center known as Dählhölzli, along the River Aar. Admission: Adults 46 cents, children 23 cents, car 58 cents.

Camping Eymatt, just outside Bern at the little lake of Wahlen.

Tourist Information

Bundesgasse 20; telephone 22 39 51.

Post Office the main post office is located just beside the train station at Bubenbergplatz.

Babysitting

Agentur Tupf, Münstergasse 6; telephone 22 60 01.
Agentur Alther, Kasthoferstrasse 44: telephone 44 30 37.
Kinderparadies, Marktgasse 6; telephone 22 46 26.

Launderettes

Masty René, Seftigenstrasse 25; telephone 45 65 75.
Gfeller Gerda, Schwabstrasse 40; telephone 56 62 85.

Levenberger V, Militarstrasse 50; telephone 41 01 54.
Pitsch Alfred, Weissensteinstrasse 32; telephone 25 93 88.
Tip Top, Schützgenweg 10; telephone 41 36 00.

With all of these you must make a reservation to do your laundry a day or so in advance. It takes about three hours to wash and dry and costs from $1.40 to $1.65.

Shopping

Migros Market in the Marktgasse, a large combination supermarket and department store.

Restaurants The following are a few inexpensive family-type restaurants.

Zum Eidgenössischen Kreuz, Zeughausgasse 41.

Gfeller, Barevnplatz 9.

Spatz, Barevnplatz 7.

Vegetaris, Neuengasse 15, is a vegetarian restaurant.

Hotel Volkshaus, Zeughausgasse 9.

The Bear Pit, just past the Fountain of Justice and next to the bridge Nydeggbrücke crossing the River Aar. Here the children can feed the bears, the symbol of Bern, and watch them perform marvelous tricks.

The Clock Tower (*Zytglogge*), located at the end of the big shopping street known as Marktgasse. Be sure and arrive on the hour in order to witness the "figure play." Three minutes before the hour a rooster to the left of Father Time crows and flaps his wings. One minute later the jester above Father Time wiggles his arms and legs and rings a bell above his head to announce the striking of the hour. The rooster then crows a second time and a little procession of bears emerge from the tower; led by a captain on horseback, the bears follow him proudly, carrying high the Bernese flag. They were no doubt intended to symbolize the military power of Old Bern. Father Time turns his hourglass to indicate the end of another hour and then slowly moves his lips to count the striking of the hour. The knight at the top of the tower then strikes out the hour with his hammer; Father Time moves his scepter and a lion nods his head to the chimes. The rooster then crows for a third time and the new hour has begun.

The Ogre Fountain or *Kindlifresserbrunnen* (meaning "eater of children"), located just around the corner from the clock tower at Kornhausplatz. This fountain is just one of the many delightful sculptural fountains built in Bern during the Middle Ages as the only source of water for the city inhabitants.

The Kursaal, reached by taking **Kornhausbrücke** from the clock tower to Schänzllhalde where you will turn left. The Kursaal is a large casino and dance hall; good evening entertainment.

Tierpark is an animal park with the animals in a natural setting.

Dählhölzli is a wonderful place for the children to run and explore.

Ice Skating Rinks

Ka-We-De, at the northwestern corner of the Tierpark Dählhölzli, Jubiläumstrase 101. In the summertime it is a swimming pool.

Eisstadion Allmend, Mingerstrasse 12. Take tramway No. 9 to Guisanplatz.

Elfenau Children's Park is a delightful play area of hand-carved figures made out of huge logs, including a log tower that the children can climb up into and peer out from above. The park is located not far from Dählhölzli on Brunnadernstrasse.

Ski Areas around Bern Beatenberg, ruschegg-Henbach Kiental, Diemtigtal, Maarbach, Gantrisch (Schwefelberg).

SIDE TRIPS FROM BERN

Aarberg, a quaint town just 30 kilometers northwest of Bern.

Guggersberg, Guggershorn Mountain is located in this little village, about 30 kilometers south of Bern. A fun place to picnic and do some hiking.

Lake Regions Thun, Brienz, Murten Bienne and Neuchâtel.

LUGANO

Camping

Agno (Ticino, La Palma, 600 meters east of town on road from Lugano to Ponte Tresa; telephone (091) 592 11 4. Open May 15–September 30 showers, shopping,camping gas, swimming. Admission: Adults 57 cents, car 34 cents, caravan and tent each 23 cents.

Marroggia (Ticino), Pizzale Mara, two kilometers south of Marroggia on Lake Lugano; telephone (091) 8724 5. Open April–October; shopping, camping gas, swimming.

Melano (Ticino), Paradiso, 500 meters west; telephone (091) 8 78 63. Open April 1–October 31; shopping, camping gas, swimming.

Lugano, Mussano Piodella di Agnuzzo, on main road from Lugano to Ponte Tresa. Well equipped with children's playground, showers, laundry facilities, camping

Tourist Information

Available from the Swiss Touring Club, located directly across the street from the promenade along the lake.

The American Express Office, located at Danzas Ltd., Piazza Manzoni 8; telephone 2 77 82.

The Municipal Park On the lakefront; very picturesque with a good children's playground and lovely wooded areas for picnics.

La Villa Favorita, a beautiful old mansion housing a vast collection of valuable paintings.

Swissminiature, at Melide, just five kilometers from Lugano, is a fascinating miniature village. Open 7:30 am–7 pm. (July and August to 10 pm), from May 11–October 3 on Sunday only.

Touring the Lake: Many tours to such picturesque spots as Marcote, Campione, Caprino and Gandria can be arranged through the Official Inquiry Office at Lugano on the Piazza R. Rezzonico, or by writing Local Transportation Companies, P.O. Box 56, 6900, Lugano, Switzerland.

Exploring the Tessin (Ticino) some of the highlights you should include in your visit are the valleys of Verzasca, La Maggia, Centrovalli, around Locarno and the Valley Bedretto on the St. Gotthard Route. Towns of special interest are Ascona, just three kilometers southwest of Locarno, Corona, Mendrisio, just north of Chiasso, and the unique little abandoned mountain village of Indemini, south of Ascona on the opposite side of Lake Maggiore.

Special Events in the Region

Wine Festival at Lugano; first weekend of October.
International Jazz Festival and Italian Opera Season, at Lugano in September
Festival on Lake Lugano with fireworks; end of July

LOCARNO

Locarno is a picturesque town on the shores of Lake Maggiore boasting the warmest climate in Switzerland and a wealth of colorful events including the International Film Festival in July. One of the most inviting sights is the superb subtropical gardens of the

Borromean Isles and the *Isle of Brissago*, reached via steamer on Lake Maggiore.

Camping

Delta, one and a half kilometers south of Lake Maggiore telephone (093) 7 60 81. Showers, shopping, camping gas, swimming. Admission: Adults 57 cents, caravan 34 cents.

Riposo, five kilometers east of Locarno and 800 meters northwest of Losone; telephone (093) 2 14 85. Open April–September 30; limited facilities. Admission: One adult and car 57 cents, caravan 46 cents, tent 23 cents.

From Locarno we drove directly to Randa where we were to take the train to Zermatt. The roads were good and the scenery magnificent, the drive taking us to Visp where you turn south for about 20 kilometers to Randa. If the road is clear you can continue to Tasch where you can also park your car and take the train to Zermatt. The fare is $1.20 adults, 70 cents children.

Swimming Pool (indoors) Maulbeerstrasse 14, near the center of town and the Bubenbergplatz.

ZURICH

Camping

Seebucht 557, one kilometer south of Zurich; telephone 45 16 12. Open May 1–October 1; showers, shopping, camping gas. Admission: Adults 20 cents, car 23 cents, caravan and tent no charge.

Tourist Information American Express, Bahnhofstrasse 20; telephone (051) 23 57 20.

Launderettes

Selbstbedienung Wascherei, 52 Acker Strasse, just off the Limmatstrasse in the area of the railroad station. You can leave your laundry while you sightsee, and it will be done for you for only $1.40 per load.

Another "Waschautomaten" is on the other side of the river, the "Sofort Reinigung" at 148 Stampfenbachstrasse, diagonally across from the Alfa Hotel. Here you do it yourself for 80 cents for six kilos.

Sightseeing

For children we highly recommend one of the best children's zoos in Europe, the *Rappellsvill Kinder Zoo*. Another fun activity in Zurich, as long as the kids hold out, is window-shopping on the famous and well-stocked shopping street of Zurich, The *Bahnhofstrasse*.

The Kunsthaus

Filled with a superb collection of 19th century art, this is a must for art lovers. Located on Heimplatz directly across from the Schauspielhaus, it is open Thursdays through Sunday 10 am–4 pm, Monday afternoon 2–5 pm, Tuesday through Friday evenings 8–10 pm.

SIDE TRIPS FROM ZURICH

Gotenbach with its deer park.

The Falls of the Rhine near Schaffhausen. Take road north of Zurich to Kloten, then Bulach, and on to Neuhausen where you will see signs to Rheinfall.

Rapperswil Take a four-hour steamer excursion on the Lake of Zurich to this quaint old town. Reservations can be made at the tourist bureau. It can also be reached by car via Route 17 south of Zurich. There are camping facilities at Rapperswil on the shore of Obersee, 30 kilometers southeast of Zurich. Open March 1–October 30.

ST. GALLEN

Camping

Altenrhein, Idyll on small road south of St. Gallen just before Appenzell. Open May–September; showers, shopping children's playground.

Side trips from St. Gallen

Appenzell, a small, typical Swiss village.
Pestalozzi Children's Village, at Trogen.

Being a woodcarver, Gary appreciated this old German
who greeted us at the door of an antique shop

Germany

We arrived in the famous German city of Munich about noon and, anxious to try some of the German cuisine, we decided to eat lunch at one of the many reasonable Munich beer halls, restaurants run by the beer companies. Our choice was the **Augustiner Grossgaststätten** at 16 Neuhauserstrasse, not far from the well-known square, **Marienplatz.** For about $4.20 our lunch was delicious and filling, including hard rolls (*brot*), liver and noodle soup (a Bavarian specialty known as *leberknödelsuppe*), potato salad, beer and milk. An hour later we walked out of this delightful Bavarian atmosphere of beer steins and laughter into the bright sunshine and crisp air with full stomachs and the resolve to find a place to stay for the night.

Our money was running low and we were now under a deadline to make it to Emden in one week, as we learned that our van must arrive in time for the next shipment of cars to New York to avoid the delay of a threatening dock strike. The nearest campground open at this time of year was at **Waldcamping**, a short distance outside of town off the Stuttgart-Munich autobahn. Before going there, we went to see the beautiful Munich zoo to compare it to the many we had seen in other European countries and so the kids could get some physical activity after being in the car for a good part of the time since we had left Bern. The beautiful woodland setting of the **Hellabrunn Zoo** was a perfect place for running and jumping as well as viewing the extensive selection of animals, arranged by geographical areas of origin.

One of the highlights of Munich is the **Nymphenburg Palace,** former baroque-rococo summer residence of German royalty. In the beautiful and spacious surrounding gardens are statues, lakes and waterfalls, and bordering the central formal gardens are rustic forests. The little **Amalienburg Palace** located not too far from the main palace is a real treat to behold with its rococo architecture. **The Hall of Mirrors** delighted the kids, and we were overwhelmed by the gaudy flamboyance of this architectural style typical of the 18th century. For 75 cents we each bought an all-inclusive ticket that admitted us to the Palace, **Martsallmuseum** (one of the finest coach museums in all of Europe), **Amalienburg, Badenburg,** (the bath house), **Pagodenburg** (a play-house structure intended to be a Chinese tea house but decorated on the first floor and staircase in Dutch tiles) and the **Magdalenenklase** (a chapel and imitation grotto built as a religious retreat for royalty). It is easy to spend an entire day at the Palace.

The **Munich Municipal Museum,** at 1 St. Jacobs Platz just two blocks from Marienplatz and the Rathaus (the City Hall), has a section of special interest to children. It is **The World of Children** devoted entirely to antique cribs, furniture, toys, games and a puppet theater collection. The exhibit traces the history of puppetry from its beginnings to the present, including all countries, with displays not only of the puppets but also of the paper scenery, props, stages and so on. Gary and I had a long-time interest in puppets, ever since we created Mr. Carrot, a favorite of the girls. Gary carved the body and I did the outfit and we both gave him a carved carrot nose. He was to be the scare crow in a puppet show version of "The Wizard of Oz," something we never quite realized, being busy working parents of young children. Whenever the girls had visitors to our house, they were happy to introduce them to "Mr. Carrot" whose strings Gary would operate with handshakes followed by a dance. So, visiting this museum was as interesting to us as it was to our young daughters.

Later, a friend in Switzerland sent us a marionette of a Swiss Mountain Goat that became Mr. Carrot's friend.

We also enjoyed a stroll through *Prinzregentenstrasse* 60, a colony of art galleries, many of them free. If you have time take in **Schwabing**, the Greenwich Village of Munich.

ULM, PFORZHEIM AND RÜDESHEIM

Heading north from Munich, we found a good turn-off point just outside of Ulm and stopped to spend the night there so that we might visit the famous Ulm Cathedral the following morning. The **Ulm Münster Cathedral** is a Gothic masterpiece most known for its magnificent tower, which tourists can ascend for a charge of about 20 cents. Several features are worth noting in this fine example of south German Gothic architecture such as the exquisite woodcarving in the chancel, the impressive "Doomsday" painting at the end of the nave, the five small, stained-glass windows of the choir all dating from the 15th century and some of the contemporary art pieces including the altar tapestry, the sculpture and new windows of the chancel. If you do decide to go up in the tower that soars to a height of about 530 feet, you will view the magnificent region that surrounds Ulm. There you can survey the plains of the Danube and the plateau of the Schwabishen Alb, and on clear days the view will extend as far as the Alps. This entire region is known as Baden-Wüttemberg and is famous as a recreation and holiday center with its picturesque surroundings, small typically German villages, castles, health spas and the beautiful Black Forest Mountains. (See "Summing Up" for highlights to visit in **Baden-Wüttemberg**)

Soon we were on our way again heading northwest on autoroute E-11. We by-passed Stuttgart and then arrived in Pforzheim, the goldsmiths' capital of Europe, shortly after noon. Our first stop was the New Goldsmiths' School at **St. George's Mount** (St.-Georgen-Steige). Unfortunately, most of the classes were dismissed for the lunch break but there was an opportunity to see a huge collection

219

of student work displayed in the lower and upper lobbies of the main building. I particularly enjoyed this visit, having taken a class in jewelry design and silversmithing the year before. I often made jewelry at my small bench in our garage on the lucky days when I could get the children napping at the same time. The few sales I made to friends and neighbors added to our trip funds.

The kids were anxious for us to get on our way as we had promised them a visit to the **Wild Animal Park** just outside Pforzheim along the Tiefenbronner Strasse. There bison, a variety of deer, wild boars, llamas, yaks, ponies and other interesting animals are bred and reared. The park is open daily, and admission is free. It's the German version of an African Safari and from a child's viewpoint every bit as exciting.

After stopping overnight in Frankfurt, we drove through beautiful countryside along the Rhine, with **Rüdesheim** our destination. Here you can visit a unique wine museum and walk along the narrow streets bordered by old houses with quaintly shaped turrets and gables. The possibilities for the photography bug are many in this lovely German town. We had also hoped to see Idar-Oberstein, a small town lying southwest of Rüdesheim and the lapidary center of Germany but looking at our map we discovered it was still 60 kilometers away, which meant we would not be able to make Cologne until late the next day. Once again choices had to be made, and off we went toward Cologne.

COLOGNE AND DUSSELDORF

The Cologne tourist office was helpful in suggesting an inexpensive hotel for the night (we had decided to forgo camping as it was about 15 degrees Fahrenheit and the snow was quite deep). Their suggestion for dinner was *Frühs*, a good family restaurant, just a few blocks away. The large wood-paneled dining room with wood tables and benches was typically German and the busyness of the waiters attested to the restaurant's popularity. The specialty of the house was *hanchen, sauerkraut und puree,* a delicious dish of pigs' knuckles, sauerkraut and mashed potatoes. The children had chicken and fries with milk. Including something to drink the total cost of the meal was about $5. Our hotel including a continental breakfast came to $7. Though our room and dinner total were over our maximum limitation, it was well worth it to have a night of luxury in a lovely, clean, warm hotel room.

In a city famous for its high Gothic Cathedral, we chose that as our first stop. After a brief visit to the interior and exterior of the cathedral, we walked a few blocks past a charming square to the **Wallraf-Richartz-Gallery,** containing a wonderful collection of Flemish and contemporary art.

We were soon back on the autobahn heading for **Dusseldorf,** just 30 kilometers away. Once in the city we went to the famous century-old restaurant, **Muschelhaus Reusch,** most known for its big plates of mussels, a specialty of the city and flown in daily from Amsterdam. The dinner was delicious and afterwards we enjoyed a stroll down the **Konigsallee,** Dusseldorf's fashionable main street.

The next morning after a brief stop with the kids at the **Hofgar-ten,** a spacious park in the center of the city, we were on our way once again going north toward Emden, arriving in Dortsmund late in the afternoon. Tired and anxious to spend the night in a warm place again with a soft bed, we found a delightful and inexpensive *gasthof* and enjoyed a delicious meal of weinerschnitzel for just $7 and a comfortable room for $7.40, including breakfast. We were going over budget at this point, counting on finding an economical way to get home. By this time, six months after our departure, the camper with its small interior, was losing its appeal when measured up to a warm roomy place to stay. During our dinner, several of the other restaurant patrons sent some beers to our table. Gary thought he should stay downstairs and return the offer, while I got the children into bed upstairs. An hour later, he walked in feeling a bit tipsy and we had some good laughs about the friendly Germans and their love of beer.

We continued heading north on the following day, and just outside of **Rheine** went in search of another comfortable *gasthaus* (guest house). On the outskirts of the city in a small village of **Ibbenburen** we found the **Gasthof of Josef Kleinhubbert,** spent the night and then drove on to Emden.

SHIPPING THE CAR HOME AND THE RETURN VOYAGE

We arrived in Emden on the day before the ship that would carry our car sailed. That night we organized our belongings, deciding what to put into our old Spanish trunk, the one we had bought in the flea market in Barcelona, to ship back with the car. Although there is the possibility of theft, there was no choice as it was impossible to take everything with us on the plane. We were fortunate that upon arriving in the States, the belongings in our trunk were intact; only a sheepskin was missing that had been left outside of it. Once organized, we delivered our car to the dock early the next day and took a train to Paris to spend our final two weeks in Europe.

There is also the possibility of going back with your car on a special freighter that carries passengers. However, we found the cost prohibitive. Because we had been unable to book a charter flight in Germany, we arranged for our flight with one of the Paris-based charter-flight organizations. *Nouvelle Frontiers* was able to arrange reservations for us on a flight to New York for just $85 each and a $10 membership fee. The one loophole was that the flight left from London, necessitating our taking the train back to England, which cost us another $60.

After a long and tiring night's train trip from Paris to the northern coast of France, then a ferry trip across the English Channel, we arrived in London and took a commuters' train from Victoria Station to the airport. The whole day was spent waiting for the delayed departure of our charter flight. This was expected though, remembering our experience at Los Angeles airport so many months before when we met our Swiss family friends. Luckily there was a small shop with children's books at very reasonable prices and a well-equipped cafeteria and snack bar in the huge airport. Our time was filled with reading stories and munching goodies. We were glad though, when it was finally time to board our plane and soon, we were winging our way back across the Atlantic toward home.

Note: I must add here in this Anniversary edition of our book that we were quite lucky when we returned to Paris, after dropping off our van in Emden to be shipped across the Atlantic, that we had a place to stay for free. A dear French friend offered us an apartment that he and his wife were not using at the time. It was located in a neighborhood we were familiar with and we had a wonderful "grand finale" to our trip, going to the open markets, buying fresh veggies to prepare at the apartment and picking up baguettes at the local *boulangerie* as well as an occasional pastry for dessert. We spent the time on short walks to parks where the girls could play when it wasn't too cold, and just recuperated a bit from our six months of camping in a van in Europe. One notable day, Gary decided to shave the beard he had grown during our travels, without sharing the decision with me or the girls. We still laugh about how the girls broke into tears when they saw their daddy emerge from the bathroom with no beard. Good memories linger and we had many from our adventures in *Europe with two kids and a van*.

SUMMING UP GERMANY

There are numerous campsites throughout West Germany, many in unspoiled wooded areas. The winding river valleys and the banks are particularly popular. Spending the night in a vehicle or trailer on the roadside is prohibited by law; however, unaware of this at the time of our trip, we occasionally did find a good spot to pull off for the night and we were never bothered. For a pleasant respite from camping you might consider a night in a castle by the Rhine. Arrangements can be made through the tourist bureaus in each major city along the Rhine; we have listed only some of the better-known castles. For a more economical rest from camping you may wish to stay in a *gasthous*, a small inn often with a restaurant and bar. There are many of these low-cost inns throughout the country.

It will help in planning your itinerary to know the major regions or states. They are **Bavaria,** whose capital is Munich: **Baden-Württemberg**, with Stuttgart as the capital, **Hessen**, whose capital is Wiesbaden; **Reinland-Pfalz**, with Mainz as the capital, **Nordrhein-Westfalen**, whose capital is Dusseldorf; **Niedersachsen** with Hanover as the capital; **Schleswig-Holstein**, whose capital is Kiel and the city-states of **Bremen** and **Hamburg.**

Prices are given in dollars computed at the exchange rate of 3.30 Deutsch marks to $1.

BAVARIA

LAKE CONSTANCE (THE BODENSEE)

A beautiful lake lying on the border between Switzerland and Germany with its eastern tip in Austria. There are three major resorts here: Lindau, Überlingen and Konstanz.

Lindau is set on an island connected to the mainland by two stone bridges amidst gardens and sunny slopes with views of the Swiss, Austrian and German Alps. Of most interest here are the old Renaissance and baroque-design buildings and the Franciscan church, which has been converted into a municipal theater.

Camping

Lindau-Zech, at Lindau take B31 in direction of Bregenz for three kilometers. Open May–September; showers, shopping.

Überlingen stands near the tip of a long, narrow, tree-encircled bay of Lake Constance.

S.C. Überlingen; telephone (0 75 51) 3483. Open May 1– September 30; showers, shopping, restaurant, camping gas, swimming. Admission: Adults, caravan and tent each 45 cents, car 30 cents.

Towns

Konstanz A German city on the south shore of the lake completely surrounded by Swiss territory.

Bodman about 100 kilometers from Lindau via route 31 and then route 34. See the **Frauenberg Castle** here with its collection of antique dolls and doll houses.

MUNICH (MÜNCHEN)

Camping

Thalkirchen four kilometers from town center near the Hellabrunn Zoo; telephone (03 11) 73 17 07. Shopping, restaurant, children's playground, swimming, camping gas.

Langwieder See, via autobahn access Rasthaus Langwieder See, five kilometers on München-Augsberg autobahn; telephone (08 11) 87 62 66. Open April 1–October 15; showers, shopping, camping gas, swimming. Admission: Adults 45 cents, car 30 cents, caravan and tent each 36 cents.

Waldcamping, off Stuttgart-München autobahn at traffic lights, at end of autobahn, left in direction of Allach-Karlsfeld, then left into Lochhauserstrasse, 700 meters; telephone (08 11) 88 58 86. Open all year; shopping, restaurant.

Tourist Information

Information und betreuiing, Bahnhofplatz 2, in the main front of the Central Station, opposite the Telegrafenamt; telephone 55 58 81.

Launderettes

The major chain of "lavamats" is called the Munz-WashsalonReinigung shops. The most centrally located branches are at:

10 Adalbertstrasse, 50 yards from the Siegestor, just off the Ludwig-strasse and near the University.

79 Landwehrstrasse, near the railroad station and St. Paul's church

10 Kurfurstenstrasse; the owners here speak excellent English.

The price is about 60 cents for four kilos of wash at all branches.

Babysitting

We suggest you call the student travel bureau of Munich in the university, ASTA-Reisen, at 15 Leopoldstrasse; telephone 3-88-61. Open weekdays 9 am–1 pm and 2–4:30 pm. They will most likely be able to suggest bilingual, student babysitters.

Restaurants There are several low-cost restaurants and beer halls in Munich. We tried the *Augustiner Grossgaststätten, 16 Neuhauser-strasse*, for lunch, and highly recommend it.

Shopping

Herties' Department Store, across from the train station.

Kaufhof Department Store on the "Stachus" (Karlsplatz). A good store for general buying, if the kids need a new pair of low-cost walking shoes for instance. Also, a good place to grab an inexpensive lunch.

For food, go to the *Viktualienmarkt*, Munich's marketplace.

Hellabrunn Zoo (Tierpark), in a splendid river and woodland setting, to the south of the city near *Camping Thalkirchen*, on road Implerstrasse, off road to Garmisch and Oberammergau.

Münchner Stadtmuseum (Municipal Museum), Jacobsplatz 1. There is a wonderful section called **The World of Children**, with antique toys, furniture, games and a puppet theater.

The English Garden, a beautiful park at the northern end of the city. The children will enjoy wandering through the wooded setting coming upon such surprises as a hilltop temple, a Chinese pagoda, the lovely *Kleinhesseloher Lake*, and an open-air restaurant. At one end is the *Haus der Kunst,* an enormous modernistic art museum that the adults will enjoy. Open daily from 9 am–4:30 pm.

The Deutsches Museum, an amazing **Museum of Science and Technology**. No doubt it will hold some fascination for the kids as well as the adults, especially the room called the "physics department" on the second floor. It is made up of glass display cases with protruding handles and levers that can be operated by the visitor and illustrate the basic laws of physics. Though the kids may not yet be fully able to comprehend the laws they'll love the action. This may be the one and only museum in Europe where they'll be asked to touch! The museum is located on the Isarinsel, an island on the Isar River. Plan on spending a whole day here. Hours are 9 am–5 pm daily; an admission fee of about 30 cents is charged. There is a restaurant (as you enter the museum, turn right and ascend a short flight of stairs) where you can purchase lunch for $1.30 each. If the weather permits, take a picnic lunch and eat it outside. The kids will appreciate the outdoor break.

Schwabing, the Bohemian sector of Munich. Take the No. 6 streetcar if you're sightseeing on foot.

Nymphenburg Palace, a magnificent baroque-rococo place. If sightseeing by foot, take streetcar No. 21 from Dachauerstrasse, near the front of the Bahnhof, a 15-minute ride. Get off at Auffahrtsalle, look to your left, (you can't miss the palace), and walk along the small canal, about a 10-minute walk from the streetcar stop. Palace hours are 9 am–5 pm (in winter from 10 am–4 pm) with some of the park pavilions taking a two-hour lunch break. Admission for all of the major sights is 75 cents.

227

SIDE TRIPS FROM MUNICH

Berchtesgaden, southeast of Munich tucked away in a valley of Alpine peaks, this resort city was once a favorite retreat of Adolf Hitler. Today, it offers ice skating rinks, steep and level ski trails, advanced and beginner's ski schools, sleigh runs, horse-drawn sleigh ride tours, and lifts and cable cars that rise up to peaks 6,000 feet high. For those less athletically inclined, there are sunny walking paths, woodland trails and deer parks at nearby *Konigsee* and *Hintersee.* Another interesting site is Berchtesgaden's salt mine.

Oberammergau, a little mountain village directly south of Munich, famous for the **Passion Play** presented every 10 years. The town is also known as a major woodcarving center.

Gamisch-Partenkirchen, a few miles beyond Oberammergau, this town is known as one of the foremost winter sports resorts in Germany. The scenery is magnificent, the activities offered vast. You can climb a mountain trail, swim, play golf, ski or skate.

Schneeferneihaus Hotel, a castle hotel with rooms that overlook the Alps just two and a half hours from Munich accessible by cog railroad. It lies at the summit of Germany's highest mountain, The Zugspitze.

AUGSBERG

Camping
Augusta, off autobahn exit Augsberg Ost; telephone (08 21) 37 05 97. Open all year; shopping, restaurant, camping gas, bungalows for rent, swimming in a lake.

FREIBURG

A special car park for 30 caravans is located in the town center on Habsburger Strasse. This park is open daily from 7 am–7 pm during the summer until October 1

BADEN-WÜRTTEMBERG

ULM

See the Ulm Münster Cathedral.

STUTTGART

The largest city in southwestern Germany and capital of Baden-Württemberg.

Camping

Cannstatter Wesen, Mercedesstraswse, between Bad Cannstatt and the Neckar near the stadium telephone (24 910 79 55. Open May 1–September 20; showers, shopping camping gas, swimming. Admission Adults 50 cents, car 34 cents, caravan and tent each 30 cents.

STUTTGART TO HEIDELBERG

The region north of Stuttgart between that city and Heidelberg is one of the most beautiful sections of Baden-Württemberg. It is made up of three main divisions. First, the **Neckarland**, rich in vineyards along the Neckar River, whose course reaches about 227 miles between Esslingen near Stuttgart and Heilbronn and Gundelsheim. The vineyards are on the sunny slopes of shell-lime cliffs that often reach heights of 100 meters. Here one can find many typical wine-growing villages and well-preserved medieval castles. The second division is the **Swabian Forest,** comprising a large number of mountain woodlands; one-third of the area, in the South, is inhabited by Swabians, the remainder by Franconians. The third division is the **Hohenloher Land** that extends between the Tauber Valley and the steep northern edge of the Swabian Forest. This is fertile land, the granary of an ancient race of peasants and noblemen. In the valley villages of Kocher, Jagst and Tauber, the many mills are typical of this wheat-growing region. For the tourist the region is rich with historical and natural sights. The area is most accessible by driving along the Romantische Strasse and the Tauber Valley or by taking the Burgenstrasse, a mountain road that goes from Heidelberg to Heilbronn and on to **Rothenburg** on the Tauber River. This is one of the most beautiful, medieval walled cities in Germany and should not be missed. There are many campgrounds in this region, and we have attempted to list the most centrally located below.

At *Bad-Liebenzell,* from Pforzheim 19 kilometers south on b463, turn left 500 meters before reaching town, toward River Nagold telephone (0 70 52) 4 55. Open April 1–October 31 showers, shopping, restaurant, camping gas, swimming. Admission Adults 70 cents.

Bad-Mergentheim Willinger Tal, on B 19 north of Heilbronn and west of Rothenburg take road to Wachbach, site near inn on left; telephone (0 79 31) 21 77. Open all year showers, chopping, restaurant, swimming. Admission: Adults 52 cents.

Buckhorn Bei Öhringer Seewiese, from Schwabisch Hall on B 14 to Bubenorbis 11 kilometers, then right in direction of Öhringer and via Geisselhardt to site by lake telephone (0 79 41) 5 77. Open all year showers, shopping, restaurant, camping gas, swimming. Admission Adults 45 cents, car, caravan and tent each 23 cents.

Ellwangen an der Jagst, on the road to Rothenbach; telephone (0 99 61) 27 30. May 1–September 30; showers, restaurant, swimming. Admission Adults 23 cents, car and caravan each 15 cents, tent no charge.

Langensteinbach, Karlsruhe-Stuttgart autobahn, exit Langenstein-bach four kilometers. Open all year showers, swimming. Admission: Adults, car and caravan each 36 cents, tent 30 cents.

Leonberg, Brühl Eltingen, München-Karlsruhe autobahn, at junction Stuttgart pass over autobahn to Heilbronn after a half kilometer follow exit to Leonberg; telephone (0 71 52) 38 26. Open all year;

showers, restaurant, camping gas, swimming. Admission: Adults and tent each 45 cents, car and caravan each 30 cents.

Neckarzimmern, NSU-Camping Cimbria from Neckareilz on B 27 at village entry turn right, 45 kilometers south of Heidelberg telephone (0 62 61) 25 62. Open April–September 30 showers, shopping, café, bar, camping gas, bungalows for rent, swimming in a river. Admission: Adults 45 cents, caravan, car, and tent each 30 cents.

Neurod Uber Karlsruhe, Albgau from Ettlingen in direction of Herrenalb; telephone (0 72 43) 37 08. Open all year showers, restaurant, camping gas.

HEIDELBERG

Camping
At *Haide,* from Heidelberg on B37 to Schlierbach, over bridge to right bank then upstream telephone (0 62 23) 21 11.

Open May 15–October 1; showers, camping gas, swimming in river. Admission: Adults and tent each 45 cents, car 30 cents, caravan 60 cents.

Tourist Information
Heidelberg City Bisitors Bureau and Information Center on corner of Sophien Strasse and Friedrich-Ebert-Anlage, 2 Friedrich-Ebert-Anlage; telephone 2 07 10 or 1 04 08.

American Express, Friedrich-Ebert Allee 16 telephone 24 6 43.

The Castle (Schlöss), reached by taking the funicular that runs every 10 minutes 7 am–9 pm.

Hercules Fountain A particularly colorful place to be in the Market Square on Wednesday and Saturday when you can buy fresh fruit, flowers, and vegetables here.

Visit the **student inns** to get a real feeling of the Heidelberg atmosphere: Roter Ochsen, Stepp'l and Schnookeloch.

Cafes and Coffee Houses Cafascö, Schafheutle and Scheu on High Street and Café Knösel near the Holy Ghost Church.

Pick up a brochure at the Tourist Information Center for suggested walking tours around Heidelberg.

SIDE TRIPS FROM HEIDELBERG

To the Bergstrasse via Schriesheim. See Castle Strahlenburg; to Weinheim, (Castle Wachenburg) and to the Castle "Burg Windeck" with its exotic gardens. Return via Landenburg, a 2,000-year-old city to **the Southern Bergstrasse** via Leimen, Nussloch to Wiesloch, and into the Angelbachtol (winegrowing communities).

Through the Neckar Valley to Bad Wimplen (former imperial palace, church of the former nightly order of St. Peter). Stop for a snack at one of the still-occupied castles such as Guttenberg, Hochhausen, Neuberg and Hornberg.

To Schwetzingen, a magnificent castle set in wide green grounds. **Go on to Speyer** and see the cathedral, historical museum and wine museum there.

Boat trip on the Neckar: From Heidelberg through Neckar Valley to Neckarsteinach; or you can take a boat trip in the opposite direction, passing Mannheim. From spring to autumn these boats leave Heidelberg daily 9:30 am and 2:40 in the afternoon.

RHEINLAND-PFALZ
RÜDESHEIM

From Heidelberg take autobahn to Weisbaden and from Weisbaden take B 42 to Rüdesheim, a Rhine town famous as an old wine center,

30 kilometers south of Weisbaden. See the Bromseiburg Castle, Ehrenfils Castle and the Wine Museum.

Nearest campground: *Heidesheim Heidenfahrt*; from Mainz go west on B 9, 15 kilometers. Open April 15–September 15; shopping, restaurant.

IDAR-OBERSTEIN

From Rüdesheim, cross river and take Route B 41 to Idar-Oberstein, most famous as a lapidary and jewelry center.

Nearest campground: *Sobernheim/Nahe*; Nahetal, about 100 meters from bridge over River Nahe from Bad Kreuznach on B 41 in direction of Idar-Oberstein 20 kilometers telephone (0 67 51) 25 55. Open April 1–September 30; limited facilities.

Sightseeing

See the Gem Museum, the castle ruins and the *Felsenkirche*, a church built before the 15th century into the rock, 195 feet above the River Nahe.

KOBLENZ

Camping

Rhein-Mosel, one kilometer east, on the left bank of the Mosel from town center via Baldwin Bridge and Neuendorferstrasse; telephone (02 61) 8 27 19. Open April 15–October 15; showers, shopping restaurant, camping gas; swimming in river.

Admission: Adults, car and tent each 36 cents, caravan 40 cents.

NORDRHEIN-WESTFALEN
COLOGNE (KÖLN)

Cologne is one of our favorite cities in Germany, and the one best prepared for tourists. It is well laid out and offers many beautiful and interesting sights. It's also a good home base for daily explorations into the picturesque Rhineland.

Camping

Between Borm and Cologne: *Rudenkirchen Bei Köln*, Berger, from Cologne Cathedral via Rhein Uferstrasse south to Rudekirchen from Rathenaustrasse turn left into Uferstrasse to boat house. Berger, telephone 30 2 21. Open all year; showers, shopping, restaurant, camping gas, swimming. Admission Adults 60 cents, car, caravan and tent each 30 cents.

At *Dünnwald: Familien-und-Jugendzeltplatz*, from town via Mulheim Road along Berlinerstrasse to Dünnwald, then right along Leuchterstrasse to Peter Baum Weg three kilometers; telephone 68 34 26. Open all year. Admission: Adults $1.50, car, caravan and tent each 45 cents.

At Poll *Poller Fischerhaus* from town via Deutz-Bridge South Siegburgerstrasse, Alfred Schütt Allee, Weidenweg to autobahn bridge telephone (02 21) 80 08 68. Open May 1–September 15; showers, restaurant, shopping, camping gas. Admission Adults, car, caravan each 36 cents, tent 30 cents.

Tourist Information

Across from the cathedral on Wallrafplatz, the corner of Hohestrasse. Open daily 8 am–10:30 pm.

American Express (Hapag-Lloyd Reiseburo), Hotel Mondial Berchergasse 10; telephone 2 08 22.

234

Post Office the main post office is on Anden Dominikanern (just two minutes from cathedral). Open Monday–Friday, 8 am–6 pm and Saturday 8 am–2 pm. There is also a post office in the Main Railway Station open 24 hours a day.

Restaurant

Frühs, located just two blocks from the tourist information office, on Sporergasse 1; telephone 23 66 16. Try *hanchen, sauerkraut und puree* (pigs' knuckles with sauerkraut and mashed potatoes).

Food Specialties

Halven-Han, meaning literally half a chicken, but when you order this you will receive a rye roll served with a large piece of mature Dutch cheese. This is a very popular snack in Germany.

Kölsher Kaviar, a roll with black pudding.

Rievkooche, pancakes made of grated potatoes, flour and onions. Mussels are popular in Cologne from September to February.

Hotel Rossner: For $10.90, we had a double room with an extra bed; price included service charge and a continental breakfast.

Check with the booking counter in the tourist information office; they can help you find a low-cost hotel or inn.

Shopping

Hohestrasse and Schildergasse are the two main pedestrian shopping streets. There can be found large department stores and numerous small specialty shops.

Rudolplatz and the Ring is another popular area with elegant shops, restaurants, street cafes and night clubs.

Ladenstadt, the theater and shopping district.

Shop Hours; Monday–Friday 9 am–6:30 pm, Saturday 9 am–2 pm. On the first Saturday of each month most shops in the city center are open from 9 am–6 pm.

Parking

If you cannot leave your car at the campground or your hotel, there are 20 multistory or subterranean car parks in the city center, open day and night. Numerous shops advertise membership in the Cologne Parking Association (*Parkgemeinschaft*). Street signs direct you to these parking lots. At the shops displaying this sign, a part of the parking fee will be subtracted from the price of purchased goods on presentation of the car-park receipt.

Sightseeing

If you plan on being in Cologne for several days and on visiting several of the museums there, see about obtaining a museum pass at the tourist office. Obtainable for about 30 cents, the pass entitles the bearer to an unlimited number of visits to the museums in Cologne on three consecutive days. Entrance for children is free. For dates and places of weekly cultural events, pick up a copy of "Kölner Leben" at the tourist office or in one of the city bookstores.

Zoo at 178 Riehler Strasse. Take the cable railway across the Rhine to the zoo. Cars cross over daily 10 am–10 pm between Easter and the end of October. See the famous aviary. Open daily 8 am–dusk.

Puppet Theater (*Puppenspieled*), on Eisenmarkt in the center of the old city. Daily performances. Check with tourist office for times and admission.

The Wallraf-Richartz Museum, An der Rechtschule. A marvelous art museum featuring European painting from the Middle Ages to present. Drawing and print collection. Open daily 10 am–5 pm; Tuesday and Friday 10 am–10 pm. Guided tours available Tuesday and Friday at 8 pm.

Kunstgewerbe Museum, in the Eigelstein Gate on Ebertplatz. Art and handicraft from the Middle Ages to the present. Open 10 am–4 pm.

Overstalz House, Rheingasse at the Heumarkt. Exhibitions of art and handicrafts; collection of textiles. Open daily 10 am–5 pm, Wednesday 10 am–10 pm.

The Cathedral Guided tours are available Monday–Friday at 10 am, 11 am, 2:30 pm, 3:30 pm, starting from the altar at the intersection of the nave and transept.

The Eau de Cologne Museum, Johann-Maria-Farina and Company, opposite Gülichplatz, 21 Obermarspforten; telephone 23 45 61. Open to the public Monday–Friday 9 am–6 pm, Saturday 9 am–1 pm.

Roman City Wall This first century A.D. wall has been preserved in several parts. Especially remarkable sections are on the corner of Komödienstrasse and Tunisstrasse, and on the corner of Zeughausstrasse and Auf dem Berlich. A brochure describing the location and details of the various ruins from Roman times located within Cologne is available upon request from the tourist office. We found this to be a bit boring for the kids, though interesting to us.

SIDE TRIPS FROM COLOGNE

There are many interesting, picturesque and easy to-get-to towns and villages around Cologne. The following are suggested areas to visit:

Brühl Castle-Bad Münstereifel: Take Brühler Strasse (B 51) to the castle and garden town of Brühl, just 15 kilometers from Cologne. The way to this baroque castle is well marked.

Phantasialand: Another sight in Brühl, more recently erected is highly recommended for the kids. On the outskirts of the town, directly on the B 51 road (see signs) lies Phantasialand, Germany's largest fairyland paradise of adventure. Grouped around a lake are hundreds of beautifully decorated and speaking fairyland figures. There's a Western Express, an Indian Village, a Punch and Judy

Show, Venetian gondolas and a South Seas restaurant. Open daily from April 1st to the middle of November.

The Ahr Valley: From Cologne proceed by autobahn to Bonn (30 kilometers) where a stop may be made to visit the capital city of West Germany. From Bonn continue along the road to Mehlem where you will take a side trip to Rodderberg, a place rich in legend. Then continue on b 9 for 10 kilometers to Ramagen where you will see the famous pilgrimage church of Apollinaris. A little way beyond Ramagen there is a major crossing where the B226 road branches off to the right for the Ahr Valley. Beyond Ahrweiler, the vineyards of the Ahr Valley become more concentrated and from Walporzheim (five kilometers onward, one passes through Germany's largest single red wine growing district. Wine has been produced here for more than 100 years; and along the winding road there are numerous small villages, some of which have ancient wine taverns.

At *Mayschoss,* a few kilometers beyond Walporzheim, the wine-growers' cooperative has a wine cellar open to the public. Next you will arrive at *Altenahr,* a 1000-year-old wine town, situated in a beautiful setting 167 meters above sea level. Return to Cologne by B 257 via Meckenheim and through the Katten Forest to Bonn and from there by autobahn. Total distance of the drive is 150 kilometers.

The Seven Mountains: In the southeast, visible from the top of Cologne Cathedral on a clear day, these mountains are part of a volcanic mountain area with 20 heights, the seven highest of which have been given the name Seven Mountains. Take the autobahn toward Frankfurt and leave it at Siebengebirge proceeding via Ittenbach to Margarethenhöhe (380 meters). From Margarethenhöhe well-marked paths lead in all directions. It is particularly worthwhile to walk to the Lohrberg or to the Olberg, the highest of the Seven Mountains.

Monastery Knechtsteden: Make an afternoon trip to the Lower Rhine area in the vicinity of a charming 12th century monastery situated in the center of a region of woods, meadows and fertile farmlands. Along the way you can visit a 100-year-old windmill at Stommeln (start out along Venloer Strasse, B 59, via Pulheim to Stommeln), Zons (The Rothenburg of the Lower Rhine, a medieval walled town and the Electoral Castle Friedestrom where June–August and the Electoral Castle Friedestrom where June–August historical plays are performed at an open-air theater.

Complete the 75-kilometer tour by returning to Cologne via B 9 and then via Dormagen and the Cologne suburbs of Worringen and Fülingen.

Altenberg Cathedral and Fairywood for Children by way of the Mülheim Bridge, cross to the right bank of the Rhine and here follow B 51 about six kilometers to Dünnwald. Just beyond the railway bridge turn right into Leuchter Strasse beyond the railway bridge turn right into Leuchter Strasse in the direction of Altenbuer. Proceed through the woods and meadowland of the Dhünn Valley to Odenthal, a small village with half-timbered houses and a Romanesque village church. Beyond Odenthal lies the Strauweiler Castle on the right (privately owned, it cannot be visited). A little further on, in the midst of wooded and hilly country, one can see the majestic outline of Altenberg Cathedral, known as the "Mountain Cathedral." Along with the Cologne Cathedral it is one of the most outstanding Gothic structures of the Rhineland. After visiting the cathedral (open daily to visitors when there is not a service in progress), proceed along the walking path from the parking ground to the special attraction for children, the *Fairywood*.

These and other trips into the surrounding regions of Cologne are described in great detail in the brochure "Ten Trips by Car Around Cologne" published by the Cologne Tourist Office and available there upon request. Spring or autumn would be ideal times to see this area.

DUSSELDORF

(Capital of Nordrhein-Westfalen)

Camping

Erkrath-Unterbach, Nord, from Dusseldorf on B 326 to turning direction Erkrath, turn left toward Unterbacher See; telephone (91) 60 20 21. Open May 1–September 15; showers, shopping, camping gas, lake swimming. Admission: Adults 30 cents, caravan and tent each $1.05, car no charge.

Castle Hotels

Haus Hammerstein, 50 kilometers east of Dusseldorf, hidden by dense woods. French cuisine.
Schlösshotel Hugenpoet, 33 kilometers east of Dusseldorf. A moated castle.

Tourist Information American Express Company, Heinrich Heine, Allee 14. Telephone 80222.

Restaurant Suggestion

Muschelhaus Reusch, in Alstadt. The mussels here are delicious and the *Mainzer käse*, a very sharp cheese, makes a good dessert.

DUSSELDORF TO PADERBORN

Campgrounds

Werden (Essen): Am Bahnhof Werden, from Essen via Werden in direction of Essen-Kupterdreh, three kilometers east of Werden, turn toward Baldeneysee; telephone 49 29 78. Open all year; limited facilities.

Deleche, from Soest or Arnsberg on B 229. Open May 1–September 30, limited facilities.

Nadermann's Tierpark, off road from Weidenbrück to Paderborn; watch for camping sign, turn off small road between Delbruck and Rietburg. This is a wonderful campground with a small zoo, a large children's playground, showers, laundry area. One of the best campsites we found in West Germany.

GÜTERSLOH

A small town just beyond Weidenbrück where the Volkswagen factory (Westphaliawerk) is located. We found this to be an ideal place to pick up camping equipment at the outset of our trip. We were able to camp in the area provided outside of the factory where we equipped the camper.

Camping Goods Stores

Sporthaus Schöppner, Berliner Strasse 77; telephone 2 22 93.
Sporthaus Fingberg, across from the train station.

Laundry facilities are handy, too, at the Washermatic, on am Noneplatz, in Weidenbrück

HAMBURG-HANOVER AREA

At the outset of our travel adventures we went directly from Nadermann's Tierpark near Paderborn to Hanover and then on to Hamburg and over the northern border into Denmark. We will give a few suggestions for campgrounds in the area.

At the end of our trip we went from Gütersloh, after picking up some equipment for the camp mobile and having a few minor repairs done, to Münster and then on to Emden via route B 70. We found few campgrounds in this region, nor was it very picturesque. Arrangements had to be made in Emden, however, for the car to be shipped back to the United States. If you have no reason to go to Emden, you can avoid this area all together and spend more time along the Rhine or in Baden-Württemberg, the Black Forest and Bavaria.

HANOVER

Since we were avoiding the large industrial cities, we merely bypassed this one. However, one of the top sights is the **Herrenhousen Castle Museum** in a beautiful baroque garden. The nearest campground is near *Celle*, an interesting village that you will want to explore.

Camping

Meissendorf Über Celle: Hüttensee-Park, from Celle northwest via Winsen and Meissendorf; telephone (0 50 56) 58. Open April–October; shopping restaurant, swimming.

GOSLAR

Another interesting sight is the quaint city of Goslar about 60 kilometers from Hanover south on E 4 and then turn to your left at the Seesen turnoff onto 248. Goslar is about 24 kilometers off the autobahn. Strolling through this town is like walking back in time seeing the various periods of architecture in front of you: Gothic, Gothic-Renaissance, Renaissance, Baroque. The natural surroundings of the "Harz country" enhance the town as well, and a rushing stream flows through its center.

Camping facilities are abundant in the area.

Göttingerode Über Goslar: Harzer, on B 6 between Goslar and Bad *Harzburg*; telephone (05 3 22) 89 54. Open all year. Showers, shopping, restaurant, camping gas, swimming pool. Admission: Adults 45 cents, car 42 cents, caravan 66 cents and tent 36 cents.

Hahneklee/Bockswiese: Am Kreuzack, from Goslar on B 247 exit; telephone (0 53 26) 25 70. Open all year; showers, shopping, restaurant, camping gas, lake swimming. Admission: Adults 66 cents, car 30 cents, caravan and teat each 60 cents.

HAMBURG

Another modern industrial city, one of its highlights is the **Hagenbeck Zoo**; another, the **Alster River,** divided in two by what is called the Lombard Bridge. In summer, there are daily boat trips on the Alster, as well as circular tours of the canals.

Camping

Hamburg-Stellingen: Heinz Buchholz, Kieler Strasse 374 near Hagenbeck Zoo. Open all year; shopping, restaurant.

Hamburg-Wilhelmsbur, Süderelbbrücke: Konig-Georg-Deich 153, via Norderelbbücke: and Wilhelmsburger Bundesstrasse, turn left before Süderelbbrücke; telephone 75 86 11. Open April 1–September 30; showers, shopping, restaurant, camping gas, tents for rent, swimming in river. Admission: Adults and car each 45 cents, caravan and tent each 75 cents.

GERMAN FOOD SPECIALTIES

Because of the German custom of serving large portions of food for each course, you are not required or expected to order (nor do the Germans) a complete meal in the sense of several dishes as in France. It is customary, for example, to order a beer and perhaps an appetizer or a cold plate to go with it. The main dish usually comes with meat, potatoes and frequently with sauerkraut, cooked vegetables, condiment and salad. These accompanying items are indicated on the menu after the word *mit* (with). The German menu is very complex having as many as sixteen food categories. The daily menu (*tageskarte*) will begin with a list of several fixed-price meals (*gedeck*), the price varying with the entrée. Soup, which is a great favorite with the Germans, will always be included in the fixed-price meals; and in addition to the entrée, a modest dessert is usually also included. Some of the main categories that you may encounter on the menu are listed below.

Vorspeisen: First courses, or appetizers.
Wurst-Spezialitäten: House specialties in hot sausages.
Wurstgerichte: Sausage dishes, usually hot.
Suppen: Soup dishes.
Fischgerichte: Fish dishes.
Geflügel: Poultry.
Hauptgerichte: Main courses or dishes.
Fleischgerichte: Meat dishes.
Grillgerichte: Dishes from the grill.
Gemüse: Vegetables.
Käse: Cheese.
Eis: Ice Cream.
Kompotte: Stewed fruits.
Nachspeisen: Desserts, sweet dishes.
Süss-Speisen: Desserts, sweet dishes.

Some of our Favorite Dishes:

Leberknöde; Munich or Bavarian specialty, dumplings of minced liver, bread, onions and spices served in bouillon.
Bockwurst: A red-skinned sausage or a pigtail-size white sausage, both boiled.
Bratwurst: A whitish to pinkish sausage of pork and/or veal mildly spiced, usually grilled.
Wienerschnitzel: A cutlet, usually veal, breaded, butter-fried golden, served topped with lemon slice, or with a rolled anchovy, black olive, chopped capers, sieved egg yolk, or parsley garnish.
Schinken: Ham. This is a good thing to buy in the market for sandwiches; it is usually boiled and reasonably priced.
Sauerbraten: Famous Munich dish, a beef pot roast marinated several days in vinegar, red wine, carrots, onion, bay leaf, juniper berries, garlic, cloves, salt and water. Browned in hot fat, then pot roasted with marinade juices, vegetables, paprika and tomato purée.

Just as the vocabulary for food and beverages in Germany is vast and varied, so is that for eating establishments. We have listed some of those most frequently encountered.

Restaurant: Complete food and drinks.
Ratskeller: Excellent for regional specialties and traditional German food. Each city, town and village have their *Rathaus*, which is its city hall. Except for villages, and a few towns the Rathaus has a *ratskeller*, a restaurant in the cellar. The ratskellers are upper-medium to high-quality restaurants, although usually not very expensive.
Gaststätte: This is the German word restaurant. They serve complete meals.
Gasthof: The village or open country word for restaurant, serving drinks and modest-to-complete meals.
Gasthaus: Same as gasthof, a restaurant of more or less modest proportion.
Imbiss: Snack. A sort of hot-dog stand.
Raststätte or Rasthaus: Restaurants and restaurant-inns along the autobahns (freeways).
Bierstube: Beer parlors serving drinks and light meals
Seinstube: Wine parlors serving drinks and light meals.
Schnellbuffet: Short order or cafeteria eateries.
Schnellimbiss: Fast snacks such as grilled sausages or hot dogs.

Note for our 50th Anniversary edition: We were quite amazed as we read over the diets we followed while we traveled in 1972–73. Several years after that time, Gary was diagnosed as "celiac" which means he cannot eat barley, oats, wheat or rye. He must be totally gluten free. Fortunately, we found on our recent travels in Europe that in most countries this is not a problem. Gluten free options are on most menus, even in Italy where one can ask for gluten free pasta but at the time of our camping in Europe in 1972–73, no one had heard of gluten free diets. Fortunately, Gary did not get ill.

Appendix

Now that you've decided you, too, want to travel in Europe with the family, we've added some new and updated information to make it easier for you to make it happen. Here we offer tips to our readers on how to travel in Europe with or without a camper, with the kids, on a budget, now.

ON THE ROAD TIPS

Traveling in Europe, by car or camper, allows a wonderful opportunity to see the countryside. Out-of-the-way places, unspoiled by hordes of tourists, are yours to enjoy, but it is necessary to understand a few things about driving in Europe. Europe uses the international system of road signs (the United States is now moving slowly in this direction) that, once understood, can be of great aid to the motorists. They are easy to identify and can be understood despite language barriers.

Triangular signs mean danger or warning.
Circular signs give definite instructions or prohibitions.
Rectangular signs are informative.

Generally, triangular signs have a red outline with black letters or figures, circular signs are usually red, but sometimes blue or white and rectangular signs are printed on blue backgrounds.

Below are the most commonly encountered signs.

Danger   Closed to   No Stopping   Overtaking   Parking
          all Vehicles   Prohibited   Prohibited

Parking   One Way   Major Road   Oncoming Traffic
Allowed   Do Not Enter   Ahead   Has Right of Way

GERMAN ROAD SIGNS

In Germany the direction signs are mounted on poles at Intersections in order of distance, with the color indicating the following:

» Yellow signs with printed information indicate distance in kilometers of cities within a short proximity of your location.
» White signs with printed information indicate local places (i.e. zoos, information offices, etc.)
» Blue signs indicate major freeways or autobahns.

ENTERING A NEW COUNTRY

When arriving in a new country stop for a few minutes at the frontier to obtain road information and directions. This is usually provided by the country's automobile club, most of which maintain offices at the borders. This information can also be obtained by writing to the major automobile clubs prior to your departure.

SPEED LIMITS

On the open road there is usually no speed limit for passenger cars, but speed must be adapted to road and traffic conditions as in this

248

country. Unless otherwise posed, maximum speed limit in cities and towns is about 50 kilometers, or 35 miles per hour. While on the open road in the countries of Sweden, Norway, France and Spain the limit is usually about 80 kilometers per hour. The only country that still has left-hand driving is England. This can be quite an adjustment and you should drive cautiously at first until you are used to it; large cities are the most difficult. In all cases, it is to your advantage to drive defensively and to give way in a tight situation.

BIG CITY DRIVING

As for the big cities, take our advice and don't drive unless it is absolutely necessary. Most major European cities have excellent public transit systems and it is wise to use them. One thing to note, however, if you do drive in the cities is to not sound your horn unless pending an accident. You can be cited for this abuse. Also, in some countries such as France and Spain, only parking lights are used in city night driving. At intersections, the practice is to blink them off and on before proceeding. Diagonal white lines on the roadway, known as zebra lines, indicate a pedestrian crosswalk. Pedestrians always have the right-of-way.

CAR TROUBLE

In the event of car trouble, contact the local police who will arrange for road assistance. In some countries such as Italy, limited road services are offered without charge to the tourist, including towing to the nearest highway exit, small repairs and towing from the highway exit to the nearest service station.

SOME NOTES ON TAXES

In countries such as France, refunds of the 15 percent sales tax imposed on items you might purchase while there can be obtained by keeping your sales tags and producing them at the border. In Germany this is also true. For example, when you purchase a Volkswagen you are allowed the refund of the 11 percent German sales tax, arrangements for which are made at the border upon leaving the country.

The Danish tax, called *Moms* (pronounced *mumps*) is an exorbitant 12 ½ percent on every purchasable item, including rooms and meals, to which another 15 percent service charge is added. There are a few things that are exempt from the Moms tax: rooms rented in private citizens' homes and self-service restaurants. In going to restaurants, check to make sure that the statement *Alle priser incl. Moms* is printed at the top. This means all prices include the taxes; however, a 15 percent service charge will still be added on to the total. In purchasing items in Denmark, if you send the article even to the next country on your itinerary you will avoid the tax.

MAKING PLANS

How to prepare for departure:

- ☐ Initiate passport application at your local post office. Allow enough time for processing. This will vary depending on where you live and where there is a passport office. Make sure you have a properly validated birth certificate.
- ☐ Make your flight reservations.
- ☐ If you've decided to camp as we did, order your camp mobile and make arrangements for payment. We put a $1000 deposit on our VW van and then paid the first six months' payments in advance so that we would not have to worry about this during our trip. This will vary in today's world. You may decide to rent a camper and if so, we have you covered in the section on renting a camper.

☐ Initiate insurance policy, car or health, or both. (Talk to your local car insurance provider and also your health providers to see what is required. We've included some information on car insurance requirements in Europe below)

☐ Take care of all correspondence in advance if emails are needed to secure decided upon campsites, places to visit, etc. (For example, some major sites such as the Ann Frank house in Amsterdam require reservations months in advance.)

☐ Receive any necessary vaccinations and have vaccination card stamped by the county health office in your area. (See travel documents section.)

☐ Start planning your wardrobe. (What to Take Section)

☐ Gather good-for-travel craft materials for the kids, light-weight, un-messy, versatile. You may also want to take along a few art supplies, if you're like me and like to draw while traveling. A small set of colored pencils, and/or a miniature set of Windsor & Newton watercolors and Strathmore watercolor postcards 4"x6" work great. Sketch your kids and send them home to the grandparents.

☐ Prepare your children for their new adventure by reading to them about children in different lands and special places you are going to see. See the children's librarian at your local library for ideas of good books.

☐ Dream like mad; it will soon be a reality.

EUROPEAN CAR INSURANCE AND PASSPORT INFORMATION

When purchasing or renting a vehicle in any EU country, you must insure it for third party liability. **This compulsory insurance is valid in all EU countries.** It covers you if you have an accident causing damage to property or injury to anyone other than the driver (as of May 25, 2021; please check current information).

Like the UK, European countries require you to have a minimum level of car insurance before you take to the roads but don't assume your UK or US policy will provide the same level of coverage in Europe as it does in the UK or US.

From the 2nd August 2021, motorists will no longer need an insurance green card.

TRAVEL INSURANCE:

https://www.squaremouth.com

Overseas insurance is an easy way to protect your car, motorcycle, or personal property when you move to a different country. Please note that overseas car insurance isn't travel insurance and doesn't include health insurance.

Note: our suggested sites for insurance in no way means we endorse these companies; they are just suggested sites for your trip research.

Campgrounds are remarkably low in theft. Campgrounds are full of basically honest, middle-class European families, and someone's usually at the gate all day. Most people just leave their gear in their vans or zipped inside their tents. A family can sleep in a tent, van, or motorhome a lot cheaper than in a hotel.

Camping in Europe is much easier than camping in North America. For one thing, there are far more campsites in Europe, and they are not isolated out in the backwoods of places you don't really want to go. Nearly every major city has a campground within city limits, or very near-by.

Can you camp in a van in Europe? The answer is a definative yes. There even places where you can camp free of charge. We suggest checking out the suggestions on the internet by typing in the question "Can you camp in a van in Europe?"

Unlike the UK, much of Europe is well prepared for camper vans and motorhomes. **Free camping** in Europe with your motorhome is easy. Often easier than finding a campsite. You can easily travel most of the European continent without ever paying for accommodation.

With that said, in the UK, other than the "Caravan Sites & Control of Development Act" – and more recent legislation covering gypsies and travelers – **there is no specific law that makes it illegal to sleep in a motorhome at the roadside.**

Can you *free camp* **in Norway?**
Yes, free camping (also known as *wild camping, boondocking, dry camping,* or *dispersed camping*) **is officially allowed in Norway.** Despite the general permission, there are a few points that have to be taken into consideration. The freedom to stay and camp anywhere in nature is based on the Everyman's Right (Norwegian: *Allemannsretten*) law. (June 12, 2020). <u>You must leave the place free of debris and garbage, and as you found it.</u>

TOP DESTINATIONS FOR WILD CAMPING IN EUROPE

 "Wild camping" in the Nordic countries, Norway, Sweden, Finland, Estonia, Scotland is more or less the most hassle-free experience you'll find. There are places in France and in Spain, also, where you can do "wild camping."

WHAT TO TAKE FOR THE KIDS (SOME HINTS AND IDEAS):

A major concern in preparing for our trip was to choose what toys and time fillers to take for the children, aware that in order to enjoy the trip ourselves we would have to make it enjoyable for them, too. Since art activities were one of the kids' favorite pastimes, this helped limit the range of items to bring. We also wanted things that would last, having heard the European toys and paper products are expensive. We made vinyl toy bags for each child, which they could carry aboard the plane and fill with all their belongings along the way. Nowadays, it's easy to find child-size back packs, the best choice. Fill them with lightweight storybooks, boxes of crayons, small blackboards and chalk, large tablets, paste sticks, construction paper and a small plastic bag of yarn and beads. Older kids, 7–12, will have their own ideas. We added to the toy supply in England at a London Woolworth. This marvelous five-and-ten-cent store can be found throughout England. In it we bought tiny five- and ten-cent books, scrapbooks that we filled with pictures clipped from European magazines and small games, spending then a total of about $3.50. Now, of course, prices will be higher. We kept some of these items aside in a surprise bag so that when the kids were bored after a long day on the road, there was always something to "fish out." For younger ones, you can do as we did and make a small fishing pole with a paper clip as a hook. By tossing the line into the front seat where the adult passenger sits, and who can clip on a small item, they will be provided the surprise. Our young daughters loved this game.

WARDROBE SUGGESTIONS:

(Check airline baggage allowances and to make life easier on yourselves and your kids, take only one medium suitcase and one backpack per person. Anything that won't fit, you can probably buy in Europe)

Fashion has changed so much in the last fifty years we've decided to leave this part up to you. One thing we will say is a must is waterproof rubber boots for the children, and a good pair of hiking boots for every member of the family if you like to hike. Sneakers or flip-flops just don't cut it when you're on rugged terrain. Thermal undershirts are also important if you'll be traveling in fall and winter. Waterproof gloves are helpful to have along. If traveling in fall or in winter, you might want to throw in waterproof pants (the kind you can pull on over your jeans).

If traveling in the summer, of course, bring swimsuits and maybe summer footwear.

What clothes would be most appropriate for varying weather, camping needs as well as for the occasional "dressing up?" These decisions were more of a problem in the 1960's than now, when dress around the world is pretty generic, when blue jeans, shirts and sweatshirts with hoods are pretty universal. You'll have your own best choices. Choose lightweight and layer in colder weather; much of this will depend on the season you decide and are able to travel.

If you are traveling for a shorter length of time your wardrobe will be smaller than ours. Or, if traveling in spring, you will not need the heavy coats that added much to our weight. One lightweight, all weather coat would suffice for late spring travel; hooded sweatshirts or windbreakers would be suitable for the kids. In general, choose clothes in darker colors that you don't have to wash frequently due to stains from spilled ice-cream cones, for example.

MISCELLANEOUS ITEMS TO TAKE:

Dish towels, a few zip lock plastic bags, some assorted utensils, a flashlight and sleeping-bag liners. In today's on-line markets like Amazon you can probably find sleeping bag liners for far less cost than the price it would take to make them like we did.

EQUIPMENT TO TAKE:

» **Fifty-foot, light-gauge nylon rope** for use as a clothesline, for tying, etc.
» **Pocketknife.**
» **Unbreakable flashlight** (batteries available in Europe).
» **Sleeping bags.** Shop at discount stores for lightweight, waterproof, well-insulated bags. The bags can instead be purchased upon your arrival in Europe, eliminating the weight of including them as luggage. The prices, though, may not be as reasonable as one can find in a discount store at home.

» **Cotton-flannel liners** for sleeping bags. They are washable saving cleaning fees on sleeping bags and give added warmth. Remember to bring along rubber sheets for kids who still wet the bed occasionally.

» **Film.** If you're the type who wants to carry along a camera and take photos with other than a cellphone, be sure and buy your film before you leave and have it developed at home. The processing establishments are more reliable. You can mail your exposed film back in prepaid envelopes and have them forwarded to a close friend or relative who can check to insure you are not having any camera problems. In this case, you'll also need a lightweight shoulder-strap bag for film, camera and important papers such as passports, insurance and traveler's checks. A bag specific for cameras is too conspicuous, thus more apt to be stolen.

» **Small sewing kit** with extra buttons, snaps, needle, thread, safety pins, patches and small scissors.

» **Collapsible five-gallon plastic water container.** These can be purchased at camping supply stores for a reasonable cost and are indispensable for filling the camp mobile water tank. You can pick these up at camp-supply shops in Europe.

» **Pharmaceuticals and cosmetic items.** Any special drugs your family may require, concentrated shampoo in plastic container, aspirin, Triaminic syrup for kids' colds, contact lens cleansers for lens, toothpaste and towelettes for the kids' dirty hands or small travel size bottles of disinfecting gel. Remember COVID masks, too. They still may be required in many areas and will make you feel safer as well when in crowded spots. If you wear glasses or contact lens be sure to take a prescription for them in case of loss or damage. These items can all be easily packed in your backpacks or in small crevices between clothing in your suitcases. We also suggest taking a plastic refillable bottle of high-concentrate biodegradable detergent that can be diluted for hand laundry, or you can pick up laundry items for travel at your local Triple A.

» **Light suitcases, and/or backpacks.** Service duffel bags work great for sleeping bags and hold an enormous quantity of other items. One trick is to pack them, then bang the bag against the floor to compact the contents. You will be amazed at what they will hold. If camping in a van or camper as we did, remember, whatever you bring needs to take up the least amount of space as possible.

» **Canvas tote bag** for picnics, shopping excursions and countless other uses.

» **A large box of plastic zip-lock bags.** These are great for holding wet washcloths, food leftovers, sandwiches on picnics and craft items. With more consideration for the environment, instead of plastic, you might take a few cloth mesh bags that can be washed out along with the laundry.

» **Plastic cups** with lids are good for storing salt, pepper, spices, crayons or for carrying beverages on picnics.

» **One bottle of chlorine tablets.** Available at your local pharmacist to be used in areas where you are at all dubious about the local water.

» **One small first-aid kit:** It should include anti-diarrheal tablets, available over the counter. They are highly recommended in case of any type of diarrhea due to a change in diet or unsanitary food or water.

EQUIPMENT TO PURCHASE IN EUROPE:

» **Tools:** Eight-inch crescent wrench, adjustable pliers, screwdriver and, if mechanically inclined, a set of metric wrenches. (Approximate cost, $12 to $15)

» **Camping equipment:** Most of this can be purchased once you get to Europe, in a camp supply store near where you pick up your vehicle. All equipment should operate with camping gas, readily available throughout Europe and not too costly. White gas and kerosene are both impossible to find, so forget your Coleman on this trip. You will need the following:

- One three-liter, camping gas bottle
- One regulator and one double bypass outlet
- One two-burner camp stove
- One light, optional if you have a VW camper
- One heater. Note: if you use this inside a tent or van, ventilate as the heater will burn oxygen.

» **Camp set for four,** including small fry pan, two pots, and a teapot; if possible, purchase a non-stick coated set as it is much easier to clean.

» **Two-quart non-stick Dutch oven,** good for stews and soups. (we bought ours in France for $7). Utensils: We suggest the camp sets, which include fork, knife, teaspoon and tablespoon. Wooden spatula for stirring with your pans.

» **Good can opener.** (The can openers we found in Germany weren't very good. Your best bet is to bring a small one from home.) REI is a good place to buy these small items.

» **Plastic containers** to store flour, sugar and powdered milk, one-quart size.

» **Melamine bowls.** We used these as both plates and bowls. When we had soup first, we washed them out for the next course. This not only cut down on the things that had to fit into our small storage cabinet, but also made the dishwasher's job easier.

» **Good-quality tarpaulin** with metal grommets. Very handy to tie over the car rack during rainy weather, to use as a lean-to, or a cover while picnicking on grass or at the beach.

» **Doormat.** A necessity in keeping some of the outside dirt from being transported into the camp mobile. At each of our camp spots we could lay this down right outside our door. We purchased ours in England. These are too cumbersome and heavy to pack in your duffle bags.

OPTIONAL EQUIPMENT:

» **Electrical tape** for small repair jobs.

» **Fold-up candle lantern,** about $8-$10 in your local army surplus store.

» **Six-mil polyethylene tarp** for ground cloth or emergency cover. It can be folded much smaller than a tarpaulin.

» **Fifty feet of electrical cord** with European adapter when you need extra light and can pull up to outlets at some campgrounds. Other travelers suggested this to us; however, we did not find it necessary.

» **Woman's portable hair dryer** convertible to either 115 or 250V. The voltage changes from country to country.

» **Battery-operated electric shaver.**

» **Money belt.** These are available at all travel stores. We recommend Triple A.

» **Elastic clothesline.** On rainy days we would string ours crisscross in the bus for our clothesline. The line was also useful at nights to hand between the front and back of the van with a towel stretched over it so our reading light would not disturb the kids' sleep.

» **Small pair of theater glasses or binoculars.** They are handy when in the London theaters and give the kids something fun to do while driving.

» **Small hand axe.** There were a couple of instances when we built small campfires that one would have come in handy.

» **Car Rack.** The one we bought was $10 in Germany, and not having the pop-top for extra storage, we found it indispensable. They will probably be more expensive now.

ENTERTAINING THINGS TO DO WHILE ON THE ROAD WITH THE KIDS

» **Play Cards.** We found the children preferred having the table up at all times as it was good for this activity and also made a great thing to hide under, a playhouse or cave, etc.

» **Draw and Color**

» **Make a puzzle for each other** Save the cardboard from containers, open it up and paste a foreign postcard, magazine cover or newspaper page to it. Let the children draw a design and cut out the pieces to make a puzzle.

» **Do a stitchery** Start with cardboard with holes punched in it and string yarn through the holes; the more advanced in age and dexterity can use the darning needles and small pieces of felt. Allow the kids to design their own.

» **Make a found-object collage** Let the kids gather seeds, pods, shells, small fibers, bits of paper, cut-up postcards, match wrappers, etc., and glue them to construction paper.

» **Put on a finger-puppet play** They can make their own puppets with small tubes that fit over the fingers made from the construction paper. By painting faces on them, adding yarn for the hair and a circle of felt with a hole big enough to allow the bottom of the tube to pass through, they take on real personality.

260

» **Make a paper chain to decorate the camper** This activity is a great time filler. First the kids cut equal length strips of construction paper and then glue and link the loops together.

CAR GAMES

» **"I Spy"** Someone decides what everyone is to look for (i.e. first one to see a red sign) and then the first one to see it says, "I Spy" and he gets to name the next item to be found.

» **"Alphabet"** Everyone watches for signs along the road with the letters of the alphabet and each one must call out all the letters in sequence. First person to call out all the letters wins. This is great for improving kids' observation powers and recognition of letters.

» **"I'm Going to Pack Gramma's Suitcase"** The person to start says "I'm going to pack Gramma's suitcase and I'm going to take a _____ (he/she must decide on one item to take, the sillier the better). The next person must repeat the same phrase adding a new item. The longer the game lasts the more difficult it is to remember all the items mentioned. If a player fails to mention one of the items or says it out of order, he's out and the game continues until all players are eliminated except for one. If kids are old enough you can name articles in alphabetical sequence.

» **"Find Something"** Mom or Dad says: "Find something in the car that starts with an "s." Children try to see who can name something first (in this case, steering wheel would be a good choice).

» **"Simon Says"** Simon says, "point to your eye." Everybody must follow the leader until he says something without putting "Simon says" ahead of the phrase. In that case, if someone follows, he is out.

» **"I'm Thinking of"** Person to start says "I'm thinking of something that is _____" He proceeds to give one clue. Everyone gets to ask one yes or no questions, such as "is it an animal?" He keeps adding clues until the thing is guessed.

» **"Mystery Bag"** Put several familiar objects in a box or bag and have kids try to guess them by feeling. The one who names the most wins. Occasionally you can put small surprise toys in the bag. If they guess what it is, they can have it.

MORE UP-TO-DATE INFORMATION ON CAMPING IN EUROPE:

We've listed a few suggestions on campsites in each country but with today's easy search engine technology like Google, you will easily find several other suggestions. Also, it's important to note you can sometimes best find places while on the road, and you may not have to reserve in advance unless you are the type that likes to have pre-reserved spots. The downside to that is you'll have to meet a schedule. Sometimes the best experiences were our "on the road discoveries." If we had campground reservations, we would not be able to stop and experience these discoveries. You will have to decide what is within your comfort zone.

Final words: Camping is a delightful way to travel with kids as they have so many more opportunities to meet other kids than on a more traditional hotel- or apartment-based trip. For those who choose not to camp but select hotels, and other accommodations friendly to kids, read Ciao Bambino, first published in April of 2013. See their website: **https://ciaobambino.com/?s=Italy%20family%20 vacations**

INFORMATION ON RENTING A VAN IN EUROPE

Google Autoeurope or call 888-223-5555 or check out these sites:

https://www.motorvana.com/rv-rental/europe
https://lovelifeabroad.com/finding-a-campervan-rental-in-europe/

SOME COMPANIES OFFER SELF-CATERING CAMPING:

Eurocamp has nearly 40 years-experience in providing self-catering holidays with freedom and flexibility. They have over 160 parks with highest quality facilities from France to Croatia, and Sicily to Sardinia. All are unique and packed with personality, from smaller hideaways in rural locations to lively beach parks with huge pool complexes and plenty of activities. **Visit eurocamp.co.uk**
   www.keycamp.co.uk

MORE SUGGESTIONS FOR CAMPGROUNDS IN EUROPEAN COUNTRIES:

Camping in England:
http://www.coolcamping.co.uk/

Camping in Italy:
There are quite a few campgrounds in Italy close to major attractions. Many have bungalows/cabins (some with AC) to rent very cheap. Many have very nice pools. Within walking distance of Pompeii is Camping Spartacus. https://www.campingspartacus.it/it/

Here's a good one near Florence: https://firenze.huopenair.com/

Campground in Rome:
Hu Camping Roma (066 623 018) https://roma.huopenair.com/
 This is the closest campground to the historic area with a bus stop right outside the entrance.

Special note: Downside of driving in Italy:
You can't drive in most of the center of Rome, Florence, etc. Yes, there are cars there, but they are citizens of the city and are allowed to drive there. As a visitor, you are not.

See https://www.autoeurope.com/italy-ztl-zones/ to familiarize yourself with the limited Traffic zones (*Zona Traffico Limitato* in Italian).

Camping in France:

In our experience, camping is one thing (among others) that the French do very well. One of our favorite parts of France is the south-west, with its amazing beaches that aren't as crowded as the Mediterranean, and some gorgeous cycle paths through pine forests – without cars! We would look into hiring bikes (there are plenty of places where you can get them) and cycle part of the coastline, depending on the age of the kids and safety considerations. There are loads of campsites, often very close to the beach with very reasonable prices.

Hautes Pyrénées département, Occitanie région, where there is a campground next to the trailhead just beyond the miniscule village of **Gavarnie-Gèdre**, municipality on the approach to the natural amphitheater known as the Cirque de Gavarnie, in southwestern France. It's a beautiful site.

Camping La Bergerie (phone: 05 62 40 05) has a fabulous location on the river with full view of the Cirque de Garvarnie. Located on a grassy slope there are some level areas for tents and a flat area for campers. Toilets, showers and dishwashing areas are basic but tidy. Its café with indoor and outdoor tables makes a good place to make new friends with fellow travelers. **Note**: Between Oct.15 and April 15 it is open only to permanent residents. **Driving Directions**: Gavarnie is 53 kilometers south of Lourdes. From Lourdes drive 15 kilometers south on D821 to Argeles Gazost. Continue south on D921 for 38 kilometers to Garvarnie. Drive up the hill through the village and then continue towards the mountains on a smaller road to camping.

Camping in the Perigord of France:

In the Périgord there are some exceptionally lovely campgrounds. They are rated using a star system (as I think all the campgrounds in France are). The 4-star ones are really something to behold

– gorgeous swimming pools, nice cafés, fancy laundry and shower facilities, and lovely affordable rooms and cabins.

Note: In France there are also very few prohibited driving zones compared to Italy.

For great information on routes, timing and cost (including gas and any tolls) try: **https://www.viamichelin.com/**

Like Google Maps (but with even more information available). **Example**: I entered: Paris to Poitiers, Centre Ville and came up with this information plus much more:

69.58 €: With a Petrol vehicle
Toll: 32.70 € | Petrol 36.88 €
Time: 03h25 with 03h04 on motorways
Distance: 207 mi with 202 mi on motorways

MORE UPDATES ON THREE OF OUR FAVORITE MUSEUMS IN PARIS, FRANCE:

Check out these museums

https://jeudepaume.org

https://www.musee-orangerie.fr/fr

https://artsandculture.google.com/partner/musee-dorsay-paris

Camping in Germany:
https://www.pure-camping.de/camping-erlebnis-zugspitze-garmisch-partenkirchen-bayern/

Near Munich (recommended by Trip Advisor)
Paradise Zugspitze: This three-star facility is located in the middle of the picturesque landscape of the Zuspitze region and is an excellent starting point for hikes and camping all year round.

MORE GOOD TIPS:

You may not want to drive in cities because:

1. Traffic can be very busy.
2. Most cities have scooters and motorcycles weaving in and out of traffic that makes driving difficult.
3. Traffic patterns can be very different than you are used to.
4. Restricted zones can garner large tickets if breached and with so many other things taking your attention many tourists miss the signs or don't know them and breach the zones.
5. Parking is very expensive and very hard to find (even hotels charge by the night to park). You can however usually park on the outskirts of a city and take public transport into the center like we often did.

CAR SEATS FOR KIDS?

Rules in Europe about seats for kids are much the same as in the US: You will need a child seat for your youngest child, a booster for 4-year-olds and maybe one for 6-year-olds, depending on how tall they are. You may be able to rent those with the car. *But remember, we're advocating for traveling with kids, 7 to 12 years of age, in which case you won't have to worry about these rules.*

BABYSITTING OPTIONS WHEN YOU JUST NEED A BREAK FROM THE KIDS:

https://www.internationalbabysitters.com/paris

GENERAL PRICES/SIZES FOR CARS:

http://www.autoeurope.com/

If you start your travels in France, there is also the option of *Achat/Rachat*, which essentially means you buy the car and resell it before you return to the US. **https://www.renault-eurodrive.com/en** You get a brand-new car that the dealer takes back from you at the end of your contract. Or you can purchase the car at the end of your trip and ship it back to the USA.

SUGGESTED WEBSITES:

This is a fun website describing a family's travels in Europe over 15 years with their now very successful daughter in her 20's who benefitted greatly from these experiences. **http://www.soultravelers3.com/2012/10/camping-europe-with-kids.html**

**Rick Steve's site on camping in Europe:
http://www.ricksteves.com/plan/tips/0899camping.htm**

Here you can find information on everything from Registration and Regulations to Services, needed equipment, safety, camping by car, RV camping, turn-key camping and free camping.

MORE BOOKS WITH CAMPING AND DRIVING TIPS GALORE:

Take Your Kids to Europe by Cynthia Harriman **(published December 2007)**

This book is an invaluable resource for parents everywhere. It provides practical information on how to plan a family trip to Europe, from car rentals to house rentals, to how to get your child to eat "foreign" food. Numerous tips on cutting costs, creating a realistic budget, interesting your children in what they are seeing and bridging the cultural differences make this both practical and inspiring. **Note: some information may be a bit outdated since the book was published in 2007.**

100 Tips for Traveling with Kids in Europe by E. Ashley Steel (published in paperback June 2016)

This book is jam-packed with tips and ideas that will help you with every step of planning and enjoying a European family vacation: designing a kid-friendly itinerary, book fun and interesting lodging, choosing the best ways to get around, packing light, saving money, enjoying the airplane ride, staying safe, and immersing yourself and your family in the many cultures of Europe.

Note: Books like these were not available way back in 1972–73 when we took our kids around Europe camping in a VW van. We are thrilled to see so many people are now doing what we did and are offering tips for others.

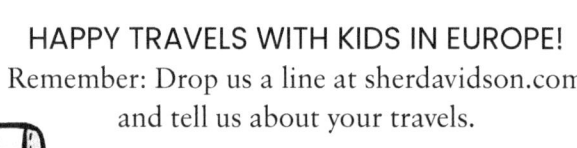

HAPPY TRAVELS WITH KIDS IN EUROPE!
Remember: Drop us a line at sherdavidson.com and tell us about your travels.

Index

Acknowledgements

As we age, we tend to look back on our life's journey. Creating this anniversary edition of *Europe with Two Kids and a Van* has truly been one of those "looking back" occasions. It has elicited more memories not even mentioned in the first book.

I want to acknowledge all those who have made this "writing journey" possible and a joy. First, there is my editor and friend, Jan Hinkski. Her editing has helped me realize the dream of a fiftieth anniversary edition of this travel memoir and guidebook. Then there is Aaron Vasquez, my cover designer who has created the clever and fun cover for this edition, much more colorful than the one produced in 1973, keeping up with new trends. Also contributing to this publishing journey has been my many early readers, and those who have kindly offered blurbs, Mark Saunders and Jan Baross. I thank them for not letting me give up on this project. It was Mark, in fact, who first suggested *Europe with Two Kids* needed a "rebirth."

I also want to thank my two daughters, Dawn and Tiffany, the two young travelers you see in the photos. They always enthusiastically support my projects.

Lastly, but not least, I want to thank my dear husband and fellow traveler, Gary, who has made this possible by doing many of the household chores like grocery shopping, cooking of meals and laundry duties. He's also been my "go-to" person when updating old information for the *Summing Up* sections of the guide. We were a team when we traveled with two kids and a van, and we are a team now! Teamwork has made this book possible.

I hope you will want to read my two novels:

Under the Salvadoran Sun
a tale of adventures and romance

and

Dark Secrets, A Legacy of Memories from 1939 Sweden
Historical Fiction and mystery

Both are available from Amazon

I look forward to hearing how you enjoyed my books.
Contact me at sherdavidson.com

www.ingramcontent.com/pod-product-compliance
Lightning Source LLC
Chambersburg PA
CBHW060908120626
46553CB00001B/245